C000138822

CARDIGANSHIRE

THE HISTORIES OF WALES
SERIES EDITOR: CATRIN STEVENS

CARDIGANSHIRE

A CONCISE HISTORY

MIKE BENBOUGH-JACKSON

University of Wales Press
Cardiff
2007

© Mike Benbough-Jackson, 2007

All rights reserved. No part of this book may be reproduced, stored in a retrieval system, or transmitted, in any form or by any means, electronic, mechanical, photocopying, recording or otherwise, without clearance from the University of Wales Press, 10 Columbus Walk, Brigantine Place, Cardiff, CF10 4UP.
www.wales.ac.uk/press

British Library Cataloguing-in-Publication Data
A catalogue record for this book is available from the British Library.

ISBN 978-0-7083-2111-9

The right of Mike Benbough-Jackson to be identified as author of this work has been asserted by him in accordance with sections 77 and 78 of the Copyright, Designs and Patents Act 1998. Every effort has been made to contact the copyright holders of visual material published in this volume; if any have been overlooked, the publishers will be pleased to make the necessary arrangements at the first opportunity.

Printed in Malta by Gutenberg Press Ltd.

In memory of M. C. S. (Mike) Evans, an inspirational teacher

Contents

Series Editor's Preface

'The Histories of Wales' series seeks to enrich our knowledge and understanding of the colourful diversity of the local and regional cultures and heritage of Wales. Gradually, as successive volumes appear, duly chronicling the distinctiveness and complexity of each '*bro*' or county, we shall be able to piece together the fascinating jigsaw, which constitutes the broader history of Wales. Each volume also aims to enhance ties of loyalty and attachment to one's '*milltir sgwâr*' (square mile) and to evoke a strong sense of locality and local identity. This has certainly been the case in my own experience with this particular volume. As a 'Cardi', or native of Cardiganshire, it gives me great pleasure to welcome this latest addition to 'The Histories of Wales' series.

Three volumes have appeared in the series already: the concise histories of *Anglesey* (David A. Pretty, 2005), *Carmarthenshire* (Dylan Rees, 2005) and *Pembrokeshire* (Roger Turvey, 2007), with this study of *Cardiganshire*, therefore, neatly completing the Dyfed trilogy. During the past century Cardiganshire or Ceredigion has, in fact, been well-served by professional and amateur historians, with works ranging from the magisterial volumes of the *Cardiganshire County History*, the erudite yet thoroughly readable, *Ceredigion, a wealth of history* by Gerald Morgan (2005), and the numerous, multi-faceted articles in the county's journal, *Ceredigion*: the Transactions of the Cardiganshire Antiquarian Society. There has also been a rich vein of vibrant biographies and autobiographies of and by members of the '*gwerin*' (ordinary folk), both male and female, written during the 1950s and 60s and published by *Cymdeithas Lyfrau Ceredigion*.

This concise history offers something different however. In it the author strides across the chronological sweep of the centuries, from prehistory to the present, halting with some events of national significance, such as the life and works of Wales's greatest poet, Dafydd ap Gwilym, of Brogynin, in the fourteenth century and the birth of the Methodist Revival at Llangeitho in the eighteenth, but also pausing to note other events of more local momentum. Mike Benbough-Jackson has a fine eye for detail and for locating these details within their geographical landscape and their historical contexts. This volume will appeal to laymen and professionals at local and national levels. I am greatly indebted to him for undertaking the task of researching and writing this concise history with such enthusiasm, diligence and scholarship. It would be a considerable feat for a mature historian, steeped in academic learning, but the author is of the generation of young Welsh historians and this makes his achievement even more remarkable. I recommend *Cardiganshire: a concise history* to all fellow-Cardis, who love this piece of paradise, but also to all those outsiders who would like to understand and appreciate further the history of the ancient county of Ceredigion.

Catrin Stevens
Series Editor, The Histories of Wales

Acknowledgements

All historical writing involves a considerable amount of distillation. Even a monograph, covering a limited time span and topic, is a blend of books, records and other sources. Yet this volume contains more distillation than narrower surveys. Like the distillers of alcoholic drinks, I hope this concoction will be to the consumer's liking and encourage them to sample more historical works about Wales and Cardiganshire.

The book's structure is based, in the main, on centuries. Turning points do not occur neatly at the start or end of hundred year blocks. Rather, centuries are convenient; they enable us to bundle together diverse features. As long as the complexities within centuries are acknowledged then their structural use need not impede the relation of historical information. Distilled liquid needs to be transported in convenient receptacles before being decanted and savoured.

Many have helped me assemble this history. The staff of the County Records Office in Aberystwyth pointed me towards vivid recently acquired sources which shed light on the county's past. Ceredigion museum, the National Library of Wales and the Ceredigion County library at Aberystwyth also contained valuable historical material and helpful staff. The county's two university libraries provided ready access to material that helped put primary sources into context.

Conversations with Neil Evans, Paul O'Leary, Geraint Jenkins, Ieuan Gwynedd Jones and Peter and Anne Borsay provided information and encouragement. I was also fortunate in having a Cardi as the series editor. Catrin Stevens helped reassure this outsider that he was not looking at the county exclusively from the wrong side of the Teifi. Any errors that remain are mine alone.

Most importantly, Shân and my parents, Michael and Ivy, have helped in numerous ways: listening, reading and being there.

Mike Benbough-Jackson
Llanybydder

I

Prehistory to the Normans

Before relating a history of the county there is value in outlining its location and prominent physical characteristics. Such factors, the 'where', often explain much of the 'what' that happens in history. Whilst people make their own history it is in a theatre set by geographical stagehands. Although some aspects of an area's geography change over time, as do perceptions of landmarks, some remain constant. The county's name, however, has not stayed the same. It is currently Ceredigion, and the territory was also identified by this name from the Dark Ages until the English conquest. For much of the period covered here it was Cardiganshire (Cardigan being a corruption of the Welsh Ceredig), and this will be used on most occasions. For many years some Welsh-speakers preferred the Welsh translation – Sir Aberteifi – over the ancient title Ceredigion. Ceredigion will be used when dealing with periods when it was the official name.

Like most Welsh counties, Ceredigion is a maritime county. Its entire western flank is shoreline and forms a substantial part of Cardigan Bay. At the northern and southern ends there are estuaries, the Dyfi and Teifi respectively. The transition from land to water is sometimes sudden; a journey along the county's western boundary is often along a cliff top. Therefore natives and visitors alike have especially valued beaches, such as Penbryn and Y Borth. Warmer waters provided by the Atlantic drift benefit these shores. The coast, through invasion, trade and leisure, has shaped much of the county's history. Ceredigion's eastern side, which adjoins Carmarthenshire, Breconshire, Radnorshire and Montgomeryshire, has also contributed to its past and present. While the west warms and opens the east protects. Even though a short journey inland can lead to drops in temperature, the eastern hills and mountains act as a windbreak against cold easterly breezes. Breconshire lambs have been moved to the county because its winters were more clement than those of its eastern neighbour. This upland area has also been credited with slowing English cultural influences. The county's highest point is Pumlumon (752 metres) in the north-east. It is composed of Ordovician rock, from 505 to 438 million years ago. The south-western portion of the county is also made of this layer; the rest of Ceredigion rests on Silurian rock, laid down in the 32 million years after the Ordovician period. Pumlumon is not a craggy eminence like the great peaks of north Wales; instead, it is part of a ridge of high land running along the eastern edge of Ceredigion.

Most of the county's main rivers and tributaries originate in these eastern highlands. A notable exception, the Aeron, flows from Mynydd Bach (Small Mountain), a cluster of upland in the middle of Ceredigion. These rivers flow westwards, dissecting the land. The Teifi, from which Cardigan town acquires its Welsh name Aberteifi, constitutes Ceredigion's southern border. Emanating from Llyn Teifi (Teifi Lake) near Strata Florida (Ystrad Fflur) abbey, significant historical landmarks and towns are found on its banks throughout its journey. Although forming a frontier, the valley has provided a focus for trade and settlement, uniting southern Ceredigion with northern Pembrokeshire and Carmarthenshire. In its later stages there are stone castles at Cardigan, Newcastle Emlyn and Cilgerran. In its less mature form it passes historic settlements like Llanddewibrefi, Llanfair Clydogau and Lampeter. From the last place, the valley broadens, before it contracts somewhat and is joined by the Cletwr and Cledlyn. Thereafter, near Llandysul, the valley widens again. From here the valley is especially fecund, and the land benefited owners of large estates nearby. Cenarth and Henllan, with their waterfalls, provide artists with material. Newcastle Emlyn, although on the Carmarthenshire side, was part of the political constituency of Cardiganshire during much of the nineteenth century. Just across the river lies Atpar, which was an important marketplace. The river enters the sea soon after passing Cardigan. The Llyfnant and the Dyfi estuary form the county's northern boundary, which separates it from Merionethshire and Montgomeryshire. To the south Llyn Llygad Rheidol, a remnant of the ice age, is the starting point of the Rheidol river. It flows below one of the county's best-known features, the waterfall at Devil's Bridge, and enters Cardigan Bay at Aberystwyth. Another major river in northern Ceredigion, the Ystwyth, reaches the sea to the south of the town, having passed through lands which were formerly part of the stately residences of Trawsgoed and Hafod.

Many ancient human settlements were established on these valleys, hills and coasts. A flint implement, found at a caravan site in Dôl-y-bont, provides the earliest evidence of human activity in the area. Other artefacts from the Upper Palaeolithic period which ended c.10000 BC are unlikely to have survived the most recent, Devensian, ice age. During its peak all of what was to become Cardiganshire was under ice. After this ice sheet retreated, a tundra-like environment emerged. Eventually, in what became known as the Mesolithic period, trees populated the land. Studies of pollen from bog land near Cwmystwyth have revealed which trees colonized the post-ice age landscape. Birch, pine and hazel led the way. The first two were outnumbered in the wetter Later Mesolithic by oak and alder, the more adaptable hazel remained. Fauna also changed as the auroch, wild pig, elk and roe deer replaced animals adapted to colder conditions, such as reindeer. Remains of the auroch, a large ox, have been found in the county. Trees fuelled technological change. Wood provided materials for bows, arrows, fishing tools and canoes. Warmer waters attracted aquatic creatures which provided an additional source of nutrition. Despite these changes the population remained hunter-gatherers.

Rising temperatures increased sea levels. Water, liberated from ice caps, flooded low-lying land. The legend of Cantre'r Gwaelod (the lowland hundred) probably stems from this prehistoric inundation. Although the blame has been attributed to a drunken dyke keeper, climate change was the culprit. Submerged forests at Y Borth and Ynys-las, provide reminders of a time when mid Wales was more rotund. Sites in the north of the county, adjacent to Cantre'r Gwaelod, offer the earliest significant traces of human activity. In this, Cardiganshire follows a general pattern. At this time, the inter-glacial maximum, the British climate would have been like that of south-western France, around two degrees celsius higher than today. As in other places, particularly Pembrokeshire, people gathered along the coast. The antler shaft, thought to be part of a stone axe, found at Ynys-las shows how fauna enhanced tool making. At the base of Pen Dinas, near Aberystwyth, there was a 'flint factory'; the stones were used to dislodge limpets from rocks.[1] Worked flints have also been found at Llangrannog. The question of Mesolithic people's diet and the degree to which it changed during the Neolithic period, which was characterized by farming, has exercised academics. A rapid shift from sea to land produce c.5,200 years ago has been identified by scientists studying the ratios of stable carbon isotopes in the bones of ancient Britons.

As the 'agricultural revolution' spread from the Middle East to western Europe it could be assumed that the limpet bashers of Pen Dinas would have been among the last to acquire those characteristics, such as pottery and enduring dwellings, which typified Neolithic farmers. However, there was contact over water in this period so change via this route cannot be ruled out. Remnants of early Neolithic-type settlements have been found suggesting that innovations came over the sea rather than a gradual diffusion across land. An investigation at Plas Gogerddan revealed that wheat and barley – two plants from the Middle East –

were grown *c*.3500 BC. This, together with pottery found at Llanilar, indicates the relatively swift arrival of Neolithic features. Evidence of settlement is rare; wood used to build dwellings would decompose. Some archaeologists suggest that the use of wood, a living substance, for people and stone, a lifeless one, for the dead presents an insight into the minds of prehistoric people.

Megalithic tombs – the watermark of the Neolithic Age – survive in the records of antiquaries but not as structures. Originally they were made by placing a large stone upon upright rocks. Archaeologists have estimated that four of the structures identified by antiquarians were Neolithic: two close to Pembrokeshire near Llangoedmor and two further up the coast. One, near Llangoedmor, was described by the seventeenth-century scholar Edward Lhuyd, as being 5 to 6 ft high, supported by four stones and situated on a 'small bank or rising'. Early in the nineteenth century it was noted that none of these stones remained, they probably ended up as gateposts or in walls. Even without these adaptations the monumental landscape of Cardiganshire would not have been imposing. Nonetheless, a scattering of tools throughout the county offers some record of the era. Axes would have been essential for any tree-felling prehistoric farmer, and some of these polished tools, characteristic of the age, have been found.

Burial practices are used as a marker to distinguish the Neolithic and Bronze Ages. After 2000 BC there was a shift from megaliths and group burial to cairns – mounds mainly composed of stone – and single graves. Earthenware vessels, a feature which gave the Beaker people their name, are often unearthed at these burial sites. One of these, an urn about 34 cm high, was found at Llanilar. Thought to be typical of the Early Bronze Age, these urns contained cremated remains and other items including pig bones, cereal and a bronze awl. But the county's most impressive urn, exhibiting considerable decorative patterns, was discovered at Pen-llwyn. Unfortunately, the Bronze Age round barrows found near Horeb in 2003 did not produce any remains.

Higher temperatures during the Early Bronze Age enabled upland areas to be utilized. These locations were not intensively farmed in later years and therefore structures were often left unmolested. Ordnance Survey maps indicate that there was a concentration of these sites in eastern Cardiganshire. An examination of a stone semicircle comprising ten stones to the east of Tregaron estimated that the complete circle would have measured some 18 metres. The builders of these structures have been described as being more bellicose than the earlier Neolithic inhabitants. Support for this may be found in the metal tools, including knives and spearheads, which have been uncovered in the county. Yet this image of warmongering propagators of the first 'industrial revolution' should be tempered by the possibility that many axes could have been used for agriculture. Moreover, it has been claimed that the bronze shield found preserved in a bog near Blaenplwyf had a ritual rather than military function. Some speculate that weapons were intentionally deposited in bogs as offerings to gods.

Metals were extracted in pre-Iron Age Cardiganshire. One mine, at Copa Hill, Cwmystwyth, has been described as the earliest lead-mining site in Britain. In addition, some Bronze Age tools including a stone chisel – an example of the usefulness of this primitive material in a metal age – have been found there. Copper mined here c.2000 BC would, when melted with tin, have produced bronze. It has been posited that copper prospectors came from Ireland where mining took place in the Wicklow Hills, the El Dorado of the ancient world. A small gold disc unearthed from a burial site on Copa Hill was a metal hungry prospector's jewellery for the afterlife.

Towards the end of the Bronze Age it became colder and wetter. This less clement weather could have led to a movement away from the highlands. Were moves to the forts visible today the product of climate change, increased conflict, or as some advocate a result of increased trading networks? Physical evidence from the late Bronze Age onwards points to a significant change in the way people lived. They became more sedentary and less inclined to construct burial mounds. Archaeologists have described this as a transformation of the human-made landscape from the sacred to the political. Cultural change occurs in all epochs, but the Iron Age c.700 BC is considered particularly significant – some suggest we still live in it today. The arrival of the Celts, or as is now more widely argued the arrival of Celtic culture, led to the gradual introduction of iron implements to the British Isles. It is thought that this continental people inaugurated a time of cultural, including linguistic, rather than racial transformation. According to the present academic consensus these changes were the result not so much of invasion, or even a ruling Celtic aristocracy, but a pre-existing people, particularly their elite, adopting continental ways. Like those at the centre of Celtic culture, between Loire and Bohemia, who emulated Etruscan craftsmanship, the inhabitants of Britain took on continental styles. An example of the renowned late La Tène style, in the form of a bronze brooch, was found at Plas Gogerddan.

Iron tools were wrought from iron ore melted in a charcoal fire, with the use of bellows to make it white hot, before being put into moulds. Warfare and domestic life was influenced by this metal. The mushrooming of hill forts has been taken to indicate the influence of the former, though these notable remnants were certainly com-plemented by less heavily defended sites whose traces have been eroded by later agricultural activities. Pen Dinas would have been a long-term residence for some 150 people. All the county's hill forts date from the Iron Age, yet during this period the same site may have served many purposes. At Henllan the discovery of sheep bones has provided a rare insight into the occupants' culinary tastes. An amber bead with a hole through it, indicating its use as jewellery, was also found there. Iron Age remains, however, are rare not only in the county but in Wales as a whole. The lack of finds limits studies seeking to define culture areas – those regions where particular objects and, more specifically, particular renderings of objects, were common.

Roman records shed a little light on the inhabitants of western Britain. Although nothing was written specifically about what was to become Cardiganshire, some remarks were made about the island's inland inhabitants; those living between the Teifi and the Dyfi would have come under this category. The Belgae, relatively sophisticated inhabitants of south-eastern Britain, described the denizens to the north and west as consumers of milk and flesh rather than corn. Despite there being evidence that arable activity did take place outside the fertile south, this image of a wild people, the oldest on the island who clad themselves in skins, gives some idea of the psychological and material gap between parts of the island. These westerners would take longer to subdue, though it could be said that there were fewer reasons to conquer them. It might be expected that those living in this area were less likely to become Romanized. Yet some 25 miles south of the river Teifi there was a significant town, Moridunum (Carmarthen). Furthermore, there was gold at Pumsaint, a site not far from the river Teifi. Areas like Cardiganshire present an interesting case study for those involved in finding out how far Roman ideas and products permeated the island. Quips that the study of Roman Britain amounts to the investigation of just 'two bricks in the corner of a wet field' can often be proved incorrect in even the remotest part of the island.

The subjugation of Wales was completed towards the end of the seventh decade AD. Flavius Vespasian, the first of the Flavian emperors, was emperor when the Romans made a concerted effort to subdue Britain. Two legionary fortresses at Chester and Caerleon overlooked Wales, and auxiliary forts were scattered throughout its interior. The presence of these forts in Cardiganshire confirms Roman activity, but the exact make-up or names of the region's tribes is unclear. Like most conquerors, in their writings the Romans paid greater attention to their vicious foes. As a result, the Silures of the south-east overshadow the Demetae of the south-west. Tacitus referred to the governor of Britain, Julius Frontinus, defeating the Silurians between AD 74–8 and taking south Wales, but omitted the Demetae. It is tempting to conclude from the lack of forts in the south of the county, also a feature of the Demetae heartland in Pembrokeshire, that this was Demetae territory. A stone at Penbryn was erected in memory of an Ordovician – a member of the tribe whose land included much of mid Wales, and whose attack on a Roman cavalry regiment brought the wrath of Agricola upon them in AD 78. The fact that his identity was noted has been taken to indicate that he was not a local. It was possible that the south of the county was Demetaeian and the north Ordovician.

A spine of Roman forts ran from south to north, eventually reaching Pennal on the other side of the Dyfi. They could indicate a need to police the more warlike Ordovicians. Yet, after thorough searches by archaeologists, the natives' main Iron Age forts, such as Pen Dinas, do not show any signs of battle or occupation by the Romans. Instead the invaders located their forts at strategic points along the road that was part of a system which enabled troops to advance quickly. Efficient roads also sped up the delivery of supplies. They would have taken far longer, to reach their objective, or might never have reached it, if the existing twisting paths were the sole means of communication. This amounted to a transport revolution and would have had a significant impact on the environment as trees were cleared, both to make room for the road and to reduce cover for ambushers. Road builders also took climatic conditions into consideration. Tacitus may have been speaking for many southern Europeans, including those supervising the construction of the roads, when he complained that the British climate was abysmal. Areas with higher rainfall such as Cardiganshire would have had roads adapted for the conditions by having higher crowns which sent rain to ditches at the roadside. It was imperative that roads could be used in most weather conditions. The Romans did not name their roads, so the route running through Cardiganshire – called 'Sarn Helen' (Helen's Causeway) – was given that appellation at a later date. Some think it originates from Sarn y Lleng – the legion's causeway, the more romantically inclined thought it derived from a Welsh princess called Elen.

Each of the three main forts in the county were positioned near river crossings – Llanio on the Teifi, Trawsgoed on the Ystwyth and Pen-llwyn on the Rheidol. They were constructed during the period of Flavian expansion. Whether these forts indicate locations where the native population was concentrated is an open question. Llanio (known to the Romans as Bremia) presents an excellent example of an auxiliary fort measuring just under 4 acres. Its street plan, in the form of parch marks, was visible from the air during the dry summer of 1976. Many of those units stationed here and in the other Cardiganshire forts will never be known by name, but we are fortunate that Llanio has divulged stones which reveal that a military unit originating from north-western Spain once resided there. In addition to the well-planned fort with its earthwork and trench defences, there was a bathhouse. This symbol of Rome's presence provided hot baths as a furnace heated up the water originating from a nearby spring. A hypocaust, as these underfloor heating systems were called, would have substantially enhanced the quality of life in first-century Llanio.[2] Those moving northwards from either the gold mines at Pumsaint, along the road which the B4343 follows today, or along the less well-investigated route from Carmarthen, would have decamped at Llanio.

Trawsgoed fort, at nearly five and a half acres, was larger than its southern neighbour. The fort has a well-defined *vicus* (plural *vici*) – a settlement outside the fort proper. It has been estimated that as many as a thousand troops could have been stationed at this fort, so various services would have been needed. A kiln for making tiles or bricks, together with evidence of bronze and iron making, was found in the mid-1980s. Remains of buildings that may have been shops were also unearthed. There are Iron Age settlements on either side that could indicate that the native population lived nearby. This trading centre depended on the fort because after the latter's abandonment in the late AD 120s activity ceased there as well. One of the most interesting discoveries from Roman-era Cardiganshire was found at Trawsgoed. This was a bronze figure – thought to be a griffin (a mythical beast believed to guard gold hoards) – probably used to adorn a cart.[3] The griffin was a common decoration on carts, although this example from Cardiganshire is one of few found in Britain.

For those who travelled by foot, camps and forts were generally a day's march apart. A soldier would march 20 miles in five hours or, at forced-march speed, 24 miles could be covered in the same time. The distance from Trawsgoed to Pen-llwyn, the final major fort in the Cardiganshire chain, was well under a standard day's march. Pen-llwyn is thought to date from around the same time as the other two forts (AD 70–130). There may well have been more small forts (fortlets) between the main forts. After the discovery of a fortlet at Erglodd, in the north of the county near Tal-y-bont, archaeologists reckon that gaps between forts, such as that between Llanio and Trawsgoed, could have been interspersed with similar bases. Pottery is often used to date the approximate construction and occupation of a place. The fortlet at Erglodd, for example, has been approximately dated by fragments of Samian ware (a type of pottery created in southern Gaul). Analysis of this and other features indicate that the military presence in Cardiganshire diminished soon after AD 130. Problems in the north of the island led to troops being redeployed; the abandonment of military bases in Cardiganshire coincides roughly with the building and manning of Hadrian's Wall and the later Antonine wall begun approximately twenty years later (AD 143).

Roman interest in the gold mines at Pumsaint raises the question of whether they exploited Cardiganshire's mineral wealth. There were mines close to Pen-llwyn fort, such as those near Goginan, that had been worked before the conquest. Yet some archaeologists are not convinced that military activity was accompanied by extensive mining operations. Such caution is based on the lack of hard evidence. Claims that Roman coins were found at Goginan mine early in the twentieth century are not sufficient evidence to conclude that a concerted period of mineral extraction took place. There was lead and silver in the Cardiganshire hills, and it is difficult to accept that the Romans did not exploit this resource. It is reasonable to expect, however, that any such utilization by the Romans would have left more traces. As is the case in many archaeological matters we must patiently wait for the next piece of evidence. Most of the traces left by the Romans originated in the second century; one of the later pieces of evidence to be unearthed was a store of coins dating from around the last decade of the third century.

The Romans brought a different culture as well as forts and roads to the area. Having a little Latin would have been valuable for those who wished to benefit from the opportunities opened up by the Roman world. Latin would have percolated down to those powerful natives most in contact with it, but traders and others could have learnt some Latin, too. Whatever the extent to which the language or other cultural features were taken up in Cardiganshire, they would have been less evident than those around Carmarthen. The fact that *vici* did not remain after forts were abandoned suggests that, for various local economic and geographic reasons, an urban focus did not develop in the county. So far no villas have been identified, and this points to a greater degree of continuity than change. There are few indicators of religious change either. Emperor Constantine's toleration of Christianity blossomed into support after he attributed a victory over a rival in AD 312 to the divine intervention of a Christian God. For the rest of that century Christianity spread, but its initial progress in the fourth century has been linked to Christian villa owners of whom there were few in Cardiganshire. By the fifth century, however, it had become more common. The memorial for the Ordovician at Penbryn mentioned above, tells us that he was a Christian. This Latin inscription also indicates the importance of the Roman's linguistic legacy.

After the Romans left the period popularly called the Dark Ages began. Owing to its peripheral location, Cardiganshire's Dark Age probably began before some other parts of Wales. We need to treat this attention-grabbing chronological headline with caution; the period did not cast a pitch-black pall over all aspects of human life. Indeed, it is ironic that the flame bearers of Christianity left their mark on the people and landscape of the county during this period. Saints provided a light in these dark times, and Cardiganshire formed a backdrop against which many acts of early Christianity were set. The enlargement of the Christian world in the west occurred as it contracted in the east of the island as pagan Germanic peoples conquered and settled in what was to become England. It would be some two centuries before most of these colonizers were converted to Christianity.

Our knowledge of the saints of post-Roman Cardiganshire is founded on accounts written long after the saints died. Although there are fleeting references to St David (Dewi Sant) before the turn of the first millennium, much of what we know about this figure, the most renowned saint with links to the county, comes from a history of his life written near the close of the eleventh century, some five centuries after his death. The author of this work, a monk at Llanbadarn Fawr called Rhygyfarch, wrote that the saint was the grandson of Ceredig, king of Ceredigion. This text demonstrates how such accounts could be used for political purposes. Rhygyfarch was keen to uphold the separate status of St Davids in the context of an assertive Norman England; he also composed a poem condemning the Norman incursions into the region. Furthermore, the tales related in this account have been ridiculed. A mound of earth rising up beneath David's feet as he refuted a conflicting theological philosophy while speaking at Llanddewibrefi is one of the most well-known of these miracles, which also included raising the dead and giving the blind sight. Incidentally, Llanddewibrefi church is one of the few that contain stones from the first millennium – those in its eastern part (chancel) are thought to have been erected in the seventh century.

Nonetheless, accounts of saints' lives, even if exaggerated or intended to promote a particular cause, bear witness to the influence of these figures almost half a millennium after their corporal demise. These saints, moreover, contributed to the cultural and physical environment. One indication of the importance of these near-mythical individuals can be seen in place-names. While these do not necessarily indicate the physical movement of a saint, they provide the historian with some idea of areas whose common characteristics differentiated them from other places. Through studying the spread of names and dedications, we can make out, albeit faintly, the areas in which the influence of certain saints – or more exactly their followers – was greatest.

Alongside the broad divide in Britain between Christian Celt and pagan invader, there were other, subtler, geographical variations in religious patterns within Cardiganshire. For instance, there are more dedications to St David in the lower part of Cardiganshire than in the north. Wells were also named after St David. One example is Ffynnon Ddewi (David's well) between Plwmp and Synod Inn, and it has been estimated that six wells in the county are named after the saint. This was quite fitting as David, due to his abstentious lifestyle, which included a diet based on water and bread, was also known as the 'waterman'. He also stood in deep cold water in order to 'subdue all the ardours of the flesh'. Such harsh methods of self-control were in the tradition of St Anthony of Egypt (*c.* AD 251–356). This cultural diffusion demonstrates how ideas spread from Africa to Europe probably via the sea. Wells were important foci for people because in addition to providing water they were thought to possess healing properties. Away from the county, David was reputed to have transformed the waters of Bath from being 'death-dealing' to ones that were 'health-giving' and warm.[4]

Padarn, who was active in the sixth century, is the county's second saint. Three churches are named after him – Llanbadarn Fawr, Llanbadarn Odwyn and Llanbadarn Trefeglwys in Pennant – all of which are north of the river Aeron. This river also marked the division of the area into Is (Lower) Aeron and Uwch (Upper) Aeron. Like David, Padarn is reputed to have performed miracles and immersed himself in cold streams. He also defied the temporal power of kings when he confronted and subdued Maelgwn Gwynedd. According to a chronicle of his life, Padarn travelled from his native Brittany to Ireland and then to Ceredigion, where he founded the 'maritime church' (Llanbadarn Fawr). He was later aided by Nimannauc who, in a demonstration of his leader's sainthood, had made the journey from Brittany to Ceredigion by sea on a rock. With his band of fellow Christians, Padarn 'became a light in doctrine and practice throughout Britain'.[5] Together with St Davids to the south, Llanbadarn Fawr became a major religious site in west Wales, just as Llanilltud Fawr and Llandaff were in the east. Archaeologists have uncovered other smaller religious sites, such as Llaneithyr close to Devil's Bridge.

Despite their prominence, Padarn and David do not occlude the many other holy men and women who contributed to the religious life of the Dark Ages. To take a few examples, there is St Cynfelin's cause way (Sarn Cynfelin), a stretch of shingle between Clarach and Borth, which commemorates the same sixth-century saint as the church Llancynfelyn. The story of St Tyfrïog (also Brïog) provides another example of links between Ceredigion and Brittany. A native of the area, Tyfrïog founded a monastic centre (Llandyfrïog), he was called

to convert people further afield. Consequently, his name is commemorated in Cornwall (St Breock) and in Brittany (St Brieuc). A
female saint has left traces which demonstrate connections between
Cardiganshire and other places, too. The Irish St Brigit (or Ffraid) is
commemorated by Llansanffraid church on the county's coast near
Llan-non – itself commonly interpreted as being a dedication to St
David's mother, St Non.

The symbolic presence of an Irish saint is not the only remnant of
contact between the county and Ireland in this period. Indeed, the
county's history at this time was shaped more by these western
neighbours than by the Saxons, who were at this time encroaching to
the east of what was to become Wales. Stones bearing the Ogham script
have been discovered in the southern portion of the county, and the
presence of this style of writing, which originated in Ireland, together
with the occurrence of the Welsh word for Irishman (*Gwyddel*) in place-
names, points towards long term-settlement of parts of Cardiganshire.
A memorial stone at Llandysul contains a bilingual Latin and Ogham
script in remembrance of Velvoria, daughter of Brohomagli.

However, this movement of people was not without conflict. One
scholar has speculated that Ogham script was often deliberately
defaced, and cited an example of this at Llanarth. The origins of the
kingdom called Ceredigion lay in a struggle between the Brythonic
Celts of Britain and the Goedelic Celts from Ireland. Cunedda, a tribal
chief from what is now southern Scotland, moved from his homeland
to north Wales around the time that the Romans left. This warrior king
is, like the more well-known Arthur who battled the Saxons, shrouded
not only in the mists of the past but in the various stories composed
much later which often raise more questions than they answer. He is
said to have vanquished the Irish in north Wales. In the course of this
reconquest, one of his sons, Ceredig, acquired the land between the
Dyfi and the Teifi, which took on his name, becoming the kingdom of
Ceredigion. As the presence of Ogham stones made long after these
conflicts show, it must not be assumed that the Irish fled across the sea.
Rather, many would have remained under new rulers.

Little is known about the rulers of Ceredigion. Yet the *Mabinogi*
notes that one of them, Seisyll, conquered Ystrad Tywi (roughly, the
eastern part of present-day Carmarthenshire and the western portion of
Glamorganshire) during the latter part of the eighth century.[6] In the
tradition of his ancestor Ceredig, this greater Ceredigion was named
Seisyllwg after its first ruler. Two kings of Seisyllwg who followed its
founder earned a mention in *The Chronicle of the Princes* (*Brut y
Tywysogion*). Both entries refer to their deaths. The first, Arthen, died
early in the ninth century, and Glynarthen in the south-east of the

county could have been named after him. Later that century Gwgon died, and this was an especially significant event in the kingdom's history.[7] Gwgon's sister, Angharad, had married Rhodri Mawr ruler of Gwynedd, and one of only two Welsh kings to have been given the title *Mawr* (Great) – the other being Llywelyn Fawr over three hundred years later. After Gwgon died, Rhodri claimed and took Ceredigion. Consequently, the kingdom lost its independence and came under the sway of a powerful dynasty, but it was still referred to as a distinct part of Wales. Soon after Gwgon died, the Saxons killed Rhodri. His lands were divided amongst his sons, with Cadell receiving the former kingdom of Seisyllwg. In the history books Cadell is outshone by his son Hywel Dda (the Good) whose domain included much of Wales and who initiated the codification of the Welsh law.

The laws recorded through the initiative of Hywel Dda can tell us something about society as a whole. They describe a model where each *gwlad* (such as Ceredigion) was divided into *cantrefi*, then *cymydau* (of which there were two per *cantref*) then *maenorau* (each of the *cymydau* would be made up of four of these). Reality did not always replicate this neat division, however. It has been suggested that in Ceredigion's case the *cymydau*, or commotes, were the primary administrative elements, rather than the *cantrefi* – only one of these, Penweddig, appears to be taken seriously by historians as others mentioned later are of questionable provenance. Even Penweddig deviates from the picture laid out in the Laws as it contained three commotes not the customary two. Each commote had a court which ensured various duties due to the lord or the king were gathered. A further departure from the Laws is seen in the use of *gwestfa* instead of *maenorau* – a term used only in Ceredigion and some neighbouring areas. Those who populated these administrative areas varied in status. After the lords, there were the freemen who owned land but still had to perform certain duties for the lord, most notably that of *gwestfa* – a payment of food or, increasingly, cash which gave its name to the areas which commotes were divided into. There were also landless bondmen, who worked on the lord's property. The latter group often lived on the lord's estate, or *maerdref*. A man possessing the enticing job title of *maer y biswail* (steward of the dung heap) oversaw their work. Some indication of the bondman's lot is contained in the Laws of Hywel Dda. Although not as low in the hierarchy as the slaves who are also referred to in the Laws, there was a rule that if a freeman strikes a bondman the fine is monetary (twelve pence to be spent on clothing and equipping the bondman), but if a bondman strikes a freeman then 'it is just to cut off his right hand', unless his lord was willing to pay compensation.[8]

In the years between Roman departure and Norman invasion conflict disturbed Ceredigion society on numerous occasions. In addition to the post-Roman struggles between Irish and Welsh mentioned earlier, there was the threat posed by the Vikings (raiders and settlers from Norway and Denmark), who controlled the north Atlantic from 950 to 1150. As shown by the relative absence of place-names derived from Scandinavian words, the only exception being *Hasti Holm* (Cardigan Island) meaning dangerous islet, their impact on Cardiganshire was not on the same scale as that experienced further south. Even so, they did strike along the coast, and Llanbadarn Fawr was plundered in 988. Coastal ecclesiastical sites offered rich pickings for them at the end of the tenth century as they had during the end of the eighth when Lindisfarne in north-east England was raided. If some scholars have correctly interpreted 'Llenwenawc' as Llanwenog in the Teifi valley, a battle was fought against the Danes there in 982. Perhaps less credence should be given to the story that King Gwgon drowned in the river Loughor while chasing the Danes out of Seisyllwg at about the same time that Alfred, ruler of Wessex, was struggling against these invaders. In all likelihood, this information, contained in *The Myvyrian Archaiology*, sprang from the imagination of the eighteenth- and early nineteenth-century scholar and forger Iolo Morgannwg (Edward Williams). The historian D. P. Kirby has speculated that Gwgon died at sea on the basis that kings of Ceredigion were 'doubtless sea-farers'.[9]

Saxons, the primary enemy in many other parts of Wales, were less of a concern in this western area. Conversely, conflicts between Welsh lords bedevilled Ceredigion. After Hywel Dda's death, clashes between the two kingdoms he had temporarily united (Gwynedd in the north and Deheubarth – primarily made up of Seisyllwg and Dyfed – to the south) were played out in Ceredigion which formed a geographical conduit between north and south. Descendants of Hywel and those of Gwynedd's Idwal the Bald fought in Ceredigion, and the latter, in the words of *The Chronicle of the Princes*, 'ravaged' the county in 954.[10] Two descendants of Hywel fought in the county during 992. Saxons made an appearance on the side of the nephew against his uncle during this familial dispute. About a generation later, in 1039, Llanbadarn Fawr was plundered by one of Gwynedd's most belligerent kings, Gruffudd ap Llywelyn. He was an arch-enemy of England's Harold Godwinson, who was presented with Gruffudd's head in 1063, three years before he fell at Hastings. In the main, strife originated from three points of the compass, Vikings from the west and the contending forces from the north and the south. With the advent of the Normans, though, trouble came from the east.

II

From Norman Assault to English Domination

The notion that the Normans overturned established social patterns in Britain has long been questioned. However, the extent to which the Normans dismantled previous governmental structures is one thing, their impact as a military force is quite another. Ceredigion provides an example of how the Normans attempted to exercise authority over an area and how the natives reacted. Nothing would be the same after the arrival of the Normans, but they did not erase native society. For much of the period covered in this chapter, Welshmen and their powerful neighbours to the east fought over Ceredigion. This pattern can be discerned in pre-Norman times, but the nature and intensity of struggles increased between 1073 and 1283. All the same, considerable cultural achievements originated in the county during this period.

Historians of eleventh- to thirteenth-century Ceredigion are fortunate. J. E. Lloyd deduced that from 1100 *The Chronicle of the Princes* paid more attention to this part of Wales than any other. Lloyd concluded that Llanbadarn Fawr then Strata Florida abbey (from 1175) were where the annals were composed.[1] The first Norman incursions into the area were in 1073–4. At this time the compilers were probably based at St David's and recorded only brief observations that the Normans 'ravaged Ceredigion' on these occasions. Roger of Montgomery, first earl of Shrewsbury, was probably responsible for these attacks. Bleddyn ap Cynfyn of Powys controlled the area, and the assaults may have been punishment for the aid he had given Saxon insurgents. William the Conqueror had granted Roger the earldom of Shrewsbury, part of the Welsh Marches. Although under the Crown, Marcher barons had considerable autonomy. Like the other barons living on the border, Roger, originally from central Normandy, was bold and determined; an earldom on the March offered opportunities in an unstable area. Roger's early raids into the county were a foretaste of later, more substantial, attempts to extend his influence.

When describing these attacks, the chronicles refer to the marauders as French (*Ffreinc*) rather than Norman.[2] This was due to the language they spoke as the collection of adventurers accompanying William included people from Brittany and Maine. Their arrival led to the inhabitants of Ceredigion finding themselves in sustained contact with a greater variety of peoples than before. As well as the French, there were Flemings, from Flanders in present-day Belgium, as well as Saxon settlers. Settlement and conflict went hand in hand. In 1093–4 Roger and Arnulf, his son, conducted a sustained assault on west Wales. The early nineteenth-century antiquarian Samuel Rush Meyrick reckoned that they attacked from the sea and began to 'inhabit the county upon the sea-shore'.[3] Yet Lloyd wrote that Roger traversed the mountains.[4] Whichever route was taken, they erected a 'castle' near the sea at Dingeraint (about a mile west of Cardigan). This was a temporary ring work (a mound enclosed by a trench) – even more rudimentary than the motte-and-bailey castles which soon peppered the county – and it was destroyed by the Welsh in 1094. This short-lived base epitomizes the fluctuations in military fortunes which characterized the period up to 1170.

Thirteen years before Dingeraint fell, a significant battle was fought between Welsh rulers. Rhys ap Tewdwr, king of Deheubarth met with his ally Gruffudd ap Cynan and a band of Irish-Viking mercenaries near St David's. They then marched for a day before meeting their opponents at Mynydd Carn. The exact location of the battle is not known, but taking into account the length of a day's march it may well have taken place in Ceredigion. Here Rhys defeated forces from Morgannwg and Gwynedd. After Mynydd Carn, Rhys consolidated his position through a truce with William the Conqueror. Consequently, the Normans did not trouble south Wales for some time. In the period of instability after William's death, three sons of Bleddyn ap Cynfyn from Powys attacked Deheubarth, which then included Ceredigion. The fortunes of Rhys ap Tewdwr fluctuated, and after regaining his kingdom from the forces of Powys he faced the Norman, Bernard de Neufmarché, a vassal of Roger of Montgomery, whose supporters killed him in 1093. His death cleared the way for an attempt to occupy south Wales.

The impact of Rhys's death was soon felt in Ceredigion, where, as mentioned earlier, a fortification was built near Cardigan. When William II left for Normandy in 1094, in an effort to undermine his brother Robert's hold there, the Welsh rose up. This rebellion continued after William returned, ending only in 1099 when Ceredigion was controlled by Cadwgan ap Bleddyn. Once again, Ceredigion was seen as a stepping-stone to lands to the south. In 1109 it presented an opportunity for Cadwgan's son, Owain, to assault Gerald de Windsor at Cilgerran, over the border in present-day Pembrokeshire. Owain took Gerald by surprise and he had to escape down the 'privy hole' – or toilet.[5] Owain then abducted his cousin Nest, the legendarily beautiful daughter of Rhys ap Tewdwr and Gerald's wife, together with her children. This audacious act presented Owain's father with a problem. It would have been foolhardy to offend the powerful Henry I.

Despite the return of Gerald's children, an attempt to avenge his humiliation soon followed. Cadwgan's power hungry-nephews were sent to capture Owain. Here the chronicles offer a detailed description of a raid into the area. The nephews, Madog and Ithel, were informed that important people were at Llanddewibrefi, and with a blatant disregard for the right of sanctuary, they 'completely ravaged' the church and 'desecrated the churchyard'.[6] The impact on the inhabitants would have been considerable. Substantial amounts of loot were carried off – they are described as 'having taken infamous spoil from the precincts of the saints, David and Padarn'. Furthermore, they burnt dwellings, agricultural buildings and corn, leaving people without food and shelter. What they could not take they destroyed. During this assault Cadwgan and Owain took shelter on an Irish merchant vessel off the coast. Following this attack Owain fled to Ireland and Ceredigion resumed its fate as both bargaining chip and bone of contention. Henry intervened and offered to restore Ceredigion to Cadwgan as long as he paid a hefty sum and swore not to contact his son in Ireland. This settlement was brief as Owain soon returned to Ceredigion. With the aid of men from the county, he attacked Dyfed to the south. In response, Henry granted Ceredigion to Gilbert de Clare, who already owned swathes of land in England. Although Henry eventually made peace with Owain – they went on a military expedition to Normandy together – Gilbert's settlements remained.

Cadwgan was murdered in 1111, and two years later Rhys ap Tewdwr's son, Gruffudd, retuned from exile in Ireland. His arrival heralded trouble. This was the time of the hotheads (*Ynfydion*), young men who joined this aspirant and audacious leader in an attempt to improve their fortunes.[7] Again, Ceredigion was a focal point for this conflict. The chronicles detail his military activities in the county and represent him unfavourably; it is there that his followers were deemed hotheads. In this, the first test for Gilbert's settlers, the climax came outside a castle near Aberystwyth. This was the first castle built near this town in 1110 to the side of Rhydyfelin. In a brief battle, Gruffudd's men were overwhelmed by a cavalry charge from the fortress – reinforcements had arrived overnight from Ystradmeurig castle to the east. The chronicler saw this as just punishment for an army which had stolen and consumed the cattle of Llanbadarn Fawr church the night before the encounter. In order to placate Gruffudd, the king granted him part of Cantref Mawr to the south of Ceredigion. Two decades later, however, Gruffudd had a second opportunity to invade the area.

During 1135 English events once again had repercussions for Ceredigion. Henry I died, and Welsh leaders took advantage of the struggle between his daughter, Matilda, and his nephew, Stephen. In the years before Henry's death, Gwynedd had begun to assume greater stature on the Welsh stage. By 1136 forces from the resurgent northern territory had struck south into Ceredigion, burning castles including Walter's Castle, near Llandre. This assault was launched after the death of the area's lord, Richard fitz Gilbert, son of Gilbert de Clare who was killed near Crickhowell as he returned to Ceredigion. These two deaths ignited the dry tinder of Ceredigion. On their second attack the forces from Gwynedd, numbering some 6,000 troops and 2,000 'mailed horsemen' were aided by Gruffudd, who assailed the Normans from the south.[8] North and south joined forces at Cardigan where they encountered and defeated a force of Normans and Flemings, many of whom drowned in the Teifi. Despite this success, Cardigan castle was not occupied.

This was a substantial set back for the colonizers, who had to defend Cardigan against another attack in 1138. The death of Gruffudd in 1137 led to Owain Gwynedd taking possession of Ceredigion and dividing it between his son Hywel and his brother Cadwaladr – the former was granted the portion south of the Aeron and the latter the northern part. In the first half of the twelfth century Ceredigion fell under the sway of Powys, the Normans and Gwynedd. Yet from around 1150 Ceredigion increasingly came within Deheubarth's sphere of influence. Disputes broke out among the house of Gwynedd, and the sons of Gruffudd ap Rhys, now old enough to assert their claims through force, took the land south of the Aeron. The following year they had taken most of the region. The 1151 campaign included a long siege of Llanrhystud castle. After one of his brothers was killed and another incapacitated, Rhys ap Gruffudd assumed leadership of Deheubarth in 1155. There is a tradition that in the same year a battle took place at Mwnt, then part of Rhys's kingdom. Flemings attacked from the sea and locals repelled their assault. Up until the eighteenth century games on the first Sunday of January (*Sul Coch y Mwnt*) were held there in memory of this victory. And even though these sports faded, place-names, such as Nant-Fflyman and Blaenfflyman, are reminders of a time when Ceredigion's coast was invaded.

In the following year Henry II, Matilda's son, became king, and Rhys ap Gruffudd assumed leadership of Deheubarth. Henry soon turned his attention to Wales and tried to bring the Welsh under control as they had been in his grandfather's day. By 1163 Rhys and other Welsh leaders had submitted to Henry at Woodstock, but this did not last for long. Rhys scored military successes in Ceredigion, where he ejected Flemish settlers, and helped initiate a general Welsh uprising. In 1165 he took Cardigan castle, honourably allowing its occupants to leave with half of their possessions. Henry II, meanwhile, was engaged against Louis VII of France. Foreshadowing, Owain Glyndŵr's contact with France in the fifteenth century, Rhys and Owain Gwynedd offered to support the French monarch. In 1171 Henry made peace with Rhys, granting him the title lord when he became justiciar of south Wales in 1172.

Changes in society and culture during this period were manifold. The arrival of new inhabitants meant castles and settlements appeared. Languages other than Welsh were heard more often as the English, French and Flemings settled there. The presence of the latter especially struck chroniclers who described them as 'folk of strange origin and customs' who sought land in Britain because much of their native territory had been flooded.[9] Arguably, this influx of settlers, rather than raiders, generated an awareness of what it meant to be Welsh. Increased contact with others led, from the early twelfth century, to the Welsh adapting the title Welsh more often than British for themselves. Despite population movements in Ceredigion during this period, by 1170 Ceredigion was in Welsh hands.

Whilst the annals do not paint as dramatic a picture of the impact of the Flemings on Ceredigion as they do in south-west Pembrokeshire – where migrants from Flanders cleared the native population – Flemish settlements were established in parts of the county. Castell Flemish, some three miles northwest of Tregaron, may well indicate their presence, though some have doubted this.[10] To the south-west there is more evidence of Flemish ethnically homogenous settlements. The chronicles mention a specific place, Blaen-porth, where the Flemings had established themselves. We get to hear of this place because Gruffudd ap Rhys burnt it during his rampage through the area in 1116. Accounts of this conflict also shed light on Saxon colonizers and the use of land in Ceredigion at this time. The Saxons had, according to the chronicler, occupied a land which was 'before almost completely empty from a scarcity of people'.[11] Perhaps the warmer climate in the period, which persisted until the thirteenth century, attracted these settlers. This ethnic group – the old English – were spread throughout the rural areas. It is important to remember that at this time the English did not benefit from many of the privileges accorded the French and Flemings. It was only later, at the end of the twelfth century, that these groups merged and became identified as English.

Although native resistance ensured that these pockets did not amount to the colonization of Ceredigion, footholds were established and different patterns of occupation and legal systems appeared. The Normans, and the English later on, are held to have introduced towns and castles to Wales. According to contemporaries and later historians such developments were proof of how they 'civilized' the Welsh. Nonetheless, this perception was based on a very particular definition of urban or civilized. While not conforming to the ordered plans of conquerors' towns, there is evidence of Welsh settlements which would, by different criteria, merit the name town. Trefilan in Ceredigion provides a good example of a native Welsh town. The forces of Rhys ap Gruffudd's son, Maelgwn ap Rhys, and his son, Maelgwn Fychan, of Deheubarth, established a castle there early in the thirteenth century. Records about this 'Welsh vil' disappear after the early fourteenth century, when documents were written detailing the payment made by its inhabitants for the occupation of the territory. The motte, situated near a stream which runs into the Aeron, serves as a reminder that the Welsh adapted to castle warfare.

Economic opportunities enticed the Flemings to the new Norman lands. These were enhanced by laws operating in the Marcher lordships which were brought by the conquerors to their enclaves in the west. Most notably, the law of Breteuil (named after a town in Normandy) enabled the creation of favoured town communities, membership of which was based on ethnic origin. No doubt this segregation bequeathed resentment. A significant pocket of outside influence was established at Cardigan. The first castle at Cardigan itself was founded by Gilbert de Clare in 1110 and held until 1165. From the description of its defenders during the battle of 1136, it is evident that the town contained a distinctive ethnic make-up. It is significant that there was no mention of the Saxons, who were also excluded from certain trading privileges by Breteuil Law in England at this time.

Distinctions between native and incomer evident in Cardigan were repeated on a less grand and enduring form in other parts of the county during the late eleventh and twelfth centuries. Although not as imposing as later constructions, mud and wood fortifications, such as those castles established at Lampeter (then called Pont Stephan) and Ystradmeurig, impacted on the lives of those around them. These structures could be speedily constructed, probably by forced labour. Moreover, they were strategically placed; there was at least one in most of the county's commotes. These were the initial steps which would, the Normans thought, lead to the conquest of Ceredigion. Therefore, when Lampeter (in the commote of Mabwynion) and Ystradmeurig (in Mefenydd) were burned in 1137 by forces from Gwynedd, this ambitious march was stalled. Enclaves like that formed in Cardigan could not be surely established inland.

Before the thirteenth century, stone castles were rare. However, Lord Rhys, in a demonstration of his influence over south-west Wales, began rebuilding in stone the Norman castle he had conquered in 1171. Roger Turvey has speculated that Normans residing in the borough contributed their knowledge and experience to Rhys's castle-building enterprise.[12] Unfortunately, due to rebuilding carried out from 1240, we do not know what this important structure looked like. In addition to demonstrating that a Welsh prince could build the primary architectural expression of power at the time, it is renowned as the site of the first Welsh 'eisteddfod'. Yet it cannot be claimed that this musical and poetic competition, held in 1176, was the direct forebear of the present festival. The term 'eisteddfod' was not used at the time; rather the event was described as a 'great feast'. All the same, this grand event illustrated the importance of music and poetry in Welsh life. It was an important event that invited contenders from all parts of Wales and beyond – invitations were sent to Ireland, Scotland and England. In a symmetrical result, the winner of the chair in the musical contest hailed from south Wales and the winning poet from the north. Of course, this was not a disinterested display as the leader underlined his importance through conspicuous feasting.

Ceredigion's religious complexion changed in this period. European monastic orders were established, overlaying or supplanting the earlier Celtic tradition. The Normans were keen to reform what they found, married clergy being one aspect which roused consternation. So, in addition to military conflict, there was an attempt to change the intellectual landscape. The Benedictines were particularly associated with the Normans. The order had its origins in Italy during the sixth century and, although there were Benedictine abbeys in England by the end of the seventh century, in Wales they were introduced by the Normans in territories they had brought under control, such as Abergavenny and Monmouth. This pattern of Norman castle and Benedictine monastery arriving together can be seen in Ceredigion. Gilbert was responsible for founding the priory at Cardigan after he had established a base there. The Black Monks (the Benedictines wore black cloaks) also appeared at Llanbadarn Fawr at this time; and some of the less favourable comments about Gruffudd ap Rhys found in the chronicles were due to this. Another example of how political power influenced religion in the county can be seen in the actions of Henry III. In 1245 Henry decided to take the advowson, the right to select rectors, at Llanbadarn Fawr. Such declarations were, however, buffeted by the military fluctuations which characterized these years. One of

Henry's clerks, Peter of Aubusson, who had been granted the living of Llanbadarn Fawr in 1251, would not have received a steady flow of revenues because the Crown's control of the area was not consolidated until 1277.

Church dedications and architecture bear the mark of Norman influence. An instance of the latter can be seen in Cellan, where the church's nave and chancel date from the thirteenth century – during this century many churches were built in Wales. Antiquarians have been particularly interested in this church's font. Although the man's face espied in the early nineteenth century is nowhere to be seen today, the font has an unusual square shape. In the years before it was restored by Herbert L. North, the font, then situated on the south wall of the nave, was used as a bin. Thirteenth-century transformations are also evinced by the history of Llandysul church which went from being a timber building to a stone structure during this period. Although some church dedications, including that of Cellan, are unknown, a brief glance at those that are reveals how there was a patchwork of religious fashions in the county. Along with the Celtic saints, like Tysul, there were dedications to other saints such as Peter (Lampeter) and Michael (Llanfihangel-y-Creuddyn and Penbryn). Many churches are dedicated to Saint Mary (Cardigan, Llanfairorllwyn, Llanfair Clydogau, Strata Florida and Tregaron). This dedication was also the most common in England, and this reflects a time when Welsh Christians were in closer contact with mainstream Christianity.

Nonetheless, Welsh Christianity continued to demonstrate distinct-iveness in these new conditions. Despite being introduced by the Normans, the Cistercians, particularly from their abbey of Strata Florida about two miles south of Pontrhydfendigaid in central Ceredigion, acted in ways deemed very Welsh and were a gadfly to the ambitions of English monarchs. In 1164, the monks from the Cistercian abbey at Whitland set up a colony near the brook called the Fflur about two miles from its later site. It was during this century that the Cistercians were at their strongest across western Europe. This settlement was set up under the auspices of Robert fitz Stephen, who controlled the area. The choice of this out-of-the-way location was governed by the ostensible rule that the order could not be granted fully developed estates. Indeed, the whole order, founded by St Bernard of Clairvaux, set out to return to something approximating the simple lives followed by early Christians, unlike those orders which, although set up with similar self-denying aims in mind, had put on extra pounds of wealth over the years. Soon after it was set up under Norman auspices, Rhys ap Gruffudd assumed control of the area and continued to nurture this religious establishment set up by his opponent; a charter sealed by

Rhys, which dates from 1184, mentions land, including some near the coast, granted by this powerful magnate. The monks kept the original name when they moved away from the Fflur, which may indicate that there was no political motivation, as some suggest, behind the move from the site granted by the Norman noble. In 1184 a new abbey was established, this building, that would play a pivotal role in Welsh history, was completed only well into the next century. An architectural reminder of its former greatness can be seen in the western door, a rare example of transitional Norman-English architecture. The continuing importance of sea transport is illustrated by the tradition that stones for the abbey came from Somerset via Aberarth, which was part of the land granted by Rhys.

Posterity has been kind to the Cistercians. Their political attachment to native princes, from both north and south Wales, will be addressed below in the context of the ongoing struggle for dominance. Another oft-admired aspect, tied to the political one, is founded on their lifestyle. A former inspector of ancient monuments for Wales, C. A. Ralegh Radford, stated that, compared with the long-established Benedictines, the Cistercians, with their 'emphasis on the ideals of simplicity and poverty, were more likely to appeal to the native temperament'. This idea of a group whose simplistic lifestyle harked back to that of the original Celtic saints has had considerable influence over the years. Gywnfor Evans's comment that this order 'fitted so well with Wales' sums up this opinion.[13]

Undoubtedly, there were some similarities between these monks and earlier manifestations of Christianity, and connections with Welsh society were strong. Living in out-of-the-way places, though rarely eschewing the grants of developed land as they were supposed to, led to comparisons being made with the early Welsh saints. It needs to be remembered, though, that this is very much an idea of both the early saints and the Cistercians, and was something which appealed as much to the imagination as to the rationality of later commentators because it served as a counter-image to the supposed degeneracy of those in power. The settlement in Strata Florida contributed to native economy through, for example, the rearing of sheep on the uplands, fishing along the coast, and barley and oats on low-lying land. Much of the work on the abbey's lands was carried out by lay brethren, men who lived as monks but were engaged in manual labour. These provided another link with the locality. Connections with Wales are evidenced in the names of the monks. All recorded names of the abbots are Welsh. With the establishment of Llanllŷr near Aberaeron, the Cistercians founded the only nunnery that the county has possessed. The women who lived there were celebrated as 'the white maidens of Llanllŷr' by the poet Huw Cae Llwyd in the later medieval period. In sum, the arrival of the Cistercians had a significant impact on the economy and culture of Ceredigion.

Records about Strata Florida provide an insight into aspects of the medieval mind. Ecclesiastical accounts, an important source for the cultural and social history of the pre-modern age, suggest that this remote monastic settlement was the site of debauchery and visions. In 1196, unruly behaviour among drunken lay brethren necessitated a visit by a senior figure from Whitland. Sometimes divisions between sections of the monastic community outweighed the benefits of having a large workforce, as the lay brethren could get frustrated because they had no role in decision making. Six years after this incident, a monk had a vision. He saw three angels spreading incense over the altar of the church that had been completed in 1201. 'Wrapped in an ecstasy of mind', this monk was taken by one of these divine angels 'towards the east' for a day and a night where more visions were played out before his mind's eye.[14] As he fell, he may well have revealed more than his ecstasy, because, according to Walter Map, Cistercians wore no underwear – supposedly to keep 'that part of the body cool', they believed that heat induced lust.[15] From a less mystic angle, this individual, who had been taken, presumably unconscious, to the infirmary by his fellow monks, had been struck by a physical illness inducing hallucination. Nonetheless, the very nature of his hallucination informs us of beliefs, such as the importance of 'the east' – Jerusalem was depicted as the centre of the world on maps of the period, and the Hereford *Mappa Mundi* placed the east towards the top. This vision occurred in the middle of a period (the twelfth and thirteenth centuries) that was the apex of dream-vision literature in Europe. So the stricken monk from Strata Florida was part of a wider culture of awe and fear of God. In addition to written records, images provide clues that help us understand belief systems. It is a pity that none of the twelfth-century seals used at Strata Florida remain, but other items, such as a bronze crucifix of Christ wearing the crown of thorns and a loincloth prove valuable. Relics like this one enable us to compare the ways in which Christ has been imagined at various times by different societies.

Gerald of Wales, who provides us with the longest and most detailed description of medieval Ceredigion, was not a friend of the Cistercians. He had been educated at the Benedictine abbey of St Peter, Gloucester (the motherhouse of Cardigan and Llanbadarn Fawr at the start of the twelfth century). Yet his disdain for what he deemed the avaricious Cistercians was personal rather than simply being the product of a different monastic order's prejudices. In fact, Gerald maintained that the monks of Strata Florida had swindled him out of his books.

In general, his account of Wales was more favourable than the one he gave of the Irish; his mother was part Welsh (the daughter of the well-known abductee, Nest) and his father, William de Barri, was Norman. As an assistant to Baldwin, archbishop of Canterbury, Gerald's role in the journey through Wales in 1188 was to further the recruitment of men for the third crusade. This intensification of the holy war between Christian and Muslim had been initiated by an appeal by Pope Clement III after the Muslim warrior Saladin had captured Jerusalem in 1187. We do not know how many of the estimated 3,000 volunteers who reputedly joined the crusade as a result of this mission came from the area. Although exact figures are not forthcoming, the account provides insights into the meanings attached to religion and life at the time. The journey through Ceredigion lasted from 30 March to 7 April and followed a route from Cardigan in the south, via Lampeter, Strata Florida and Llanddewibrefi to Llanbadarn Fawr in the north. This portion of the journey provided Gerald with instances of divine intervention and examples of devotion among the populace. A woman, 'one of the matrons of Cardigan', who prevented her husband going on the crusade was 'punished' when she rolled over and suffocated her son in bed. Cautionary tales like these stressed the duties of Christians and God's ability to intervene in this life as well as the next. Evidently, fear was felt to be as good a way to compel people to join the crusade as faith alone. The role of women in impeding, facilitating and giving their sanction to this cause is also illustrated by an elderly woman from the same town who expressed her pride when her only son and 'sole comfort' went to fight.[16]

Gerald tells us more about the salmon and beavers that occupied the Teifi than about the common people who occupied the land. Yet he mentioned how sick people went to a field outside Cardigan where Baldwin had preached and were cured there. But details about the lives of the lowliest inhabitants are not elucidated. According to the medieval historian T. Jones Pierce, though, significant changes were taking place. By the end of the thirteenth century in Ceredigion serfdom, or villeinage, had declined. This 'early ending of absolute servitude' was suggested by the lack of reference in contemporary records to *tir cyfrif* – the arable strips given out to bond males. Pierce argued that this indicated 'an intrinsic cultural difference between two regions', Ceredigion and north Wales – where such practices persisted for many years. Perhaps fewer bondmen made the area a better re-cruiting ground for the crusade. Sermons from Urban II onwards were aimed at those termed the 'fighting classes', not the enervated poor. At Lampeter, Gerald informed readers: 'Many persons were induced to take the Cross'. In his history of the town W. J. Lewis cast doubt on this claim. The Welsh, he contended, were unlikely to have flocked in great numbers because those who were calling them to fight were Normans.[17] Yet it is not unreasonable to assume that this conflict, between believer and unbeliever, was something which could unite local enemies in the call to arms. After all, Lord Rhys accompanied Baldwin and Gerald through his lands from Cardigan to the river Dyfi. The sanction of this eminent Welshman might well have encouraged many to embark on a crusade.

Some of those who listened to the recruiting sermons of 1188 may well have ended up fighting fellow Christians, both Welsh and English. Unlike their father, who had cooperated with his brothers, the sons of Lord Rhys struggled amongst themselves. Moreover, at one point he was incarcerated by his offspring. Fortunately, for Lord Rhys, one of the sons who imprisoned him, Hywel Sais, had a change of heart and released his father. Yet Rhys himself was restless, too, and his ambitions may have heightened the appetite of his sons. With the death of Henry II in 1189, and his son Richard's overriding interest in overseas ventures, there was an opportunity to increase their sphere of influence. Rhys grasped this and carried out a series of successful attacks on Norman fortifications, such as St Clears. There followed years in which inter-family conflict contributed to the decline of Deheubarth, and led, in part, to the centre of power in Wales shifting northwards. Some rips, which contributed to the tearing apart of a once pre-eminent part of Wales, took place in Ceredigion. The main contenders among Rhys's sons were Maelgwn and Gruffudd; the latter was the heir in waiting, Maelgwn, his half-brother, the aspirant. Both had concentrations of support in parts of their father's land, Gruffudd in Ystrad Tywi and Maelgwn in Ceredigion. Although Deheubarth long-standing distinctions between parts of Rhys's territory enabled his sons to found pockets of influence. Ceredigion was defined as being culturally distinct by Gerald of Wales, when, in his *Description of Wales*, he recounts the area's reputation for speaking the best Welsh because it was 'the heartland of Wales'.[18] Such distinctions no doubt contributed to the local patriotism that enabled the sons of Rhys to establish bases.

Ystradmeurig castle was an important site in this struggle. By this time it was a stone construction, and in 1193 Maelgwn overwhelmed it. Siege engines, 'slings and catapults', were used in the attack, their first recorded use in Wales.[19] Both types of weapon were employed in the east during the crusades. Two years later Rhys made use of this castle to imprison another two of his sons, Rhys Gryg and Maredudd, who had attempted to usurp their ageing father's authority in the south (Rhys was now about sixty-three). After campaigns against the Normans, which involved the burning of Carmarthen, Rhys died in 1197. Again, the fortunes of Ystradmeurig castle illustrated the shifting fortunes of nobles. About a decade after his father's death, Maelgwn, confronted by an aggrandizing Llywelyn ab Iorwerth of Gwynedd who had already taken over southern Powys, took apart this castle lest it fell to the northerner. Up until this retreat from the northern part of his territory, Maelgwn had experienced a period of ascendancy. He had cooperated with Gwenwynwyn of southern Powys, and taken Aberystwyth where they also captured Gruffudd. Despite continuing his advance, taking Cardigan and Ystradmeurig, Maelgwn was faced by Gruffudd once more, and lost all territory except the aforementioned strongholds. Cardigan, known as the 'key of Wales', was also to prove a key to a short period in which Maelgwn held most of Ceredigion. At the end of 1199 he sold the castle to King John of England. In return, John gave Maelgwn the rest of the county – with the exception of the half commote of Is Hirwern next to the castle – and Cilgerran and Emlyn. Soon after this, Maelgwn's fortunes were furthered when Gruffudd died. However, his position depended on the support of Gwenwynwyn. When his ally was imprisoned by John in 1208, the other northern ruler, Llywelyn, took southern Powys. Two sons of Gruffudd were allied to Llywelyn, and he rewarded them when he struck into Ceredigion. Keeping the most northerly *cantref* of Penweddig for himself, Llywelyn gave Gruffudd's two sons, Rhys and Owain, the land north of the Aeron. In 1210, Maelgwn attempted to cross this long-standing geographical divide. Not far into his opponent's territory, at Cilcennin, his force was routed in a night attack.

When John and his Welsh allies brought Llywelyn to heel in 1211, he inadvertently set in train circumstances which led to Llywelyn's revival. The English, with no powerful Welsh leader to counter them, were now dominant. There was an attempt to found a castle at Aberystwyth. Maelgwn's reaction, an attack on this encroaching royal influence, heralded an alliance with his former enemy. Indeed, Llywelyn's fortunes rose as John's declined. Whereas the latter was compelled to accept the Magna Carta, Llywelyn was at Aberdyfi deciding who would get portions of land. This partition saw the two rival branches of Lord Rhys's bloodline, Maelgwn and the sons of Gruffudd, receive parts of the region. Until 1240, when Llywelyn died, Ceredigion orbited Gwynedd, but it was not a steady orbit. Cardigan attracted the Norman adventurer William Marshall, and later it passed from him to the Crown and the care of Hubert de Burgh, first Earl of Kent, only to fall to a Welsh force led by Maelgwn's son in 1231. In addition, Strata Florida remained, in D. H. Williams's words, at 'the forefront of Welsh affairs' even though the centre of power had moved from south to north Wales.[20] Here, in 1238, Llywelyn attempted to secure his lands for his son, David, by gathering various Welsh leaders there to declare their allegiance.

In the past, the Welsh had profited from the deaths of English kings. When Llywelyn died in 1240 the tables were turned, and the waves of English influence, which Llywelyn had held back, began to wash against the area. Gilbert Marshall's forces took Cardigan. Yet a new barrier to English influence, Llywelyn ab Iorwerth's grandson, Llywelyn ap Gruffudd, arrived in 1256, and his presence ensured that nine and a half of the region's commotes remained in Welsh hands. Dependence, although offering security, left the minor rulers vulnerable when their lord was defeated in 1277. These descendants of Lord Rhys were too weak to oppose the English. Allegiances switched from Llywelyn to Edward I, except for Rhys ap Maelgwn who fled to Gwynedd. The English met no resistance. Rhys's men abandoned the commote of Genau'r-glyn with such haste that they 'left their land and their corn waste'.[21] Such food reserves would have fuelled the forces sent to the north by Edmund, Edward I's brother, in 1277. He commenced building the castle at Aberystwyth at the site where the ruins stand today. This marked a turning point in the area's history. Over sixty years earlier an attempt by English forces to found a base here had been foiled by Maelgwn, but with the arrival of Edmund the hitherto delayed era of increased English influence began.

III

From Conquest to the Arrival
of Owain Glyndŵr

The establishment of a castle at Aberystwyth (known as Llanbadarn in the period covered by this chapter) signalled a new era in Cardiganshire's history. There were rebellions before the end of the thirteenth century, but the English had never been in such an advantageous position in the area. Cardigan had been in English hands since 1241; the town and part of the commote of Iscoed were being referred to as a 'county', or shire, from the 1240s. In time the term would encompass the adjoining areas, thus transforming Ceredigion into Cardiganshire. Aberystwyth castle pegged down the northern part of the region. More importantly, it blocked the route along which Gwynedd's leaders had previously struck south. Located by the sea, it could withstand a siege far better than if it were situated inland. Indeed, it was too close to the sea as by 1280 parts of it were being undermined by the waves. This castle of stone was part of what a specialist on medieval fortifications, C. J. Spurgeon, called an 'unparalleled programme of castle building' in the twenty years after 1277.[1] Put simply, this attempt to shackle the ambitions of Welsh leaders was initiated by Edward I; inspired by his experiences in Gascony; often designed by castle architects from Savoy (one of these, Master Giles of St George, came to Aberystwyth in 1282); and executed by craftsmen from the west of England.

It was an irony not lost on Ralph A. Griffiths that a town now welded to Welsh cultural identity owed its inception to the ascendant Edward I; it was no Trefilan.[2] The year in which the construction began, 1277, saw Llywelyn ap Gruffudd ensconced in Gwynedd. Although he was there only from July to September, Edmund, Edward I's younger brother and duke of Lancaster, contributed to the foundation of the borough and the evolution of the entity that became Cardiganshire. In 1265 Edward, before assuming the throne, had given Cardigan and Carmarthen to Edmund. Both towns and the territories accompanying them were effectively marcher lordships – local officials were chosen by Edmund not Edward. Fortunately for the king,

Edmund sought lands elsewhere and in 1279 he received tracts of
Derbyshire in return for Carmarthen and an embryonic Cardiganshire –
but the castles were still under the control of Lancaster. Edward held
the commotes north of the Aeron – Pennardd was given to Geoffrey
Clement. The final triumph of 1282 led to the erosion of Welsh
lordship in the lands south of the Aeron. Cardiganshire, therefore,
owed its origins to two wars against the Welsh and a transaction
between English royal siblings. At the same time, however, it was
founded on an ancient land called Ceredigion. Nonetheless, some parts,
the lordships of Caron and Llanddewibrefi which became components of
the county after the 1536 Act of Union, were not mentioned in the
settlement of 1284.

Edmund would probably have received the hospitality of the rector
of Llanbadarn Fawr, Anthony Bek, during his stay. Historians have
regarded Bek as being more of a soldier than a holy man. Later, Bek
pursued his ambitions further and became the bishop of Durham in
1284 and patriarch of Jerusalem in 1305. Evidently, the sword in
tandem with the cross reaped rewards. He was renowned for his
extravagance and was one of many eminent royal favourites who
became rectors of Llanbadarn Fawr – another was the academic
M. Thomas Bradwardine who acquired the living in 1346. Bek, the
warrior clergyman, was a fitting resident in 1277. Edward I may have
been the first English ruler to establish himself securely in the former
Welsh region of Ceredigion, but this foothold needed to be protected.
A wall, costing £200, was built around the town in 1280, only to be
breached in 1282 when the Welsh conquered the incomplete castle – it
was something that could be taken but not defended, so they
demolished the work in progress. After twelve years, and £4,300, the
castle was completed. International finance contributed to the English
war effort. Italian bankers financed a substantial part of the cost of
Edward's conquest. For example, the Riccardi of Lucca provided
money to pay troops in the area during 1277.

Once the risk of Welsh rebellion receded in the fourteenth century,
the county faced the less bloody, though no less capricious, vagaries of
trade and harvest. Questions about medieval towns have preoccupied
historians, and it is worth relating the situation in Cardiganshire to
these debates. In a comparative study of English and French towns,
R. H. Hilton argued that 'the town has to be distinguished from its rural
hinterland and not, as some historians have tended to do, to be
assimilated into the agrarian economy and society'. Hilton highlighted
three features which defined medieval towns: a 'permanent market';
'occupational heterogeneity'; and an 'institutional dimension', which
set its inhabitants apart – this usually took the form of certain freedoms

granted to a section of the urban population.[3] Cardiganshire towns were small and scarce. Maurice Beresford has calculated which counties were the 'most intensely urbanized' in England and Wales c.1348, albeit by a rather crude method of dividing a county's area by the number of towns within its borders. According to this measure, the county came forty-first out of fifty-four.[4] Neighbouring Carmarthenshire was tenth and Pembrokeshire, just behind Glamorganshire, was thirteenth. The town of Carmarthen was the seat of the justiciar. At first judicial proceedings moved between Aberystwyth, Cardigan and Carmarthen, but by the 1320s the latter entirely absorbed the judicial role.

Still, measured against Hilton's yardstick, Cardiganshire's towns merit the title. Their small size, however, makes the issue of how distinct they were from the surrounding area a moot point. Both the port towns, Cardigan and Aberystwyth, possessed markets. A day set aside for trading did not guarantee success, and concerns about the economic vitality of towns provide an insight into their relationship with their hinterlands. Regulations concerning markets illustrate the third of Hilton's characteristics of a medieval town. Commercial jealousy resulted in some inhabitants acquiring privileges in trade. Therefore, a legal distinction was drawn between town and country, or rather a privileged group and those without rights to trade. Even though it is hard to calculate the effect of these regulations, protests that they were not being obeyed and the frequent grant of rights of trade to non-burgesses indicate that the burgesses could not monopolize commerce. The payments of money for non-burgesses to trade were called *censes*. At the end of the thirteenth century, Aberystwyth burgesses were granting *censes*, costing 9 *s.*, to trade in Llanilar. Similar privileges existed for the twenty-one who bought this right in Cardigan in the early years of the fourteenth century. Others could easily circumvent this restriction, as protests by burgesses reveal. Tension existed between purportedly privileged townsfolk and those who refused to comply with regulations. In 1305 most of the trade in the land between the Aeron and the Dyfi, became the sole preserve of Aberystwyth's burgesses and those who paid for the privilege. Cardigan probably had a similar sphere of influence south of the Aeron. Yet these assertions did not eradicate traders operating without the permission of burgesses. A protest dating from the 1330s complained of those who traded in areas beyond Aberystwyth, and that this hamstrung their Monday market.

Both Aberystwyth and Cardigan grew in the early fourteenth century. Later a long period of stagnation and decline set in. Even during its better days Cardigan's inhabitants were not eager to hand over money. They responded to a request for men and contributions towards supplying a ship for Edward I's campaign against Robert the Bruce with a letter underlining their poverty, stressing local dangers and the need to keep men in Cardigan. Perhaps they did protest too much. Even so, these towns were not conspicuously wealthy. Archaeologists have concluded that the dearth of items discovered in their environs indicates that Cardiganshire's ports were not flourishing. Returns of the wine entering Cardigan recorded in custom returns collated by E. A. Lewis provide some indication of the town's consumption of luxuries compared to other places. In 1307–8 five ships carrying wine arrived at Carmarthen, and one at Cardigan. In 1315–16, three docked at the former, while none called at the latter.[5] It appears that the burgesses of both Cardiganshire ports did not inhabit especially wealthy places. Indeed, a petition to the monarch sent by the burgesses of Cardigan dating from the mid-1380s, protesting at the cessation of a county court held there, described the town and castle as being 'in decay'.[6]

Another defining feature of Welsh towns was their ethnic composition. Like Caernarfon and Conwy, most of Cardigan's burgesses had English names. Aberystwyth, however, was an exception. Welsh names constituted almost half of the 112 burgesses recorded in a list from the first decade of the fourteenth century. By contrast, Cardigan, in 1301–2, had only five burgesses with Welsh names out of 102. Names provide only an approximate guide to origin, but the differences between the towns are significant; there were no instances of the patronymic 'ab' or 'ap' in Cardigan. This difference has been explained by the fact that Cardigan was older than its northern neighbour. However, in a Welsh context, new towns like Conwy and Caernarfon were almost entirely English. So there may have been other factors at work in Aberystwyth, which was one of few Edwardian towns containing a substantial Welsh population. Maybe the inhabitants of the area were deemed trustworthier, or the north Walian towns simply offered greater economic opportunities for English settlers.

Besides these ports there were towns which, though lacking castles, were still significant. Tregaron, part of the lordship which Edward I gave to Geoffrey Clement, and therefore technically outside the county, held a market on Tuesday; this right, together with the permission to hold two fairs during the year, was given by Edward in 1292. Tregaron's streets differed from the grid-like pattern of Aberystwyth, and I. Soulsby has taken this as evidence that Clement did not fundamentally alter the form of the original Welsh settlement.[7] Lampeter, to the south, had been established as a borough in 1285 and held a market and yearly fair. Information from 1302–3 tells us something about the town when it was held by the Crown. The rent and survey of 1302–3 name the burgesses of Lampeter, the majority of whom (nineteen of the twenty-one) bore Welsh names. And it must be remembered that this was at a time when the town was under royal control after the rebellion of its former lord. The original grant had been given to Rhys ap Maredudd, who lost the property in the aftermath of his rebellion in 1287. In 1309 it passed to Rhys ap Gruffudd, a steadfast supporter of Edward II. Atpar was a sizeable borough. In 1326 there were ninety-six burgesses (two of which were shared between two people). Like Lampeter, their names indicate that the majority were of Welsh origin. Moreover, twenty-five of these burgesses were held by females, like Eva, daughter of Ieuan ap Cadogan and Lleucu daughter of Adaf. This borough was in the hands of St Davids, and fortunately this meant that agricultural activity in 1326 was recorded in the *Black Book of St David's*.[8]

What of Cardiganshire outside the towns? Few remaining records indicate the nature and extent of agricultural activity. All the same, there is evidence to support R. R. Davies's comment that the Welsh landscape in 1350 was more like that of 1650 than 1050.[9] An archeological investigation near Llanfair Clydogau detected traces of rabbit farming, in the form of a breeding mound, dating from the late fourteenth century. The majority of rabbit warrens in Wales have been dated later than this, so these remains – which also include the remnants of a warren keeper's dwelling – support Davies's argument. In other respects, however, the county lacked those features which fuelled medieval commerce. The fulling mill, the sole indicator of investment in the textile industry, did not appear in Cardiganshire until the fifteenth century, and during the fourteenth century the industry was concentrated in eastern Wales. There were mills in the county, and wool was gathered from flocks, but this component of medieval industrial evolution was absent.

Records of the arable crops grown on one of the manors of the bishop of St Davids in the county – Llandygwydd – show that wheat, rye, oats, barley, peas and beans were grown. But it is difficult to generalize about the features of fourteenth-century arable farming in Cardiganshire from this as we have returns for only one year, 1326. Livestock returns for the same year indicate the type of pastoral activity carried out in the county. In a survey of medieval farming in Wales, R. Ian Jack stated that the 'principal question about Welsh stock-rearing is the balance between sheep and cattle'.[10] After studying available returns Jack concluded that there was a north/south divide: sheep predominated in south Wales and cattle formed a more significant fraction in the north. Information for Cardiganshire revealed that the numbers of both were similar. Llanddewibrefi forest contained some 240 head of cattle – more than any other manor mentioned in the

Black Book of St David's – whereas in Llandygwydd there were 200 sheep to twenty-four cattle. Extracts from correspondence reveal the value of cattle in medieval times. Robert Tibetot, who was then constable of Cardigan castle, boasted how he returned to Cardigan with 3,000 cattle after attacking Trefilan in 1282. Atpar returned twenty-four pigs out of the total of thirty-six. These returns represent only a fraction of the economic activity carried out in the county, but they constitute a valuable vignette. Although fishing is not mentioned, this pursuit, whether carried out at sea, by the river or using long-standing fish traps, such as those near Aberarth, must have formed part of the rural economy.

The victories of 1277 had been won with few swords being unsheathed in Cardiganshire. Yet in the years following the establishment and extension of royal power there were bloodier conflicts. The area was a significant theatre during the rebellion of 1282–3, which was incited by resentment of English power asserted after 1277. An example of how the behaviour of the English authorities and their Welsh supporters caused resentment can be seen in an episode played out in the northern commote of Genau'r-glyn. Not long before the revolt of 1282, Llywelyn ap Gruffudd wrote to Edward I reporting how, while he was hunting in Meirionnydd, a stag fled from his party and crossed the river Dyfi into Genau'r-glyn. After following their quarry, those who governed the area for the king confronted them, and they called together the local population to face the hunting party. The stag was taken from Llywelyn and they behaved aggressively towards his men. Therefore, Llywelyn requested that the king reprimand the aggressors.[11] The incident of the stag in northern Cardiganshire did not provoke war, but the details relayed by Llywelyn reveal how local friction was an important matter, and that Llywelyn was acting in a deferential, though assertive, manner towards his liege lord. Indeed, Llywelyn did not start this rebellion, although he soon became involved and came to lead it. His brother, Dafydd, initiated the violent expression of discontent in north Wales that boiled over because Welsh law and custom were being overridden.

Assaults in Cardiganshire succeeded in the north, where Aberystwyth was taken and its inhabitants put to the sword. These initial occupants paid dearly for their ambitions. Bogo de Knoville, the constable, was captured through the common ruse of an invitation to eat with someone (in this case the Welsh leader Gruffudd ap Maredudd) who sprung a trap and captured his guest. In the years leading up to the revolt some of the native leaders were not allies. Two brothers based at Trefilan, Gruffudd and Cynan ap Maredudd, laid claim to the northern commotes held by Rhys Fychan. John E. Morris, in his history of Edward I's Welsh campaigns, describes a series of sudden strikes and a 'fury' which made the English unsure of where the next blow would fall.[12] For a short time, these Welsh rebels were the arrow of the English as Edward was the hammer of the Scots. Gruffudd, Cynan and Rhys, drove their enemies to Dinefwr, in Carmarthenshire, and Cardigan. Initial success was not sustained, however. Cardigan did not fall. Royal forces and allies took the lands of the two brothers – this was when Tibetot acquired the vast herd of cattle. Their cousin, Rhys ap Maredudd, who was granted their lands, benefited from loyalty to king over family. After the death of Llywelyn ap Gruffudd on 11 December 1282 the insurrection withered. By January 1283, Aberystwyth had been reached, Roger de Mortimer was established as constable there, and Cynan and Rhys capitulated. Gruffudd escaped and joined Dafydd in north Wales, but by June he surrendered. With these men incarcerated, the only influential native lord was Llywelyn ab Owain – Maredudd's and Cynan's nephew. His youth absolved him from Edward's desire for revenge, and as well as portions of land in southern Cardiganshire, the king granted Llywelyn the right to hold a market and fair at Llandysul. Significantly, Owain Glyndŵr was Llywelyn's great-grandson, and this provided the later rebel with an important base in south Wales.

Other rebellions resounded through Cardiganshire before the arrival of Glyndŵr. Firstly, only four years after the last rebellion was smothered, one of those who had benefited from the defeat of this rising, Rhys ap Maredudd, revolted. This brief uprising began and ended in 1287. Rhys was based in Carmarthenshire, but held land in Cardiganshire. As well as being disappointed by the amount of territory he had received, he was, more importantly, frustrated by the lack of liberty to impose his will on these lands. The justiciar, Tibetot, was a powerful figure, and his influence irritated Rhys, who was hanged at York for instigating this uprising. Support for him was not forthcoming from Cardiganshire; he had, after all, benefited from a rebellion against men with greater links with the area than he had. Leaders able to garner more support in the region, and conduct an uprising founded on more than personal pique, led a rebellion in 1294. Cynan ap Maredudd, and the son of Rhys Fychan, Maelgwn, found Cardiganshire ripe for rebellion. Other risings occurred in north and south-east Wales, which compelled Edward to cancel a French expedition. They were, however, not as fortunate as the insurgents of 1282. Resentment towards the English officials may have been intense, but Aberystwyth was not taken, although the land around it was occupied. The rebellion in Cardiganshire crumbled as the king moved southward after defeating Madog ap Llywelyn. In 1294–5, the initial royal leash of 1277 was tightened and this marked, according to Ralph A. Griffiths, the end of the Welsh lords' ability 'to assert to themselves as the traditional, hereditary, almost natural leaders of Cardiganshire society'.[13] This era of dynastic influence ended in a succession of defeats, as battling against English military and administrative might proved futile. If 1277 marked the beginning of the end of traditional leaders, 1295 was the end. Cynan, despite dressing as a leper to conceal his identity, was captured at Brecon. Ingenuity and initiative could only take the Welsh rebels so far. An illustration of how the royal forces exercised control over the county, consequently changing the landscape, can be seen in the orders given to Strata Florida in 1294 to clear woods on their extensive lands, thus limiting the opportunity for ambush.

Increased English influence in Cardiganshire during this period is evinced the establishment of a collegiate church at Llanddewibrefi in 1287 by the bishop of St Davids, Thomas Bek. Overshadowed somewhat by Strata Florida and Llanbadarn Fawr, where his brother Anthony had been rector, this institution was one of only six of its kind established in medieval Wales. It provides an example of how an older Celtic religious centre was altered into something in keeping with English tastes and more useful to the Crown. This site of St David's earlier victory at a synod held there was not transformed into a continental-style monastery; instead this old centre was turned into a college – as at Llangadog in Carmarthenshire. The emergence of a college at Llanddewibrefi was linked to the English conquest because Edward and his advisors saw the potential profitability of extending Canterbury's control over the Welsh dioceses. Glanmor Williams has suggested that Rhys ap Maredudd's rebellion in 1287 may have stimulated efforts to transform Welsh cultural institutions.[14]

A collegiate church was made up of secular canons much like a cathedral chapter. The canons lived in a community and were supported by prebends from tithes. Numerous churches in the locality contributed their tithes to its upkeep. One of the reasons for establishing institutions like this was to offer regular prayers for the souls of the dead and living. At Llanddewibrefi these included the souls of Edward I and his successors. Collegiate churches also provided ways to reward clerics through dispensing patronage. St Davids was a large diocese, so the base at Llanddewibrefi would have aided the spread of the cathedral's influence. During the Hundred Years War, the Crown needed to exploit its resources and expand its power. At Llanddewibrefi, the king chose canons who owed their positions to him and were thus likely to return favours. This placement of king's men occurred during periods when the bishopric of St Davids was empty. In 1361, for instance, eight individuals bearing non-Welsh names appear to have been chosen by the king. Perhaps the plague was the reason why so many posts had to be filled. Richard III also placed men at Llanddewibrefi in 1389.

For native leaders any advancement in their status would not come through rebellion. Consequently, the story of Cardiganshire's native leaders was, in the main, about loyalty to the English monarch rather than rejection of his authority. Local notables were unlikely to rise to the highest positions in the region or even occupy prime administrative posts; when particularly successful they owed their position to the king. This is not to say that the Welsh elite in Cardiganshire were English puppets, they still held a privileged position in Welsh society which meant having influence, if not carte blanche. The most influential native during the early part of the thirteenth century was not based in the county, but in Carmarthenshire – a reminder of Carmarthen's significance at this time. Rhys ap Gruffudd inherited his father's lands in that county during 1308, and then received the stewardship of Cardigan. He was granted Lampeter, and he also, towards the end of his life, held property in Llanrhystud in the north of the county. This connection between local lord and king led to men from Cardiganshire being drawn into conflicts such as that of 1316 against the Glamorgan rebel Llywelyn Bren. Later, early in 1322, the year that Edward's forces defeated Thomas, earl of Lancaster, Rhys was ordered to prepare the men of Cardigan between the ages of sixteen and sixty to act as a reserve to serve the king's cause wherever needed; 1,000 men from Carmarthenshire and Cardiganshire marched to Newcastle upon Tyne in April.

Many medieval people travelled substantial distances in order to trade, visit shrines or to fight. It is likely that Cardiganshire men served under the king's banner in Scotland. The loyalty which Rhys ap Gruffudd evinced for Edward II contrasted with the machinations of Marcher lords, notably Lancaster and Edward's nemesis Roger Mortimer. Like a number of Welshmen, Rhys who was deputy justiciar of south Wales in the 1320s, remained loyal to Edward. This loyalty may have derived from the fact that Edward was born in Wales. After Edward was killed in 1327, Rhys's fortunes fluctuated. He was forgiven, but then supported a rebellion and fled. Nonetheless, when Edward III disposed of his mother's paramour, Mortimer, in 1330, Rhys did not suffer for his previous loyalty to the new king's father. When a rebellious individual played an important role in governance defeat did not necessarily mean ruin. Indeed, Rhys was knighted and continued to raise troops from the lands entrusted to him for France in the 1340s. In 1346 they took part in the battle of Crécy, where cross-bowmen with wet strings and tired cavalry were defeated by archers. He died in 1356, but Dafydd ap Gwilym immortalized his name. Instead of berating the old Saxon foe, Welsh poets of this period, including Dafydd ap Gwilym, expressed antipathy towards the Scottish and the French. Rhys's record was one of loyalty, which was of especial value during the turbulent fourteenth century. But, as will be seen in the following chapter, the emotions stirred by powerful Welshmen could work against English monarchs as well as for them. Aspirations could be thwarted and satisfied by English kings.

Records listing royal officials reveal that Cardiganshire had more Welshmen in influential positions than Carmarthenshire. This may indicate that there were fewer English in the former county. Nonetheless, loyal and ambitious men were in good supply. One man, bearing the lengthy name of Rhys ap Gruffudd ap Llywelyn ab Ieuan, was paid 50 *s.* in 1394 for having raised money for the king from the county. Nevertheless, the ambitions of Welshmen in Cardiganshire were also stymied. Despite being chosen as the deputy constable of Cardigan castle in 1348, Adda ap Llywelyn was removed from the post when his superior was reminded that the appointment breached Edward I's instruction that Welshmen should not hold a key post in any castle. Adda, however, continued to hold responsible positions and was involved in the movement of troops to fight in France.

Culture and power were entwined. Just as Lord Rhys heard his generosity sung at the musical gathering over which he presided in Cardigan, fourteenth-century poets often wrote about county notables. Praise was thus broadcast and presumably believed by many; bardic patrons could be assured that their deeds, fictional and factual, would be sown in the poet's wake. Dafydd ap Gwilym is the best known of these wandering poets, indeed, he is considered to be the greatest Welsh medieval poet. He was born around 1320 in Brogynin, between Aberystwyth and Tal-y-bont. Poets like Dafydd were not humble peasants extolling the qualities of those infinitely greater than they were. Dafydd was of some standing; he was the son of one of Rhys ap Gruffudd's cousins, and an uncle, Llywelyn ap Gwilym, was constable of Newcastle Emlyn castle. The latter is believed to have been a potent educational influence on Dafydd. The poet described himself as being of the *clêr* (wandering scholars) many of whom had been members of religious orders. Although the term was also used critically to denote poets who simply mocked and praised people for a living, Dafydd was using it simply to describe a group who earned a living in this way.

Poets' paeans to men of standing are useful because they elucidate patterns of power and demonstrate the ways in which magnanimity was expressed during the period. When Iolo Goch described the notables who welcomed him in Cardiganshire he provided a sketch of those who had influence in the county at the time, including an abbot of Strata Florida, Llywelyn Fychan. The personal perspective in some of Dafydd's work, however, lights up more corners of the medieval world than those provided by sycophantic eulogies. Descriptions of nature permeate his poems. The seasons which inspire aesthetic contemplation were integrated into the fortunes of individuals. Perhaps for those in his occupation, the summer, in whose honour he composed a poem 'Mawl i'r Haf' (Praise of Summer), facilitated travel to various nobles' houses, and was therefore not celebrated for the same reasons by poorer people. Yet his poems demonstrate the importance of seasons in the lives of others, for it was the time when, in another of his poems simply titled 'Yr Haf' (The Summer), 'Good crops, unblemished in their flesh, / in summer come from the old earth'. For Dafydd, the clement months were patrons worth honouring, without them life would be like his bleak description of January, 'mis dig du' ('a sad black month').

Many of Dafydd's poems focused on the area of his birth, northern Cardiganshire. He implored the river Dyfi to allow him to pass so he could reach his love, Morfudd. This lady was married to a merchant at Aberystwyth, and a poem, 'Morfudd a Dyddgu' (Morfudd and Dyddgu), indicates the wealth of this lady, for in it he described 'her glass-windowed home' – before the fifteenth century only the wealthiest had glass windows. References like these indicate which possessions distinguished the affluent sectors of medieval society, and hint that although Aberystwyth was not extremely wealthy some traders possessed a feature which distinguished the well off.

During Dafydd's time the parish church was a social focal point, indeed, the parish would for many centuries remain central to people's lives. Amorous Dafydd bemoans his inability to woo any of 'the parish girls' ('ferched y plwyf') and this may hint that relationships were often between men and women from the same parish. Moreover, opportunities to espy members of the opposite sex took place in church on Sundays. Another of Dafydd's poems sheds light on the competition between males for female attention. Naturally, in this poem Dafydd champions the poet as being a more suitable partner than a soldier. Allusions to conflicts in France and Scotland reveal the regularity of struggles in far away lands during the fourteenth century and how they attracted many young men. The culture of conflict eventually entered into the framework of relationships between men and women and how men defined themselves. Dafydd's poet concedes his cowardice in conflict, but his ability to charm is not questionable. It would be rash to see this competition between men who fought and those who possessed less aggressive instincts as unique to Dafydd's work because this sort of debate was common in French poetry. Thus Dafydd's tale may owe more to literary fashion than actual relations. Nonetheless, he refers to discrete episodes, the conflicts of Edward III that drew many men from Cardiganshire, which may have influenced notions of masculinity, and added an extra dimension to the competition for female attention.[15]

Artistic and intellectual energies also converged in southern Cardiganshire during the fourteenth century. Rhydderch ab Ieuan Llwyd of Glyn Aeron was a significant patron of poets. This ensured that Iolo Goch and Dafydd ap Gwilym praised him. He also contributed to literature through the *White Book of Rhydderch*, which contained a variety of prose texts by a handful of scribes and was compiled for Rhydderch. The texts include legends and Christian topics – demonstrating a varied cultural tradition. This patron of culture also held administrative positions, including that of steward of the county in 1386. Before the fourteenth century, Cardiganshire had two stewards, one for Uwch Aeron and one for Is Aeron. But this role grew less important as castle constables and the justiciar exercised increased influence. Stewards acted as senior figures in courts held in each commote every month. A celebrated clergyman and scholar, Einion Offeriad, whom academics now believe came from southern Cardiganshire, wrote a Grammar which proved influential in Welsh poetry and contained pieces which praised Rhydderch's mother, Angharad.

Some contributors to this patron-fuelled culture were anonymous. All we know of the anchorite of Llanddewibrefi is that he transcribed a collection of prose texts for a patron from Carmarthenshire in 1346. The subjects copied and translated from Latin to Welsh by this hermit, who seems to have had no connection with the collegiate church, included the lives of St David and St Beuno. Through his translation of the Apocalypse of Paul, the anchorite transmitted visions of hell in the Welsh language. This dissemination was happening in other areas of western Europe, so a solitude-loving scholar in Llanddewibrefi was part of a Europe-wide diffusion of beliefs and images which included the fabulous tale of Prester John and the Eastern Christian kingdom that contained a fountain of youth and ants that dug for gold. Less fanciful, but far from unprofitable, activities were carried out by Cardiganshire men in legal affairs. In a study of the legal men of the county, which included Rhydderch, Llinos Beverley Smith observed that the special knowledge possessed by these men was commended by Welsh poets and English royal officials alike.[16] Individuals from Cardiganshire contributed to a number of fields that constituted the cultural resurgence of post-conquest Wales in the fourteenth century.

Although poets and patrons resided in the county, Cardiganshire did not provide posterity with an account of the Black Death which started to sweep through the British Isles in 1348 after arriving in ports on the south coast of England. The want of an equivalent to the Italian, Giovanni Boccaccio, chronicling the minutiae of this horror in fourteenth-century Cardiganshire, means that less graphic sources have to be relied upon. The plague – it earned the moniker the Black Death only in the seventeenth century – exacted a tremendous toll. An estimated 20 per cent of adults died, but among the elderly this figure rose to 60 per cent. Such estimates, based on manorial records, conceal regional variations, with East Anglia being the worst affected. On the other side of the island, a lack of evidence and studies of Cardiganshire at this time prevent detailed comparison with other places; generally, information about low-lying areas is greater than upland regions. Yet the plague did reach out-of-the-way places; it arrived in western Ireland in 1357. Academics continue to put forward hypotheses explaining its origin and means of transmission, ranging from multi-causal explanations which include 'undersea out gassing' leading to hydrogen sulphide entering the atmosphere, to those who question whether it was the bubonic plague in its modern form at all; some have even suggested that it was anthrax. Its persistence in winter suggests that it took on a pneumonic as well as bubonic form – in other words, it passed between humans through coughing and sneezing which infected the lungs, as well as from fleas. Death was more likely in the former – killing at least 95 per cent of its victims, the latter killed 50–60 per cent.

There has been much debate about whether this plague – which returned on two occasions in the 1360s – altered society or merely accelerated existing trends. In spite of there being little information about the plague in the county, Cardiganshire provides an example of how the plague impacted on society through accentuating pre-existing features. Information from the county also suggests that its effects were not necessarily long lasting. By March 1349 the plague fanned out from Carmarthen, and by summer it had ravaged Cardiganshire. Nearly all of the *gabularii* – tenants who paid rent instead of performing a service – around Cardigan had either died or left the lands they rented by midsummer. This group had fewer ties to the land than others, so they probably fled. Another sign of distress can be detected in the fact that few men were willing to take on the role of reeve or beadle at the time. In order to fill these posts some were chosen by the Crown. Furthermore, the benefits accruing from the posts were reduced. This involved an attempt in 1353 to take away the 'aid' or *cymorth* which had been a perquisite of local officials in Cardiganshire from pre-conquest days. Records of men taking up the positions of beadle and reeve in Cardiganshire during the 1360s indicate that the attempted ban had not deterred ambitious men from taking up the posts. Evidently the tendency for local men to pass over positions during the days of the plague was short lived. But the actions of the Crown, such as its attempt to extinguish *cymorth*, were repeated later in the century. This caused friction which contributed to the rising led by Owain Glyndŵr, an event which William Rees, the only historian to explore the plague in any detail in Wales, argued 'was far more disastrous to the economic life of Wales than even the ravages of the Pestilence'.[17] As early as the 1360s and 1370s fear concerning a possible Welsh uprising, led by Owain Lawgoch (a descendant of the royal house of Gwynedd who fought on the French side during the Hundred Years War), meant that orders were sent to the castles at Cardigan and Aberystwyth calling for vigilance in identifying anyone who expressed support for this Welshman who was residing overseas. Yet it would be three decades before these imposing structures faced something more substantial than threats and rumours.

IV

The Fifteenth Century

When Owain Glyndŵr was declared prince of Wales in 1400 the event was the culmination of long simmering discontent among the Welsh as well as a more personal *casus belli*, namely a territorial dispute between Glyndŵr and Reginald Grey. The rebellion ignited by this north-Walian squire lit up the first decade of the fifteenth century and contributes to expressions of present-day Welsh identity. The ways in which Cardiganshire was affected by the revolt, and the part played by the county in its fortunes, will be considered here. An examination of events in Cardiganshire can tell us something about the dynamics of the insurrection.

Two royal bloodlines, Powys and Deheubarth, ran through Glyndŵr's veins. His mother, Helen, was descended from Lord Rhys. It was through her that he inherited land in southern Cardiganshire, parts of the commotes of Gwynionydd and Iscoed. Ironically, Glyndŵr would find more enduring support in the north of the county, and some of his strongest adherents came from another southern commote, Mabwynion. Connections with southern Wales enabled Glyndŵr to make a more convincing claim to stand for Wales as a whole than earlier leaders. Despite this, such advantages needed to be reinforced by a vision and demonstrations of aptitude; in order to be led, followers had to be persuaded that they were destined for something more than defeat. An important part of Glyndŵr's initial success therefore lay in his being hailed as the *mab darogan* (son of prophecy), who would ensure that the Welsh (the native Britons) would become an independent people, free of trammels imposed by the English (Saxons). Poets nurtured this belief, as did legends such as Merlin's prediction that the Welsh would eventually vanquish the Saxon invaders. Previously, Owain Lawgoch, who had been assassinated in 1378, was heralded as the son of prophecy. Glyndŵr was set on the plinth that this mercenary leader had vacated. Initially the rising in north Wales – based in the north-east and Anglesey – was a failure.

This early setback compelled the son of prophecy to retreat into the empty spaces of central Wales. In the meantime, Henry IV invoked laws against Welshmen that reiterated the limits stipulated during Edward I's reign, such as preventing Welshmen acquiring land in England or in plantation towns in Wales. Troubled times had returned.

When the revolt started in the north there was no simultaneous rising in the south, though the stark statement of penalties against the Welsh probably sent a tremor through the rest of Wales and heightened the likelihood of the current rebellion spreading. Glyndŵr crossed into south Wales and had to triumph there before men from Cardiganshire flocked to his banner. This crucial shift in fortune, which spread the embers from north Wales, took place in an upland area on the Cardiganshire–Montgomeryshire border. A Welsh chronicle of the rebellion, believed to have been written before 1450, described how the leader and his band of 'reckless men and robbers' based themselves in 'the uplands of Ceredigion' during the summer of 1401. According to the chronicle his force numbered 120, but later historians have estimated that it amounted to roughly five hundred. From this natural fortress the force struck south and west, plundering more fertile parts. These raids must have penetrated far south because they provoked the men of southern Pembrokeshire, as well as those from 'the lowlands of Ceredigion'. A force of some 1,500 men from these areas made their way up to Owain's fastness. The resulting clash became known as the battle of Hyddgen. Ian Fleming has assessed various accounts of this battle and convincingly argued that it amounted to a siege instead of the English ambushing the Welsh in a valley, as accounts from J. E. Lloyd's book on the Owain Glyndŵr rebellion suggested. On top of Mynydd Hyddgen the avenging lowlanders surrounded the rebels. It is possible that this stand-off lasted for days, before Glyndŵr's company sallied forth, using their desperation and the advantage of downhill momentum to scatter the numerically superior force. Subsequently, the victors attacked Aberystwyth, where, unable to take the castle, they burnt the town.[1]

The chronicle concludes that this victory won Glyndŵr 'a great force' ('*llu mawr*'). Even so, it is possible to over-emphasize the long-term influence of Hyddgen. By the end of 1401 most of county's notables had turned their backs on Owain and accepted the king's pardon. Henry IV's second anabasis in October 1401 succeeded in temporarily extinguishing the rebellion. This military expedition traversed the vale of Towy in Carmarthenshire up to Strata Florida in Cardiganshire. Garrisons at a number of Welsh castles were reinforced. Of these, Cardigan and Aberystwyth received the greatest addition, indicating concern about the loyalty of the surrounding area. Adam of

Usk's account of the English army's advance reveals that the intention of the expedition was to frighten those who might sympathize with the rebels. He wrote that they 'left the country desolate' and 'carried off' over a thousand children 'whom they forced into service for them'.[2] Equally, such actions may betray frustration, or, if the case of the abducted children is genuine, an attempt to entice opponents into battle. At the same time, however, no decisive military victory was achieved. In fact, actions such as the theft of plate and the stabling of horses at Strata Florida abbey, where the king also decamped, may have increased resentment. Even if those distressed by the pillage were not in a position to express their anger at the time, they were prepared to do so when the opportunity arose. By stationing eighty men-at-arms and 200 bowmen at the two castles, the Crown acknowledged that the incursion did not guarantee long-term quiescence. The following year, after a signal victory had been gained at Bryn Glas close to Pilleth in Radnorshire, the Welsh rebels were emboldened. By 1403 a force of Cardiganshire men, led by Rhys Ddu, joined Glyndŵr's army and headed to the Tywi valley.

In order to effect the transformation from guerrilla leader to head of a nation, Glyndŵr needed to acquire the trappings of royal power. Transmogrification from elusive, possibly magical, rebel to a ruler of a territory involved acquiring castles. Of the two key castles occupied by Glyndŵr's forces during the peak of the revolt, one, Aberystwyth, was in Cardiganshire. The other, Harlech, became his base, but Aberystwyth was the other pillar on which he became, in Lloyd's words, '*de facto* ruler of Central Wales'.[3] According to most histories both were taken in 1404, but Rhidian Griffiths has drawn attention to the fact that records identify that Thomas Burton was in charge of the Aberystwyth castle garrison from March to November 1404 and from April to July 1405. Griffiths proposed that this information may 'cast doubt on the statement of the Welsh chronicle that Aberystwyth fell to the Welsh in 1404'.[4] Yet Burton was described as being custodian of both castles in the county, so his position at Aberystwyth may have been in name only. Glyndŵr's dominance of the surrounding area was demonstrated by the frantic attempts to resupply the castles by sea – the two Cardiganshire castles received their victuals from Devon and Bristol. Possession of fortresses was followed by other steps toward statehood, such as the parliaments at Machynlleth and Dolgellau, the treaty with Charles VI of France and the congregation of learned men who provided the nation's administrative backbone. Among these was a former sheriff of Cardiganshire, Rhys Ddu, who became constable of Aberystwyth castle. Others from the county who joined Glyndŵr included Philip ap Rhydderch and his brother Thomas – sons of the cultural beacon

Rhydderch ap Ieuan Llwyd – Maredudd ab Owain, who married Rhys Ddu's daughter, and Rhys ap Llywelyn ap Cadwgan who had also been sheriff of Cardiganshire. Like other rebels, the last mentioned forfeited his lands when he joined the uprising, in his case they went to John Merbury, one of the king's staunchest supporters.

In the popular imagination Glyndŵr and those who joined his revolt are often taken to embody Wales. Doubtless, he attracted a wide range of followers, but Glyndŵr did not receive universal support from his countrymen. Furthermore, support ebbed and flowed. Whereas a man bearing a name like Merbury might be expected to align himself against the Welsh, there is no ethnic explanation behind the rewarding of the lands forfeited by Rhys Ddu to William ap Llywelyn ap Hywel in 1401. William, who had held the position of constable in the commotes of Creuddyn, Caerwedros, Mabwynion and Gwynionydd since 1399, illustrates how men of Welsh lineage did oppose this son of prophesy. One of the most well known of these was Dafydd Gam from Breconshire. Most of Glyndŵr's Welsh opponents came from the east and south of the country, but there were exceptions, like William, who profited from lands lost by Glyndŵr's supporters in the west. An interesting sidelight on the matter of loyalty to Glyndŵr in Cardiganshire and Wales in general is cast by the actions of Llywelyn Fychan ap Llywelyn Goch. This former deputy justiciar in Cardiganshire is thought to have come from the commote of Anhuniog, and with another loyal servant of the Crown, he lent Prince Henry (the future Henry V) £400 towards the defence of Carmarthen. Llywelyn was noted for his knowledge of native law, and thus provides an example of one who, though undeniably a cultured Welshman, opted to oppose champion of the culture in which he was so well versed.

As important, few were willing to support him when the scales tipped in the Crown's favour. In 1406, according to the Welsh chronicle, much of Cardiganshire had submitted to Henry IV; but perhaps it is unrealistic to expect men to continue fighting to the end and risk losing everything, and surrender in 1406 was not ignominious. After all, as Glanmor Williams put it, the falling off of support in south Wales that year was due to fatigue, a 'loss of heart coupled perhaps with a shortage of food', rather than any military defeat.[5] Morale would have been sapped by the lack of consistent French support, the failure of another ally, the earl of Northumberland, and the imprisonment of the young Scottish king. For the rebellion to succeed substantial and sustained support was needed. Although there was a thrust into England by Glyndŵr and his French allies in August 1405, it was not repeated. This advance to Worcestershire followed the fall of Cardigan to Glyndŵr's forces – a result of loyal forces in Pembrokeshire being unable to support Cardigan. A greater blow to rebel spirit was delivered in 1408 when both Aberystwyth and Harlech fell. The sons of Rhydderch made their peace with the Crown after this. By 1416, Maredudd ab Owain was in the service of the Crown. However, his wife's father, Rhys Ddu, remained with Glyndŵr and, after being captured during a raid into Shropshire in 1410, was hung, drawn and quartered in London. Strange to say, Rhys Ddu could have ended his days at the hands of Glyndŵr, albeit in a manner less painful than the fate he eventually suffered. During the siege of Aberystwyth in 1407, Rhys offered to surrender the stronghold to the English at the start of November. The Welsh chronicle of the rising records that he travelled north to ask Glyndŵr for permission to do this, but his lord 'threatened to cut off Rhys's head, unless he might have the castle'.[6] As a result of Glyndŵr's determination, the English, who felt that the siege was as good as won, had to resume the assault in 1408. This was unexpected as the 1407 attack, which involved a mighty canon called *Messager* (Messenger) that exploded, and a collection of notables including Prince Henry, was expected to be the finale of the revolt. Evidently, Glyndŵr retained the ability to confound his enemies even when he was on the defensive.

Towards the end of the struggle in Cardiganshire, Glyndŵr's influence retracted northwards; the north of the county was closer to the rebel stronghold of Merionethshire. Sparse taxation returns in this period attest to the north's less stable condition. By the second decade of the century, however, this charismatic leader had left the brief entries of the chroniclers and entered the broad acres of legend. Here, the national saviour flowed into a reservoir of expectation; the next leader might achieve what Glyndŵr had sought. Few would have believed that the whole island would return to the Welsh, but there was hope that the Welsh would regain some standing. After the Lancastrian victory under the part-Welsh Henry Tudor at Bosworth in 1485, and his consequent transformation into Henry VII, a more modest version of the prophecy appeared to have materialized.

While ambitions, fashions and conventions drove people just as they had in earlier periods, the fifteenth century offers some important indicators of the part religion played in personal and political life. This century was the last one in which England and Wales were Catholic, though traditions persisted. Religion played a part in international, national and individual spheres. It could be used as a means to declare independence from powerful neighbours, as seen in Glyndŵr's declaration of support for the Avignon pope in 1406. With this allegiance came plans for a Welsh Church separate from England with an archbishopric based at St Davids; moreover, churchmen were to be Welsh-speakers.

Such ambitions were, no doubt, in keeping with the hopes of the monks of Strata Florida who had a long tradition of sympathy for the aspirations of Welsh princes. They were also smarting after their monastery had been, according to Adam of Usk, 'completely stripped of its plate' by the king five years earlier.[7] Henry IV supported the pope in Rome, so the schism between rival popes contributed to the struggle in Wales.

Lollardy, a broad term used to describe those who expressed discontent with the corruption and teachings of the Church, briefly entered the county's history as Glyndŵr's rebellion flickered out of existence. Although not a stronghold, or even a district with a faint connection to those who espoused Lollard beliefs, Cardiganshire's distance from centres of authority may have offered a convenient base for the Lollard rebel, John Oldcastle. This aristocratic rebel, who at one stage was thought to have colluded with Glyndŵr's son, Maredudd, rose in 1414 and was executed in 1417. Oldcastle, who formerly sat in the House of Commons for Herefordshire, and his supporters were described by contemporaries as 'heretics'. Their activities prompted the king to pay for troops to guard Cardigan castle in case Oldcastle, or his 'adherents who were presumed to have left England for Wales, should take the said castle by night'.[8] Likewise, during 1415 Aberystwyth castle was ordered to prepare in case of Lollard activity. At this time Richard Oldcastle, John's father, was in charge of defences there. Cardiganshire, however, would hardly have provided a solid foundation for a Lollard base, and no attempt was made to take either castle. Rebels involved in the 1414 rising came from southern English counties, notably Oxfordshire, Buckinghamshire and Northamptonshire. Although a historian of the phenomenon, Richard Rex, contended that 'there is no evidence at all for Lollardy in Wales', the activities of the authorities as regards Cardiganshire's main castles provides evidence that some feared that Lollardy might spread to the principality.[9]

On a personal level, religious belief encouraged individuals to travel on pilgrimages. An example from the county illustrates this manifest-ation of human action and belief which characterized the age. We are fortunate that in Wales the late medieval period was the age of the *cywydd*, a particular form of Welsh poetry with its own rules, used to praise the Welsh gentry and request largesse. Such a work, by Lewis Glyn Cothi, mentions a lady called Elliw from Glyn Aeron, who travelled by sea from Santiago de Compostela on the north-west of the Iberian Peninsula, to Pembroke and then, also by sea, to her home county.[10] This second leg of her journey indicates that, for many, journeys by sea were preferable to land travel, although the sea could be treacherous too. Another poet, Deio ab Ieuan Ddu of Creuddyn,

Cardiganshire, reveals this when he describes how a man from his county was captured at sea by the French.[11] The less traumatic journey of Elliw to Santiago de Compostela would have been just one of many to the site where it was believed the body of St James lay. Beheaded at Jerusalem, St James was the first apostle to be martyred, and his miraculous conveyance to Spain, on a boat made of stone, inspired many to journey there. This site became the most important destination for Christian pilgrims after Jerusalem and Rome. A route by land was popular, but despite the many discomforts mentioned in a fifteenth-century English poem, the sea route was cheaper and quicker than passage on roads and tracks. In the late medieval period those who had ventured to the site wrote many narratives, and Glyn Cothi's reference to Elliw from Cardiganshire adds another example of how this spot drew Christians.

There has been a tendency for the century to be seen as a time of religious lethargy, when Roman Catholicism became increasingly distant from the uneducated population, those without the means or opportunity to undertake voyages to Santiago de Compostela. However, a convincing case can be made that, for many, the Church had a purpose. Perhaps later Protestant historians have, given their affiliation, underestimated the vitality of the Catholic Church. Indeed, this perceived ecclesiastical anemia does not tally with the fact that many new churches were built and existing ones improved, something which, in Wales as a whole, became particularly noticeable from the 1460s. There are signs of the Church's strong pulse in Cardiganshire, though activity was not as great as in some other parts of Wales which experienced considerable building and restoration. St Mary's church, in Cardigan, has a font dating from this century. Llanarth's western tower dates from the fifteenth century, and Llanwnnen church also has a tower built during this era. More remnants may have survived were it not for the zeal of nineteenth-century church builders. An antiquarian, writing in 1888, described how the church at Llanfair Clydogau had 'bits of fifteenth-century work; but it has this year been pulled down and rebuilt, and all the old work has vanished'.[12] Perpendicular architecture, defined as a branch of English Gothic, was in the ascendant during this period. Windows partitioned by vertical and horizontal lines (the former called mullions) gave the style its name. While not containing as many examples of this style as East Anglia, where wealth from the wool and weaving trades helped build churches, there are examples, such as the windows in Llanbadarn Fawr's chancel, which indicate how this style permeated Cardiganshire. On the subject of fifteenth-century architectural influences found in the county, Richard Suggett has considered the presence in Cardiganshire of an architectural form called the king-post ('a post standing on the tie beam and reaching to the roof ridge').[13] Relatively rare in Wales as a whole, this feature, seen in Mwnt and Penbryn churches, became more ornamental in places far from the north of England where it was most common. Something practical, part of a building, acquired greater importance, possibly as a status symbol, where it was seen as being innovative.

Records about the church at Penbryn provide an insight into some issues which preoccupied its congregation in the last quarter of the fifteenth century. A dispute arose over the appointment of a successor to a post made vacant by the death of the former vicar. On 25 August 1488 two men were appointed to investigate the disputed succession in the church. They initiated their investigation by calling together the parishioners, both male and female, and selected from these twenty-one men who, after taking an oath, considered the means by which vicars were appointed to Penbryn. Together they cast their minds back eighty years, when Glyndŵr was 'feigning himself Prince of Wales'. After the years of rebellion, there followed a dispute over who should appoint the parish priest between the abbot of Talley monastery, Carmarthenshire, and the bishop of St Davids; men in these positions were behind the dispute of 1487–8 as well. The importance attached to the process of appointing men to such positions can be seen in the fact that the earlier dispute was settled at the Court of Rome. Eventually, the bishop's right to select the incumbent was confirmed. Yet, as well as illustrating how parishes could be drawn into struggles over patronage, this incident conveys the importance placed on what was called 'the common voice and talk', or the memory of inhabitants – although, incidentally, their calculations regarding the time served by ministers was somewhat awry.[14]

Not all ecclesiastical matters were resolved so amicably. As repositories of wealth and influence, monasteries attracted criminals, among whose number were some abbots. During the early 1440s, for instance, Strata Florida was occupied once again, though not on this occasion by royal forces as it was at the start of the century, but by John ap Rhys abbot of Aberconway. This incident reveals how central authority became entangled in local affairs as a result of avaricious schemes. John ap Rhys claimed that the present, recently appointed, abbot had 'unjustly occupied the abbey and done much damage thereto'. This prompted Henry IV to 'preserve the abbey under royal protection'. But this was the last thing that happened. Grasping this self-orchestrated opportunity, John ap Rhys descended on Strata Florida with a band of 'many evildoers' and did just what he had accused the current abbot of doing, and more. Before ejecting the abbot, John ap Rhys and a number of other monks 'entered the abbey by force and spoiled it of its goods and jewels'. The dispossessed were 'imprisoned in the castle of Abrustuth [Aberystwyth] till they were freed by one William Thomas'. Despite the act of this Good Samaritan, John ap Rhys still held the abbey 'by force'. This action led to the king taking the abbey, and the appointment of two Cistercian abbots, one from Whitland the other 'of Morgan [Margam]' to steward the abbey. These guardians were to prevent any more losses and to 'make an inventory of the goods as speedily as possible and cause them to be preserved for the use of the abbey'.[15] Thus order was imposed, property secured and the conflict between would-be abbots stifled by the intervention of the Crown and other members of the order. A Caernarfonshire-born poet, Dafydd Nanmor, extolled one of the men looking after the abbey in a poem which described improvements carried out there. Among these improvements, many no doubt rendered necessary as a result of previous neglect and pillage, were costly walled enclosures like those seen in England.[16]

Like religion, warfare continued to play a significant part in the lives of Cardiganshire's population. In keeping with the rest of Wales, the county supplied men to fight against the French. Whereas those engaged in the struggles of the previous century might have supplied a reserve of fighting men for Glyndŵr and his opponents, those who fought in the war, which resumed in 1413 with the ascension of Henry V, returned to a land where nobles established their own forces. Some of these would be deployed in the War of the Roses. Significantly, these troops amassed for the fifteenth-century campaigns in France were paid, not simply drawn upon as part of a levy. It was, therefore, more akin to a professional fighting force composed of paid volunteers rather than pressed men. Among those who embarked on the Agincourt campaign were 102 archers and five men-at-arms from the county. The latter were heavily armed individuals of some standing who dismounted when on the battlefield, pages taking their horses to the back. Bowmen, who played a pivotal part in the battle of Agincourt itself, are better known to posterity, having benefited from being the object of both Welsh and English national pride. The deadly flurries of arrows sent by some 5,000 archers into the French forces won Henry V a famous victory later immortalized by Shakespeare in *Henry V*. Archers using the 6-ft-high longbow made from the yew tree were necessarily tall and strong. The string needed to be pulled back to the right ear before the arrow was sent on its journey of up to 300 yards. Troops from Cardiganshire would have been involved in more operations than this battle as the success needed to be consolidated by an offensive campaign lasting many years, which included the conquest of Normandy, sealed at the Treaty of Troyes in 1420.

Names of some of the men from the county who fought in France at this time have been recorded. Gruffudd ab Adda ab Ieuan ap Gruffudd hailed from Uwch Aeron and served as an archer in the Agincourt campaign. Although it is thought that most archers were from the less wealthy ranks, he had served as a reeve and beadle in Mefenydd during 1417–18 and in 1423–5 respectively, so relatively speaking he was a man of some consequence. Whilst holding these positions he would have collected various fees and fines in the commote. As reeve, Gruffudd would have collected monies paid for the right to trade in markets. Similarly, Gruffudd ap Maredudd ap Rhys, an archer in the 1415 campaign, was reeve of Genau'r-glyn from 1419–20. Those archers who were in a position to occupy posts such as reeve were probably defined as mounted archers, and were in receipt of 6 d. a day. Men-at-arms received 1 s. and the foot archers 4 d. Mounted archers did not fire from horseback, as central Asian horsemen did, but dismounted for battle in much the same way as the men-at-arms. In addition to this pay there was the prospect of booty. Perhaps Jankyn ap Rhys ap Dafydd's frequent forays into continental Europe as a man-at-arms helped fund his acquisition of property in the south of the county. Conversely, the cost of war meant many in Cardiganshire were called upon to contribute to its upkeep. A beadle of Iscoed Is Hirwern, Gwilym ap Rhys ap y Coeg collected a subsidy for that purpose. Such a prolonged war also meant that officials were called upon to remain vigilant in case the French attacked. Although it was not at the forefront of the war, the fact that one in every fifty of the archers at Agincourt hailed from the county, in addition to the financial implications of war, meant that it left some impression on the area. Demands generated by this long conflict, and the role taken by the Crown, have lead some historians to challenge the conventional idea that changes from a feudal to modern society began with the Tudors and to assert that they can be traced to this earlier period.

With the demise of strong leadership after the death of Henry V in 1422, however, central control slackened. Lawlessness, a leitmotif in historical writing about pre-Tudor Wales, may have been exaggerated by those keen to stress the order established by the early Tudor, but a glimpse at Cardiganshire in the fifteenth century reveals an element of truth behind the generalization. Anarchy is too strong a word to describe the state of the area in this period; even lawlessness would be an exaggeration. It was not a free-for-all. Rather, certain figures who attempted to scoop up power and influence were not as inhibited by possible legal sanction as they could have been. In particular, there was Thomas, the violent and ambitious son of a Carmarthenshire magnate, Gruffudd ap Nicholas of Dinefwr. Family aggrandizement led to

Thomas, and two others, causing disorder in the Teifi valley. One of Thomas's associates reputedly entered Llandysul church and made copies of its seal, which thereby enabled him to illicitly obtain £89. Forceful tactics were not typical, though. Marriage enabled Thomas to gain influence in Cardiganshire. His wife's father held property in Llangybi, Betws Bledrws and Llanrhystud. From this union Rhys ap Thomas, ally of the future Henry VII, was born. The activities of Thomas who, while deputy sheriff of Cardiganshire in the early 1440s was fined for allowing a prisoner to escape, were representative of those grand perversions of justice in which the English barons indulged during the period. Those who supported the local potentate were often given their aid in courts of law. Frequently during Henry IV's reign the Court of Great Sessions would impose a general fine on a county. This obviated the application of law to areas in return for a blanket payment. Between 1422–85 only seven of the forty-seven sessions in Cardiganshire continued beyond the payment of a fine. This, the most widely cited indicator of lax law by historians, suited both the landed interest in Cardiganshire and the Crown. It ensured lack of interference in what was done, on the one hand, and ready cash without having to struggle to procure it from a reluctant populace on the other.

The social, economic and demographic features of the fifteenth century presented a number of opportunities for the ambitious gentleman. Depopulation and cheaper land enabled more property to be bought or leased. As the church-building enterprises mentioned earlier reveal, the latter part of the century was not one of widespread scarcity. The roots of this wealth, the cattle and the plough, appear in the poems of Cardiganshire poet Deio ab Ieuan Ddu, and a legal document now in the National Library of Wales contains a drawing of the latter.[17] An English chronicler noted how, when the after effects of the Glyndŵr rebellion faded, 'the Welsh began to live in the manner of the English. They accumulate riches [and] they fear losses'.[18] After the penal legislation passed against Welshmen during the Glyndŵr rebellion and renewed in the first half of the century, ambitious men from Cardiganshire, or those with interests there, felt that their aspirations were unduly restrained. As a result, they sought to remove the disabilities of being Welsh. Once men like Dafydd ap Thomas, a landowner from the south of the county, had been granted denizenship in 1427, at the request of Parliament for loyal service to Henry V and VI, jealous English burgesses in Welsh towns could not carp about the influence acquired by the 'foreign' Welshmen.

Similarly, Gruffudd ap Nicolas received equal legal footing with Englishmen. His family benefited from the period of weak Lancastrian rule. When the York faction was in the ascendant from 1461, soon after Gruffudd's death, the family was thrown on the defensive. Yorkist attempts to impose authority on west Wales were hampered by the fact that Thomas and his brother Owain had crossed swords with York at Mortimer's Cross. On the ascension of Edward VI a sum of 600 marks (a mark was two-thirds of a pound) from Cardiganshire was given to the new ruler as a token of loyalty. Yet in the 1460s Cardiganshire proved to be a recalcitrant territory. Thomas and his son Rhys may have fled to Burgundy as the tide turned against them, but in 1469 two of Thomas's sons – Morgan and Henry – captured Cardigan castle. The Yorkists, headed by Richard, duke of Gloucester and the future Richard III, re-established their authority after this brief insurrection, and the family were denied administrative posts in the county. Before 1483 Cardiganshire was, on the surface, under the influence of the Yorkists as never before. When Richard III took the throne, however, there appears to have been a softening of opinion as Rhys, who had by now returned from exile, was provided with an annuity of 40 marks from the king. Yet a great shift in fortune was about to occur. Although Rhys was not rash in proclaiming support for the pretender Henry his decision to throw in his lot with the Welsh-born Henry consolidated his position and elevated his fortunes beyond even those held by his father.

After Henry Tudor landed at Mill Bay in southern Pembrokeshire, the king-to-be set off on a circuitous route that ended in glory at Bosworth Field. Among the notables present there was Rhydderch ap Rhys of Cilbronnau in the south of the county. Most diagrams of Henry's march plot part of his course through Cardiganshire. Local tales told of stops at Cardigan, where he is said to have written a message to the Stanleys outlining his plans, and also Ffynnon Ddewi where they watered. The latter tradition tied one Welsh figure, St David, with another who also came to be known for his faith. An overnight stay at Llwyndafydd at Cwmtydu appears to conflict with another story that he spent a night at Wern Newydd only 4 miles away in Llanarth parish. In the north, he was reputed to have stayed at Llanilar. Some have cautioned against assuming that we can ever know the actual route. In a history of the Wars of the Roses in Wales, H. T. Evans reminds readers that 'local tradition apart, there is no data which will enable us to describe his itinerary between Cardigan and Shrewsbury'.[19] Indeed, a nineteenth-century antiquarian attempted to reconcile the story that Henry slept at Talley abbey in Carmarthenshire during his advance by suggesting that he could have ridden from western Cardiganshire and back again. Whichever route was taken, the cartographic consensus is that Henry travelled through Cardiganshire while Rhys ap Thomas marched further east.

This momentous event spawned many local tales. Indeed, through these local traditions we see something of what Miri Rubin called 'the desire for settlement' which Henry VII represented.[20] Those families who claimed that Henry spent nights in certain places, and even sired children on this journey, were writing themselves into, if not the history books, then the tale of a man born in Wales who changed a kingdom. Supporters of the Tudors were keen to emphasize the new, to underline that they were different from what had gone before. The celebration of a new beginning, which, as Rubin pointed out, concealed much continuity, was given structural form at Llanwenog. A history of the parish postulates that the church's tower, built during Henry's reign, was in memory of the men from the area who fell at Bosworth. There is a shield over one of the windows in the tower which contains the arms of Rhys ap Thomas who is thought to have ordered its construction to commemorate the victory. Cardiganshire men who supported Henry were rewarded during his reign. Rhydderch ap Rhys, for example, became constable of Cardigan castle. The Tudor age had dawned, but the full heat of that dynasty's most infamous individuals was felt in the following century.

The Sixteenth Century

By the start of the sixteenth century western Europe was beginning to pull ahead of other parts of the world; countries were gathering together resources that allowed them to play a role in world history out of all proportion to their size. Scholars have long mulled over why this came about. Immanuel Wallerstein, for instance, held that a lack of government interference, which enticed individuals and groups to exploit economic opportunities, contributed to the change.[1] Indeed, moving from the broad canvas of world history to a smaller picture, Wallerstein's general statement finds some support in Cardiganshire's history. Although the first written record of lead mining in Cardiganshire, near Llanbadarn Fawr, dates from 1305, it was during the reign of Elizabeth I, when the Mines Royal Society was established in 1568, that this extractive industry began to be systematically developed. Even then, it was not a case of instant 'take-off'. To entice people into mining, the Crown resuscitated ancient laws which exempted those engaged in mining from taxes and serving on juries, as the 'labour of such work is so advantageous to the publick'.[2] Through forgoing some obligations, the authorities could benefit by way of enhanced productivity. However, it needs to be borne in mind that a few restrictions on people were also imposed, some laws obligated the children of mineworkers to follow their father's trade. Thus carrots alone did not encourage profitable activity; there were sticks too.

In 1564, four years before the establishment of the Mines Royal Society, some German miners arrived in the British Isles. One of these valuable human imports, Daniel Houghsetter, played an important part in the history of Cardiganshire mining. Initially, mines at Tal-y-bont, Goginan, Cwmystwyth, Trawsgoed and Great Darren were worked, but they did not reward the society so they were let to other entre-preneurs. Although the following century was to witnesses a more fruitful commercial exploitation of the county's mineral resources, the mines did contribute towards satisfying the prevailing desire for silver coinage; notably after the arrival of Customer Smith and the unearthing of a vein of lead and silver at Cwmsymlog. Silver was prioritized; lead was cheap although it was still exported to continental Europe. If the proportion of silver in the lead was low, mining operations were discontinued. The environmental impact of mining in Tudor Cardiganshire was palpable. It was not so much the mining as the smelting of the ore that transformed the landscape because timber was needed to stoke the fires. The Pembrokeshire antiquarian, George Owen, related rumours that an alternative source of fuel – peat – was being used by smiths in Cardiganshire, though it is not stated whether this was through choice or dearth of wood.[3]

Even some thirty years before the establishment of the Mines Royal, Leland noted in his *Itinerary* through England and Wales that the Ystwyth valley was denuded of trees. Similar stripping probably occurred in the Rheidol valley. We can only conjecture about the impact this had on the people and wildlife of the area; no doubt profit accompanied loss. Leland's comment that the melting of lead 'hath destroyd the wooddes that sometime grew plentifulli thereabout' hints at the perceptual impact of this change that must have been even more evident for those living in the area. There were other factors which contributed to deforestation. North of Tregaron, Leland, who bore the title of 'King's Antiquary', noticed that the hills had, in the past, been 'well woddid, as evidently by old rotes apperith'. Three reasons were put forward for this, none of them related to smelting. Most importantly, in Leland's opinion, wood was never coppiced and this explains the decline across Wales as a whole. In addition to this there were goats – sheep were not the sole masters of the hills as they are today – who ate young trees. Finally, thieves could ensconce themselves in woods, so law-abiding men removed this hiding place. Evidently, environmental change in Tudor Cardiganshire sprang from a number of causes.[4]

An increasing population may have also contributed to a decline in trees, as wood was a vital source of heat and shelter. The historical demographer relies upon sources such as the muster roles of able-bodied men made during Henry VIII's reign, the 1563 records of the number of houses in each diocese, and another ecclesiastically inspired source, the number of Church of England communicants of 1603. Leonard Owen used these and other materials to compute the population of Welsh counties during the sixteenth and seventeenth centuries.[5] Of the 1563 returns, only three Cardiganshire parishes are not extant. The subsidy list compiled by tax commissioners during the reign of Henry VIII is also almost complete, only Creuddyn being absent. From these, Owen estimated that during the middle of the century Cardiganshire had a population of 17,320. For every householder he postulated five inhabitants. This total was less than any other county in southern Wales – Carmarthenshire to the south was the highest with 34,375. Compared to the counties to the north, however, Cardiganshire had a greater population than any bar Denbighshire. The population of Wales began to increase from the late fifteenth century, so the figures related by Owen for the middle of the sixteenth century represent this revival in numbers, which may have contributed as much to the disappearance of trees as the smelteries did. Owen also provides figures for the county's hundreds and Cardigan town. The latter had a population of 216, a figure, which, when taken with Leland's remarks that this town's market was far inferior to that at Aberystwyth, indicates its relative poverty. It is difficult to draw any conclusions from the hundred data about the distribution within the county, yet there was a concentration of population in the northern hundreds, areas with less fertile soils than the south. This pattern could have been the result of mining activity. Indeed, it is significant that Leland mentions a dearth of woodland only in the northern half of the county.

Economic improvement has often been attributed to the Acts of Union (1537 and 1542–3), between England and Wales. The administrative and cultural consequences this legislation had on the county will be addressed below. With order came greater profit, though this pithy truism must not obscure the fact that profit was earned before the Henrician administrative reforms. Amongst Cardiganshire's exports was the aforementioned silver exhumed in the county, which was sent eastwards to the mint, and cattle. There were also indicators of increased economic activity in the then key woollen industry. This was carried out on a small scale in many places. There was little of the concentration seen in Yorkshire. After weaving, fulling 'cleansed' the material. Fulling mills, powered by water, were relatively rare at the turn of the sixteenth century. But by 1536 there were, according to R. Ian Jack in his study of Welsh mills before 1547, four in the county. One of these, at Pontrhydfendigaid, was leased by the monks of Strata Florida to a man for 40 *s.* a year. This was in 1537, two years before the monastery was dissolved. Jack suggests that it was a 'grist-mill' that may well have had a fulling mill attached. A similar double use of water power occurred at Rhuddlan Deifi.[6]

During Henry VIII's reign regulations were passed regarding the Cardiganshire cloth trade which reveal concerns about quality. This in itself is an indication of increasing commercial activity. The Act 'for the true making of Frises and Cottens in Wales' justified its imposition by their being 'foreigners, husbandmen, and grasiers dwelling in the country' who 'make theyre owne woollin fryses and cottons after the most false and deceytefull mannner that maie be'. This piece of legislation regulated the weight and size of pieces of frieze and cotton. Doubtless the regulation was broken in many out-of-the-way mills. The desire to protect the consumer also protected what were termed 'all true cloth-makers'.[7] The tone of the regulation hints at some economic competition between town and country – foreigner at this time was often used to describe those who were not members of a guild in addition to those from another county, parish or country.

Attempts to facilitate legal trade by sea are illustrated by the commission appointed by Lord William Cecil Burleigh for the suppression of piracy. One of its objects was to make Cardigan Bay less dangerous. Commissioners were asked to list all havens and landing places. These provide us with brief accounts of coastal locations in 1566. Starting from Cardigan, they listed creeks where ships could unload goods at Aber-porth, Penbryn and Llanina. The 'small Crike or landinge place at Aberayron' and Llansanffraid near Llanrhystud were further up the coast, followed by Aberystwyth and Borth. The four commissioners indicated the relatively poor nature of the towns – both Cardigan and Aberystwyth having as many houses 'in decaye' as inhabited. Correspondingly, the trade was insignificant, the commissioners recorded that there were no vessels apart from small fishing boats, with six to seven men in each, used for herring fishing. They stated that 'no mariners' occupied these boats, only fishermen. This distinction is important, for it suggests that there were none who made their living through trading on the sea alone, although the produce of the sea was amply exploited. Trade did occur with Ireland, however this was limited by the sand bars that prevented those ships which weighed over 10 tons from frequenting the ports. The bleak descriptions provided by officials about the condition of the coast, such as the comments of Thomas Phaer who wrote that from St Davids along the county's coast there 'is no trade of merchandise but all full of Rocks and daungiers', should be adapted to take into account the activity, legal and illicit, which did occur.[8] Maybe there was a tendency to compare the scanty, though locally significant, activity with trading elsewhere. Coastal trade was increasing during this period; collier vessels weighing over 100 tons traversed the Bristol Channel and the North Sea.

Unlike its predecessor, the sixteenth century has been generally viewed as being a time of order and development. This is usually attributed to administrative reforms. One of the measures set in motion by Thomas Cromwell in 1536 was the establishment of the post of Justice of the Peace (JP), a position which in England dated from the thirteenth century, and which enjoined the gentry to administer local justice. Though it was not reimbursed financially, the influence gained in a locality ensured that many took up the post. On the whole, there were fewer of these positions in Welsh counties compared to their English equivalents. The English county with the fewest justices, tiny Rutland, had thirteen in 1580. Cardiganshire, with nine JPs, had fewer than any other Welsh county. The county's relative poverty may account for this. In 1575 there were ten fewer holders of this office in the county than there were in Caernarfonshire which had fewer inhabitants. In a comparison of the two counties during the Tudor period, W. Ogwen Williams thought this discrepancy stemmed from Cardiganshire's lack of gentry who possessed the financial where-withal to qualify for the position.[9]

Before the Acts of Union, Cardiganshire presented a problem for central authority. Rhys ap Gruffudd was not granted any position of influence after the death of his illustrious grandfather, Rhys ap Thomas. A nationalist historian, W. Ambrose Bebb, has suggested that the selection of Lord Ferrers, Walter Devereux, as chamberlain of south Wales, instead of Rhys's heir, led to resentment. Ferrers related how, in 1526, the inhabitants of Cardiganshire and Carmarthenshire refused to accept summonses to court, declaring that they would rather 'run into the woods'.[10] Little is known about this incident but, as Wolsey had ordered that no subpoenas should be implemented in Wales, it seems that the Cardiganshire and Carmarthenshire rebels did not have to escape into the forests. Bebb hailed this as the last demonstration of an independent spirit in the principality. Nevertheless, this incident was not followed by any other demonstrations of resistance on the arrival of the English system. Indeed, there were benefits for the gentry which would have made these intrusions palatable. The denial of a position to Rhys ap Gruffudd, taken as a slight by many in south-west Wales, contrasts with the political and administrative shifts which enabled substantial numbers of the gentry, who would have been the leaders of any opposition, to satisfy their ambitions.

Accompanying the greater 'annexation' of Wales by England there were smaller rationalizations carried out in 1536 and those parts not included in the shire in 1284 became part of Cardiganshire. Two lordships in the county – Llanddewibrefi, held by the bishop of St Davids, and Caron – had their own system of jurisdiction, so when the first Act of Union was formulated they had to be included in the county. In the words of the law, these were to be 'united annexed and ionyed to and with the Countie of Cardigan as a membre parte or parcell of the same'. The Act also stipulated that the entire county was to be governed 'according to the lawes customes and statutes of this Realme of Englande and after no Welshe Lawes'.[11]

A uniform legal system did not eradicate criminality. Later in the century the remote former lordship of Caron and the surrounding area called 'Cymystwyth' was identified by George Owen, in his 'The dialogue of the government of Wales', as being an especially dangerous area because it was a refuge for those deemed criminals for not attending the county's Great Sessions. Despite being incorporated into the county, this remote border area retained, or perhaps acquired, its unenviable reputation of being an area blighted by vagabonds. Also according to Owen, some people of standing contributed to this lawlessness by accepting money from those fleeing justice. They then embarked on careers as inverse Robin Hoods as they 'lyyve upon the spoile of the Poore & honeste laboureinge people'. Owen's account qualifies statements made by some historians like W. Llywelyn Williams who noted that thirty years or so after the Acts of Union had been passed Wales had been transformed into a law-abiding country. Even at the end of the century small corners, such as eastern Cardiganshire, could remain thorns in the paw of the Tudor settlement. H. Noel Jerman, speaking at the National Library of Wales before the Cardiganshire Antiquarian Society on the subject of Tudor Cardiganshire in 1937, said that the county's 'physical configuration' meant that the passing of the Acts of Union did not affect Cardiganshire as much as other areas. As the case of Caron demonstrates, there is some foundation to this argument. On the whole, though, W. Ogwen Williams's assessment that 'the Tudor settlement of Wales had a more profound effect' on Cardiganshire than the three counties of north-west Wales is the sounder judgement.[12] After all, the 1536 Act stated that the county would abandon all its Welsh laws and adopt those of England in 'suche form and fassion as iustice is ministred and used to the Kinges subijects within the thre Shires of North Wales'. With the Act of Union, the county was coming into alignment with patterns established elsewhere in Wales.

Cardiganshire politics was shaped by another piece of Henrician law. Legislation concerning the representation of boroughs requested that smaller settlements, or contributory boroughs, should be incorporated into the borough electoral framework. This happened in less than half of such constituencies in the sixteenth century because large families dominated the towns and smaller places did not feel it was worthwhile to pay for the upkeep of the elected member. Cardiganshire's borough elections in the period, however, included towns in addition to Cardigan. In 1545 Aberystwyth and Talsarn took part in elections, as did Tregaron and Talsarn eight years later. There were relatively few large families in the county, and this made it practicable for smaller settlements to enter contests. As a result of this, from time to time some exciting elections took place. One of the most stirring contests in Tudor

Wales was played out in Cardiganshire during 1547, and this contest has been examined in detail by Philip S. Edwards.[13] Cardigan and Aberystwyth each tried to return a different candidate in the election. The former chose a Gloucester man, John Cotton, but Aberystwyth selected Gruffudd Dwnn of Carmarthenshire, and the sheriff chose the latter. This slighting of Cardigan town's wishes was not an insult to the county town – until an act of 1553 the county court was held more often at Aberystwyth. At the end of the Tudor period, the 1601 election for the borough was similarly contested. On this occasion, Cardigan's candidate, Richard Delabere gained the seat and held it until 1604. At times Cardiganshire's history is a tale of two towns. From 1553 the county court was held alternately at Cardigan and Aberystwyth. Although the borough elections were held in Cardigan, Aberystwyth was the wealthier town and was closer to the seat of the county's most important family – the Pryses of Gogerddan.

After the Acts of Union granted electoral representation to the Welsh counties, men from various backgrounds represented the county and the borough constituencies. Commentators note how many 'strangers' held these positions. In 1543, for instance, Morgan Rhys ap Philip died, precipitating what has been called the first by-election in Wales that led to the arrival of an outsider, Thomas Eynns, secretary to Prince Edward. Nonetheless, the county seat soon became the virtual preserve of the Pryse family of Gogerddan. The borough seat, however, attracted a variety of representatives. A significant figure who sat for Cardigan borough during the late 1550s was the Englishman Thomas Phaer. Considered the father of paediatrics, Phaer was also a lawyer. His translation of the *Aeneid* into English was the first attempt to do so, and for a man who taught himself Latin it was an admirable one. His lands lay in northern Pembrokeshire, but he held Cardigan borough from 1555–63. Before he was elevated to the House of Commons, he reported on the coast of Wales, providing the description of the county mentioned above. He was certainly one of the most talented men who occupied the seat during the sixteenth century. Among the grander personages from outside Cardiganshire who held the more prestigious county seat was Thomas Jones of Abermarlais, Carmarthenshire. Some caution needs to be made when describing these men as outsiders. Firstly, a person in a neighbouring county, like Thomas Jones or Phaer, could have considerable influence because they also owned territory in Cardiganshire – Jones was the county sheriff on two occasions. Secondly, in a political system founded on associations among the gentry, a person could be part of a group without having to be attached to the land he represented. An example of the latter is the Pembrokeshire man Thomas Perrot who held the seat for two years from 1586.

The relative dearth of native members of Parliament has been taken as an indicator of Cardiganshire's poverty. If this was true of the upper ranks, then the conditions of those lower down the social hierarchy can be readily surmised. In comparisons of the fifteenth and sixteenth centuries, the former, despite experiencing two major conflicts, is usually depicted by historians as being the least unpleasant. Unlike the previous century, there was a significant increase in population in the sixteenth century, and that had some negative repercussions. There was 'land hunger' which put pressure on those tenants who occupied property on the basis of annual leases. In addition, inflation meant that the purchasing power of labourers and craftsmen fell. A variety of factors contributed to these price rises including the debasement of coinage and increased government spending, but the primary reason was population growth. These circumstances produced an employers' rather than employees' market. Of course, the experiences of those not in the nobility or gentry varied enormously. That the county was not divided into haves and have-nots, but also contained some have-somethings, is illustrated by the garments owned by a yeoman's wife which included a 'frise gown, a red petticote, a blue mantle and a white dublet of fustian'. Another, equally colourful but unpleasant, insight into the lives of women in Tudor Cardiganshire is provided by an account of an abduction which culminated in the county's sheriff rescuing a young woman from Betws Bledrws, whose uncle attempted to force her to marry a man of his choice. There were often financial motives behind these marriages, and some family members risked much by persuasion, trickery or force to bring them about.

The generally unfavourable economic trends of this period would have had some impact on the lives of all whatever their station. Conditions would have been particularly poor in 1564 and 1579, years blighted by bad winters. There was a decline in temperature from the mid-sixteenth century to the late eighteenth, now known as the Little Ice Age. Conversely, a plentiful harvest could lead to relative abundance, especially in the agriculturally blessed parts of Wales. One of these was the 'barley belt' between Aberaeron and Llanrhystud. The majority, though, would have eaten oatmeal bread, as it could grow on acidic soil, and rye was common in upland areas.

Turning to the wealthier portion of society, the gentry on whose tables could be found meat, we find a group who were expanding their estates and influence through divers means; for example, by marriage, the end of partible inheritance and money made in trade or the law. With this increased influence in the administration of local government and seats in the national government came grander houses. Cardiganshire's premier family, the Pryses of Gogerddan, like many others, traced their descent to early times, in their case Gwaethfod, lord of Cardigan, who died in 1057. Maybe this preoccupation with pedigrees, in which the Pryses and most other Welsh gentry participated, compensated for their relative poverty; an ancestral line was culturally valuable. Some insights into the lives of Cardiganshire gentry can be garnered from a study of the Lloyds of Gilfachwen, a family of some standing in the parish of Llandysul. Although undeniably a member of the gentry, David Lloyd, who died in 1568, was an active farmer who left a list of livestock in his will. The will of his son Jenkin also survives – interestingly, Jenkin permanently switched to the surname Lloyd and his abandonment of the 'ap' patronymic indicates how English cultural forms were gradually supplanting the traditional ones. Jenkin contributed to the infrastructure of the area by leaving some money for the repair of Llandysul bridge. The Lloyds also traced their family back to the middle ages.

Yet the Cardiganshire gentry, especially ones as prominent as the Pryses, did not rely on past glories alone. They further established their prominence through conspicuous acts of generosity, such as those carried out by Richard Pryse and his son John which were praised by the poet Sion Cain. John Pryse become the first Pryse MP, beginning a tradition that lasted for centuries. A less respectable member of this family was Richard Pryse, the son of John, who followed his father as MP for the county in the later 1500s. His activities illustrate what J. Gwynfor Jones, in his study of the Tudor gentry, perceived as a tension between the expectation that members of the gentry should provide a moral role model and an increasingly competitive society.[14] Cases in which Richard Pryse was cited as being the offender had been before the Star Chamber in the late 1590s. In one he was accused of appropriating the county militia's weaponry for his own use. Even though this was the first century during which Cardiganshire's population did not witness substantial military operations, Pryse deployed force for his own ends. In 1599, together with three other JPs and reportedly 500 armed supporters, Pryse compelled a number of men to pay the traditional payment of *cymorthfa* which, despite being outlawed by the Acts of Union, continued to be exploited by avaricious landlords. On gathering at Tregaron church as requested, the group were accosted by this force and threatened with the prospect of military service in Ireland if they did not pay. The financial pressures of high inflation could have prompted such measures, which in this instance raised £100. Despite his transgressions, Richard Pryse was knighted in 1603.

The *cymorthfa*-gathering incident – which necessitated bringing together a scattered population at one point – reveals how the church was a focal point in Tudor Cardiganshire. Religious debates, though, did not loom large in the county's history at this time. In spite of the enormous religious dislocations during the Tudor period, Cardiganshire did not play an active part in these developments. The Tudor period included Henry VIII's break from Rome, the dissolution of the monasteries, his son Edward VI's Protestant crusade, then Mary's Catholic counter-attack, and Elizabeth's 'compromise' between these extremes. Yet in Cardiganshire there were no robust reactions such as the Catholic uprising in northern England during 1536, or the Prayer Book rebellion in south-west England in 1549. The Welsh gentry's firm allegiance to the Tudor dynasty has been put forward as one possible explanation for this passivity.

Despite the lack of uprisings, the dislocations wrought by the succession of religious changes must have touched the lives of many in the county. The fortunes of a religious statue from the county encapsulates some of the characteristics of this turbulent period. During the first decade of Henry VIII's reign, William Barlow, bishop of St Davids, removed a wooden statue of the Virgin Mary holding Christ from a shrine at Cardigan. This centrepiece included a miraculous taper which, the faithful believed, never died out after being lit. Worshippers may have felt aggrieved on seeing traditional religious landmarks erased. Yet, in the eyes of many in authority, these graven images were undesirable remnants of Catholicism. According to Gilbert Burnet's history of the Reformation, the shrine was the most visited religious site in this part of the country, and local people swore oaths on it during civil law cases.[15] Later, during Elizabeth's reign, this image was purportedly tossed into the Teifi, where it was believed to have miraculously appeared during the thirteenth century. If this was the case, perhaps Cardigan's Catholics had managed to preserve the figure through Edward VI's reign as well as that of his father.

Another change in religious policy that affected people in the county occurred during the Catholic backlash. In Mary's reign ministers were unable to practise if they were married. In the diocese of St Davids, of which Cardiganshire was a part, some sixty-five left their positions after this change was introduced in 1553. Yet the material trappings of ecclesiastical life were most vulnerable at times when the Protestants were on the offensive. An Act was passed during Edward VI's reign in 1549 which outlawed the use of old liturgical books, like the service book of Llanbadarn Fawr. Moreover, Edward's ruling of 1547 that the gold vessels used in Mass were to be replaced by silver communion cups, and a similar later demand by Elizabeth, were not complied with in the county until the early 1570s – one of these symbols which demonstrated an external acceptance of the Elizabethan settlement was granted to Llanddewibrefi church in 1574. Therefore, the absence of a dramatic reaction must not be taken as an indication that the switches in religious stance by monarchs did not have an effect here. There are some indications of what Glanmor Williams called 'non-militant Catholicism' in the county.[16] Yet, in all likelihood, the Welsh translation of the Bible by William Morgan, who had been vicar at Llanbadarn Fawr in the early 1570s, contributed to the waning of Catholic sentiment in Cardiganshire.

Accounts of this period are often dominated by the dissolution of the monasteries. The termination of Cardigan Priory, Llanllŷr and Strata Florida mark the largest single material changes in the county during this period. While these religious sites were not what they once were, their disbandment could have been more significant than has often been presumed. Only twelve monks resided at Strata Florida, and the incarceration of one of their number for minting false coins has been taken as a sign of the abbey's degeneration. A change in the aural soundscape as the bells fell silent, and the possibility that monks continued to perform some medical functions, suggested in the enduring belief that they possessed a healing bowl made of olive wood said to be part of the cross on which Christ was crucified, offer two clues as to the possible loss felt at the abbey's demise. Strata Florida managed a stay of execution when it paid a fine in 1536. But three years later the axe came down, and the Devereux family took possession of it. Later, in 1571, the Steadmans bought it. Parts of the already neglected abbey were taken, its bells went to the parish of Caron and lead was stripped from the building thus hastening the structure's decline. Just the heads of these houses received a pension, the last abbot of Strata Florida was granted £40 per annum and the abbess of Llanllŷr £4. Observations made by John Leland during his journey through Wales provide an easily accessible source of information about the twilight years of these religious communities. Of Cardigan Priory, which was bought by John Cavendish in 1539, Leland wrote that there were only two black monks there. It is somewhat ironic that Leland was commissioned by Henry VIII to record the antiquaries of England and Wales and, as a result of Henry's policies, these religious institutions soon joined castles and other ancient sites whose *raison d'être* had come to an end.

Cardiganshire had its own contemporary antiquarian. While not quite in Leland's position, he was something more than his later scandalous reputation as the 'wild wag of Wales' implies. A 'natural' son of Sion ap Dafydd Wynn of Gwydir, Thomas Jones (Twm Sion Cati), entered legend as a gentleman rogue. His supposed youthful adventures embarrassed later antiquarians who admired his genealogical work; a nineteenth-century antiquarian was certain that 'he never practiced or performed' the 'many exploits' attributed to him. Thomas Jones, of Fountain Gate near Tregaron, was renowned as an expert on the pedigrees and heraldry of the Welsh gentry. A contemporary, Dr Sion Dafydd Rhys, described him as the greatest genealogist and one whose death would leave a gap that could not be filled by anyone else.[17] Thomas Jones's interest in the pedigrees of the upper portion of society provides another indicator of the importance of lineage in Cardiganshire society at the time referred to earlier. In 1590 he recorded the Pryse line, and perhaps his connection to Richard Pryse, who had criminal tendencies, lends support to the tales about him being a 'wild wag'; though whether he in fact threatened to cut off the hand of a woman, Lady Joan Devereux of Ystrad-fin, Carmarthenshire, unless she gave it to him in marriage will never be known.

Gentlemen were not necessarily 'gentle' in Tudor Cardiganshire. In his detailed account of the game of knappan (believed to be connected to the verb to 'knock') played in Pembrokeshire and southern Cardiganshire, George Owen noted that as well as prearranged days for the games, 'two gentlemen' when they so desired could call together teams representing parishes, hundreds, or shires. That men of standing could initiate an event which involved masses of men fighting and literally tearing each other's hair out over a wooden ball, boiled in tallow to make it difficult to hold, would shock later sensibilities.[18] Revealingly, Owen, although providing graphic descriptions, did not censure these events. This lends some support to the cultural historian Peter Burke's idea that popular culture in the sixteenth century was not so strictly divided on class lines as it became during the following two centuries. What Burke described as the 'withdrawal of the upper classes' from the cultural activities of the majority had evidently not reached its lowest ebb in Cardiganshire when Owen recorded his observations.[19]

According to Owen the largest regular knappan games took place on Ascension Day and Corpus Christi at 'St Meygans' in Pembrokeshire. In these events the Cemaes men faced those of Emlyn 'and the men of Cardiganshire'. This inter-county contest drew more players than the other Pembrokeshire-only events. Up to two thousand men, besides those on horseback, took part in the game which lasted until the ball 'be soe farre carryed that there is no hope to retorne it backe that night'. Owen noted that the knappan was more violent at this time than in its classic form. Reputedly a means to maintain the martial spirit among men during peaceful times, the knappan also provided a means for localities to earn glory and offered commercial opportunities for victuallers who set up stalls selling food and 'drinke and wyne of all sortes'. At another level, this event, after which there was to be peace until the next meeting, provided a means to ventilate pent-up social tensions.

Other forms of popular culture in Tudor Cardiganshire emerge from the records. As is often the case, however, the activities we read of are those considered a problem by those attempting to maintain social and moral order. Thus we hear of tennis being played in a churchyard at Cardigan in 1580, which, unlike the knappan, was deemed to have disturbed the peace. So attempts to regulate activities were sporadic and uneven, though we can discern, from the late fifteenth century, efforts being made, particularly by members of the clergy, to alter the cultural activities of the lower orders. Alehouses were often linked to illegal activity, like gambling and 'women of light conversation'.[20] Such centres of misbehaviour, it was argued, led to the beneficial pastime of archery being neglected. In 1577 the Council in the Marches of Wales requested JPs to list the alehouses and attempt to reduce their excessive number. Not many responded, but fortunately those for Cardiganshire did and identified forty-one in the county. Despite being far fewer than Carmarthenshire's 196, Cardiganshire's alehouses, like those of Anglesey and Caernarfonshire which had the least at thirty, need to be related to differences in their respective populations. More reliable than an indicator of morality is their use as a sign of commercial activity in various parts of Wales. However, these figures are sketchy and are probably of most use in indicating a concern with public behaviour. Far more fundamental attempts to combat such disagreeable practices surfaced with the advent of Puritanism in the following century.

VI

The Seventeenth Century

Nonconformity, that multi-textured alternative to the established Church, first established roots in Cardiganshire in the seventeenth century. In future it became one of the county's defining characteristics, yet later success should not overshadow its vulnerable beginnings in a less hospitable climate. In religious matters Wales was a conservative land during this century. The reasons given by historians for this – geographical isolation and the absence of a large middle trading class – were particularly applicable to Cardiganshire.

Puritanism – a term defined in part by a desire to avoid the impurities of ceremonial forms of worship practised by Catholics – was most often generated in environments where the economy was driven by an enterprising middle class. In addition, tensions between the new and older ways of worshipping the same god occurred in places where the puritans' antithesis, the High Church Arminians who sought to return to Catholic forms of worship, were strongest. James I and his son, Charles I, supported this stance and promoted Arminians in the Church of England. Neither of these contributory factors figured large in seventeenth-century Cardiganshire. The county possessed few of those people described by the historian Geraint H. Jenkins as 'serious-minded middling sorts in urban communities'. Some indication of the relative poverty of Aberystwyth's wealthier inhabitants is provided by figures from the 1670 Hearth Tax collections. Roy Lewis and Sandra Wheatley found that only just over half of the town's houses were taxed and that a mere 8 per cent possessed more than one hearth, figures far lower than many English towns. Few in the town, then, had to part with more than the 2 s. for a single hearth or oven.[1]

For all that, the county was not entirely bereft of this history-making section of society. After his appointment in 1646, the early Welsh Puritan Evan Roberts was active in the parish of Llanbadarn Fawr and adjoining parishes. It is possible that he was the 'one Roberts' ejected by the bishop of St Davids in 1634 for 'inconformity'.

He was appointed during the Interregnum and it is recorded that he preached in Welsh and English. Roberts was to 'preach diligentlie' to some four thousand souls and in return was paid £100 per annum for carrying out his duties. In 1649 Evan Roberts's translation of *The Foundation of the Christian Religion* (1590) by the theologian William Perkins was published. Roberts was one of fourteen preachers appointed by the Puritan new order to serve in Wales during the late 1640s.

This attempt to bolster the Puritan cause was headed by preachers from outside Cardiganshire, notably Vavasor Powell and Walter Cradock, who promoted their faith in the county. In fact Powell sent four preachers from Brecon on a preaching campaign to Cardiganshire. Radnorshire-born Powell was a Fifth Monarchist. This group believed they were preparing the earth for the second coming of Christ. When Oliver Cromwell took the title of Lord Protector in 1653, the Fifth Monarchy men opposed his assumption of near kingly status. In choosing Llanddewibrefi as the starting point of a preaching campaign, during which he attacked Cromwell's assumption of greater authority, Powell was echoing St David, who had contended with an alternative belief at the village centuries earlier. Unlike St David, Powell did not stage a miraculous counter-attack and his vehemence repelled many Puritans who felt Cromwell was better than the unknown; the other Puritan leading light, Walter Cradock, supported Cromwell.

Changes were inaugurated in 1650 by the Act for the Better Propagation and Preaching of the Gospel in Wales. In effect, the Propagation Committee was the real government of Wales during the years 1650–3. Reformers emphasized the failings of the established Church, particularly its lack of preaching. The Propagation Act was used to remove three Cardiganshire ministers from their positions in the county because they kept alehouses – the vicar William Meredith at Lampeter, Morris Powell, rector of Betws Bledrws, and Griffith Evans, the vicar of Llanrhystud. Of the 196 ministers removed in south Wales, twenty were from the county. A number of those who did not keep 'common alehouses' evidently frequented them for ten were rejected for being drunkards. Most grounds for removal were moral and not founded on religious suitability. However, three of the ministers were found guilty of using the Common Prayer Book. This text, an Elizabethan compromise, was deemed by the Puritans to have not broken away from the Catholic style of worship. After ejection, the wife and children of each removed minister received 20 per cent (called a fifth) of the living they had held. Generally speaking, the lot of removed clergymen in Cardiganshire was better than elsewhere. According to Thomas Richards, 'Cardiganshire was by far the most generous and consistent' in the provision of fifths among the Welsh counties.[2] Although not amounting to proof, this could be interpreted as evidence that there was a special affinity for the old order in the county.

Throughout Wales concern was expressed about the quality of the new ministers. In 1654 the Cromwellian government instituted a test which had to be passed by all preachers before they took up their posts. This was important as the perambulating preachers were to be replaced by stationary ministers. In all, eight successful candidates were rewarded with Cardiganshire parishes. One of the Cardiganshire men about whom we know most was John Lewis of Glasgrug. A Puritan landowner, Lewis wanted to improve clerical standards through the establishment of a Welsh training college. Among the locations suggested for the institution were two in the county – Cardigan and Aberystwyth. Financial support for this vision was not forthcoming, however, and it would be many years before ministers were trained in the county.

As well as the state, or Presbyterian Church, there were Congregationalists (Independents) in the county during the middle of the century. Notes taken from the Cilgwyn church book – which disappeared towards the end of the nineteenth century – reveal that congregations first gathered at Lampeter in 1654. Its organization was separate from that of the parish churches; they had taken a step further away from ecclesiastical tradition. The 'exceeding rude' reception given to the Quaker George Fox at either Lampeter or Cardigan (his journal does not specify which) during a tour in 1657 reminds us that alternative religious groupings were not always tolerated at this time. Some of those who voiced disapproval may well have been Puritans. The Interregnum was a time of toleration from above while confrontation occurred between the various groups who were able to voice their views. In his 1656 work, *Eyaggeloigrapha*, John Lewis mentioned that Quakers were holders of 'strange opinions and crased extravigancies'.[3]

After the restoration of the monarchy in 1660 toleration from above was replaced by periodical persecution. The Act of Uniformity of 1662, which required every clergyman to accept the Book of Common Prayer, led to many who had not already been removed leaving the church. Thirteen were dismissed from the county as a result of this, but the harshness of the restored monarchy reinforced the Nonconformist cause as Presbyterians and others now had a common enemy. This contrasted with the earlier period when governmental tolerance led to confrontation. In addition to removing ministers, there was an attempt to stifle Nonconformist worship by the Conventicle Act which forbade more than five to meet for religious worship unless it was in accordance with the Book of Common Prayer. After being caught doing this for a third time the penalty was transportation – punishment for the second offence was imprisonment and there was a fine for the first. Until 1670, when the powers of the arresting magistrate were extended beyond their county, Nonconformists held meetings near county boundaries. Consequently, the Teifi valley, a boundary between Cardiganshire, Carmarthenshire and Pembrokeshire, became a choice location for meetings

Persecution was continual rather than continuous; it was often repeated, but not incessant. The law was applied more vigorously at particular times than others. Furthermore, in 1672 the short-lived Declaration of Indulgence meant that all penal statutes against Nonconformists were lifted. Records of the licences granted to preachers include one Morgan Howell, born in Betws Bledrws. A tale, typical of religious conversion stories, explains how Howell started a game of football in an attempt to interrupt the great Walter Cradock while he was preaching. After sustaining an injured ankle during the game, he listened to Cradock, heeded his instructions and then joined the Congregational church at Lampeter. Eventually, the Act of Toleration (1689) entitled most Nonconformist ministers to practise. William III acknowledged that the Nonconformists had worked with the Anglicans in their opposition to the Papist James II. Yet the Test and Corporation Acts were not banned, so private belief still prevented Nonconformists from assuming public office.

By the end of the century, however, Cardiganshire was not a Nonconformist county. As E. G. Bowen noted in his work on the Teifi as a 'religious frontier', by 1696 all of the county's Baptists could gather at one church at Glandwr, in Carmarthenshire.[4] Undoubtedly this denomination's strength lay on the south side of the river. Nonconformity remained strongest in southern Cardiganshire during this period. The north was virtually bare of meeting houses until the emergence of Methodism in the eighteenth century. Still, at the end of the seventeenth century Welsh dissent was about to turn a new page. As some Anglicans were aware, the growth of dissent in Wales went hand in hand with the publication of literature and educational drives which developed after the Act of Toleration.

In a survey of seventeenth-century Wales, Philip Jenkins argued that there are a number of 'convenient myths' about Welsh society during this period. Among these were 'the hostility of the Established Church towards the Welsh language'.[5] There is evidence from southern Cardiganshire which could support Jenkins's view, while at the same time identifying some of the weaknesses within the Anglican Church. Welsh-language hymns called *halsingodau* were written by Anglican ministers. These were popular in the south of the county from the latter part of the seventeenth century until the arrival of Methodism. *Halsingodau* were intended to fill a gap in Welsh religious life after the retreat of Catholicism. Yet this form of worship, which educated singers and listeners, also helped compensate for the absence of sermons in churches; it was a means to satisfy spiritual hunger where ecclesiastical provision was wanting.

Welsh loyalty to the monarchy during the Civil War has been explained by the relative lack of religious dissent. This broad-brush picture of Welsh loyalty to Crown or Parliament during the Civil War places the bulk of Wales with the former and the more 'progressive' mercantile areas like Pembrokeshire and Denbighshire in the latter camp. Some individuals and localities did not fit this pattern, however. In Cardiganshire, a supporter of the Parliamentary cause, John Lewis expressed his support in *Contemplations upon these times, or the Parliament explained to Wales*. This was published in 1646, the year following significant Parliamentary victories when the Royalists lost the Midlands. This left the Crown in control of only the west of England and Wales, areas too poor to provide financial assistance. Lewis's timely call for support noted how 'the favours of God have broke in upon our Armies', and condemned the Common Prayer Book as promoting '*Conformity* to *Ceremonies*' rather than '*Conformity* to *Christianity*'.[6] Lewis demanded its abolition, it was only of use – like a full moon at night – during 'the times of Superstition', now the rays of the gospel were emerging it had no place.

When a Royalist commander observed that the counties of south-west Wales would probably give up on 'the first danger' appearing, he was noting a key aspect of the war – a tendency for self-preservation over loyalty to ideals. Yet these simplifications and accusations of lack of principle hold water only if viewed from a certain perspective. John Vaughan, although not rushing to either side, revealed a fundamental belief which could be judged as being just as principled as outright loyalty to Crown or Parliament. At the start of the conflict, he wanted advice on the course that would cause the least harm to the country. This wily man, who had expanded his estate through the purchase of lands formerly belonging to Strata Florida, was a Royalist who was not afraid to criticize or oppose the king's wishes. Even after the Restoration, in 1667, he made a stand against Charles II's requests for capital.

Subtleties of thinking in the minds of individuals like Vaughan were rudely disturbed by a conflict which compelled polarization. While some, such as Walter Lloyd of Llanfair Clydogau, kept their heads below the parapets, others were drawn into the conflict. The second earl of Carbery took most of Cardiganshire and Carmarthenshire into the war under the king's standard. Throughout 1643 his forces made inroads in Pembrokeshire. In 1644 his campaign faltered when Rowland Laugharne broke out of Pembroke, regaining lost territory and gaining new footholds. Cardiganshire appears to have demonstrated more loyalty to Charles I than Carmarthenshire at this time. When Laugharne called, or 'summoned', both counties to change sides, the latter expressed more willingness to side with him than the former. On being advised by some supporters to request Cardiganshire to change sides again, Laugharne refused and set out to convert the Cardiganshire Royalists by force of arms instead of words.

Replacing Carbery with Charles Gerard rejuvenated the Royalist cause. After taking Carmarthenshire, Gerard attacked Cardigan castle, which had been taken by Parliamentary forces. According to J. Roland Phillips, in his nineteenth-century history of the Civil War in Wales, before Gerard arrived in 1644 'the County of Cardigan had been at this time much distressed by the Pembrokeshire men'.[7] Phillips referred to a Royalist source which claimed they had taken the town and castle along with 200 prisoners. A Parliamentary source, *The True Informer*, also mentions the capitulation of Cardigan castle. While in south-west Wales Gerard ruled with an iron hand, located many troops there, established governors from outside the area and created a belt of barren land to hem in the Pembrokeshire Parliamentarians. This policy alienated many in the region, and this, as much as the removal of Gerard and his army to England in August, explains the rapid gains made by the Parliamentarians towards the end of 1644.

Captain Beal was sent to reinforce rebel forces at Anglesey, but stormy seas took him to Pembroke where he joined Laugharne. Then Beal headed north to join the northern rebels. They came to meet him on 2 November at Lampeter. Cromwellian forces had penetrated northern Cardiganshire in 1644 when Myddelton sent soldiers to Llanbadarn Fawr. From here they launched raids on Trawsgoed – Vaughan wrote that his property had been completely ransacked – and the property of other Royalists. In response, Royalists launched an attack on the base at Llanbadarn Fawr early in the morning, but were defeated in the skirmish.

The weather once again played a part in the war, as rains prevented Parliamentary forces from marching on Cardigan until shortly before Christmas. Cardigan town submitted without putting up any resistance, and this was in all probability due to the prominence of James Philips who resided at the priory. Yet the castle, commanded by Major Slaughter, held out under a barrage of cannon fire, which took three days to pierce the walls. After this breech was entered over one hundred troops were captured, and 200 fatalities had been sustained during the siege. Royalist prisoners, including the former chaplain to the Crown Dr Jeremy Taylor, were taken. An attempt to regain the castle by the Royalists took place before Gerard arrived. To forestall Parliamentarian reinforcements from Pembrokeshire they destroyed the bridge over the Teifi. Laugharne's troops made rafts to cross the river and in a bitter struggle killed 350 and took 150 prisoners – including men of some standing – and four brass cannons. Contemporaries placed great emphasis on artillery during this conflict, but castles still offered substantial protection, as the sieges of Cardigan and later Aberystwyth revealed.

In an effort to put Laugharne back in his Pembrokeshire cage, Gerard, together with what were described as 'his Irish and Popish forces', returned from England. They travelled through mid Wales, plundering Tregaron and Lampeter on the way. This march down the Teifi ended when they met the Parliamentarians as the latter were attacking Newcastle Emlyn. In this struggle the Roundheads were overwhelmed by a larger force, and 150 fell there. Cromwell's supporter in Cardigan did not suffer the same fate. Using the sea as an escape route, they returned to Pembrokeshire. They soon returned to the offensive because the Royalist cause in England needed the notoriously ruthless commander Gerard in May 1646.

Laugharne struck again, and by September all the counties of south Wales had joined the Parliamentary cause. Control of Cardigan castle changed for the last time, when the surrounded Royalists vacated it. Garrisons in Aberystwyth and Newcastle Emlyn, however, held out. The latter fell to Colonel Lewes in December. Aberystwyth, commanded by Colonel Richard Whitley, was resilient. Eminent men gathered around this problematic castle as they had in Edward I's day. Colonel Rice Powell led the besieging forces, and the local notable John Jones of Nanteos, who had raised Royalist forces earlier in the war, contributed to this assault. While waiting for the castle to fall, these adherents of Parliament, old and new, launched attacks into Merionethshire, the bastion of the Crown in north-west Wales. These raids from northern Cardiganshire had serious consequences for some who resided in what had been a relatively undisturbed part of the principality. On 8 December 1645 John Jones launched a night assault on Peniarth during which his forces abducted two Royalists 'in their beds and carried them to Cardiganshire'. A maritime raid on Barmouth by 'Cardiganshire men' occurred on 3 January. They 'plundered' the settlement in this assault. These attacks were the result of local initiative and Laugharne condemned them, promising to punish these booty-hungry raiders.[8] Eventually, the troops defending Aberystwyth castle surrendered in April 1646. In spite of the siege, the castle was only brought down in 1649. This was probably due to its having become a place where former soldiers lurked and stole from the locals.

On 1 March 1648, before the Second Civil War broke out, the Cardiganshire forces were disbanded at Lampeter. The Royalist uprisings of this second troubled period did not affect the county. Nonetheless, Cardiganshire, through the MP for Cardigan borough, Thomas Wogan, played a vicarious part in the execution of Charles II after the Second Civil War. Wogan, a Pembrokeshire man and lieutenant in the Parliamentary army in that county during 1644, was an ardent Roundhead who had performed well at the battle of St Fagans in 1648. He was MP for the county boroughs between 1646–53 and was one of only two Welshmen who contributed to one of the most significant events in British history when they signed the king's death warrant.

During the Interregnum numerous committees were set up in the counties. Their aims included promoting Puritanism and the more mundane, but crucial task of collecting money. These committees included some new men, often from the minor gentry or ex-soldiers, and were resented by those who had long been involved in the administration of the county. An especially disliked figure was Thomas Evans of Peterwell, Lampeter, who was sheriff of the county in 1653. He was married to a niece of John Vaughan of Trawsgoed, but unlike the latter had made a more committed switch in allegiance during the war. This staunch Cromwellian commanded cavalry units, and his son David led foot soldiers, as part of the Committee for Safety revived in 1659. After the Restoration he was described as being a very violent man who was eager to fill important positions and cruel when he acquired them. Even when the tide was turning, in 1660, he tried to incite men to take up arms against General Monke's Royalist forces. As Cromwell's agents in Cardiganshire, Thomas and his son were thought to have acquired great wealth and correspondingly plentiful amounts of resentment.

Letters written in 1652 provide evidence of the tensions in Cardiganshire during the Interregnum. From Tregaron on 10 November the county commissioners wrote to London regarding a problem they faced. After summoning Thomas Evans, registrar to the late subcommittee of accounts for Cardiganshire, Evans objected to having his papers examined or handed over to the county commissioners. They committed him to the mayor of Tregaron, Oliver Lloyd, but the mayor later refused to hand him over 'and used opprobrious words in affront of our authority'. They then arrested Lloyd. Another Tregaron rebel, Thomas Lloyd Bishop announced that 'some of us were traitors and delinquents, and were incapable of our place'.[9] Problems of this nature reveal how strong local opposition towards the new order could be. This discontent sparked a rebellion in the county during 1651. Rowland Dawkins, MP for Carmarthenshire in 1654, quelled an insurrection at Llanbadarn Fawr. This was sparked off by rumours that Charles was near at hand. A brother of John Lewes of Abernantbychan led the rising.

Some of the money sequestered from the Church was used to fund educational institutions. Two Propagation Act schools were established, one at Cardigan and the other at Lampeter. Of the sixty-three established in Wales by 1653 only twenty-one are thought to have been in operation by 1660. If these schools are taken as indicators of those places where Puritanism was strongest, then evidently the north of the county was less Puritan than the south – this may also help explain why there was a rebellion in Llanbadarn Fawr at the northern end of the county. In 1647 James Philips of Cardigan gathered support for a school in the town and asked Parliament to establish a school funded by an annual grant of £100 'out of the impropriations sequestered from the delinquents in the county'. Points made by Philips in support of the request reveal a town where English was rarely heard – 'None save the best sort of gentry can read or speak the English tongue' – and where preaching was conducted in that language the majority could not understand 'for want of breeding'. By 1653 it was agreed that the fees would come from the impropriated tithes of Llansanffraid parish. While this source of income was removed with the return of the monarchy, the school continued, probably by reducing the number of scholars who were given a free education and increasing the fees of those who paid.[10]

Most high-ranking Parliamentary commissioners were English. One exception, the aforementioned John Lewis, came from Cardiganshire. Though never denying his Welshness, he used 'we' when describing the Welsh, Lewis's attitude reveals how some Welsh Puritans could accept the prominence of outsiders. Lewis thought that the county and Wales as a whole 'deserved harsher means, and rougher hands to reduce us, than we had'. Evidently, there were ideological ties which were valued more than national attachments. For others, though, losses were sustained. At the end of the century parishioners in Llanwenog recollected strange kinds of trout occupying a well. It was said that these fish had gold chains around them and that they had been destroyed during the 'Oliverian Revolution'. Whether these bizarrely adorned fish were genuine may well be doubted, but the tale symbolically represents the Puritan attack on adornment and old beliefs.[11]

Political instability wrought by the Civil War and its aftermath deterred investment and this had an adverse affect on Cardiganshire's mines. Earlier in the century, however, Hugh Myddelton had further exploited the mines of Goginan and Cwmsymlog. He originally came to the county in 1617 to find coal. Though disappointed on that front, he discovered plenty of lead. What was more, he challenged conventional wisdom that the quality of lead declined the deeper one found it. This enterprise brought profit; silver and lead were produced until his death in 1631. An equally intrepid individual, Thomas Bushell, one of Francis Bacon's favourites, took over the mines in 1636 and he improved drainage and ventilation. While engaged in the costly exercise Bushell asked the king for a mint to be established at Aberystwyth castle – this would reduce the cost of transporting material and provide quick returns for mining work as silver could be minted nearby. Determination and innovation reaped rewards; his first success was at Tal-y-bont, where he also set up a smeltery.

Bushell lost control of the mines after the king fell. During the conflict he supplied Charles I with money and provided medals with which to reward loyal Royalists. Money was minted at Aberystwyth until 1643, but the fall of London meant that the king needed his money to be closer to hand. As a result it moved to Shrewsbury then Oxford, though the silver still came from Cardiganshire. Parliamentarian ships targeted vessels carrying cargos of lead destined for Royalists. Silver went overland but was also frequently intercepted after war was declared. Although mines were worked later, it was not until the explorations near Esgair-hir from 1690 by Carbery Pryse, that mining in the county experienced its next period of expansion. After winning the right for landowners to operate their own mines, even if they contained silver and gold, he established a company to work the mines. Humphrey Mackworth of Neath bought his shares after Pryse died. Mackworth's manager of the mines William Waller promoted the potential of the mines when he put forward a scheme in 1698. Waller coined the description 'The Welsh Potosi' after the mines in Peru. Shareholders were promised a profit of £171,970 per annum from lead alone. In his *Essay on the Value of the Mines* Waller declared: 'There are in the North of England many rich Mines discovered; but there is none either in England or Wales, that can pretend to come near the Value of the famous mines of Sir Carbery Price.' In order to fire the imaginations of potential shareholders, a map of the South American mines was included in his description. Despite advances in mining methods, the following century did not entirely live up to these expectations. Waller's predictions that 'these Mines of Cardiganshire will give occasion for erecting as large a Town as that at Potozi' were not fulfilled.[12]

Poor transport links and the absence of coal meant that industrial activity did not take root in the county. Yet there is considerable evidence of trading activity and the sea offered an alternative to arduous journeys overland. As Waller noted in his essay, Cardiganshire mines had an advantage over those of Peru because they were closer to the sea. To the south, slates left Cardigan for Ireland at the end of the Stuart period. Indeed, Ireland was the destination for 60 per cent of all Welsh exports. Yet trade with Ireland had a negative aspect as Irish cattle threatened the Welsh, and no doubt Cardiganshire's, bovine trade. Earlier attempts to limit the importation of Irish cattle in the reign of James I had failed, but in 1666 the native cattle trade was given protection when Irish imports were forbidden. Traces of more welcome imports, parts of bowls thought to originate in the Barnstaple-Bideford area, were found at a mud-walled farmhouse in the Rheidol valley near Capel Bangor during the early 1950s. It is likely that this was a common export because its shape, a flat-bottomed pan 16 inches in diameter, could be easily stacked. Apples from Gloucester were another English import to the county during the seventeenth century.

Fairs played an important part in Cardiganshire's agricultural economy. At the start of the century, twenty-seven fairs were held every year in Cardiganshire; this was more than any other county in Wales except Carmarthenshire and Glamorgan – the former had the greatest number, forty-two every year. Even Llangrannog had a fair – an indication of the brisk sea trade. As in other parts of Wales, most were held between May and October, but nine took place between November and April. Trade with north Wales included livestock – yearling sheep were sold in May to hill farmers in Montgomeryshire and Merionethshire. Crops – namely, oats, barley, wheat and rye – were also sent northwards. The county may have been a peripheral one in some respects, but it was well placed for trade both with Ireland and between north and south Wales. Additionally, cattle bought at Ffair Rhos went to English markets. In general, the county's land was not as fertile as Carmarthenshire's. Richard Blome in *Britannia* (1673) recorded others' praise of the latter which was 'esteemed by some the strongest county in south Wales' being 'generally of a fertile soil'. Acidic soil, which made up much of Cardiganshire's land, was not as productive. Blome put this simply, writing that it was 'of a different soil', while also recording that there were 'very fertile' parts in southern and western parts. Like Carmarthenshire, the county was 'plentifully served' with fish. Though Blome thought that fishing for cod and herring would have been more profitable and productive 'were its inhabitants industrious'.[13]

Once again, the county's poverty, seen in its inhabitants' desire to avoid too much taxation, figures in this century. John Vaughan tried to shift the weight of taxation to north Wales because he felt Cardiganshire was being overtaxed. The upper echelons of Cardiganshire society were not particularly wealthy and they evidently guarded what wealth they possessed. After only a few years on the throne, James I had exhausted his coffers. This previously cautious monarch of a poor country, Scotland, lost inhibitions about spending when he succeeded Elizabeth and became ruler of a wealthier land. Among the ways in which he sought to replenish his reserves was the imposition of the 'mise' – a sum to be paid by Wales when there was a change in monarch. The reaction to this demand from Cardiganshire illustrates the relative poverty of the county, although it must be remembered that a reluctance to pay this belated tax – which was asked for in 1606, some three years after James came to the throne – was widespread. In 1606 Edward Vaughan wrote to the Earl of Dunbar, chancellor of the Court of Exchequer, to explain that the county was too poor to offer up the first instalment of £111. Soon after this, Crown tenants in Wales were asked to make a payment towards the cost of Prince Henry's knighthood celebrations in 1609.

Nevertheless, the opposition raised by James I's financial demands was negligible in comparison with those incited of his son Charles I. John Lewes, MP for the county from 1604 to 1611, headed a petition presented in 1635 which complained about the county's excessive ship money rating of £654. A later request for this amount led to a passive rebellion. Cardiganshire people's goods were taken but no income was forthcoming because they were not collected. At a loss at what to do, Richard Pryse, the county's sheriff, wrote to the Council of Wales and the Marches. Five years earlier the king requested all freeholders whose income was £40 or more per annum in land or rents to be present at his coronation and be knighted. However, this came at a cost – £50 in fees. Few leapt at this opportunity and Charles decided to call those who did not pay before a commission. A list of men called before this commission includes the various reasons they gave for not accepting the honour. Primarily these were poverty, incapacity (David Lloyd of Aber-mad was said to be seventy-two and 'decrpit') and not having received a summons.[14] It is a pity that the result of these inquires is unknown, but they do show a reluctance to part with money for the sake of a knighthood, possibly less from principle than from economy, or perhaps a combination of both.

Economic matters provide some information regarding the position of Cardiganshire's women in the seventeenth century. Freeholders could find themselves paying a 10 *s.* fee to the lord of the manor 'for evry of his daughters which Marrieth or Miscarrieth' in the lordship of Iscoed Uwch Hirwern in southern Cardiganshire.[14] The extent to which this outlay influenced reactions to the birth of daughters and the consequent value placed on them can only be guessed at. Successive dowries, economic accompaniments to marriage, were paid by the female's family and would have also placed a strain on resources. They may, indeed, have encouraged people to limit their families. In Cardiganshire, dowries generally consisted of livestock instead of money which was relatively rare. Nevertheless, as Gerald Morgan has written, many women did lead active lives 'not necessarily restricted to home and farm'.[15] Some lent money. For example, when she wrote her will in 1681, a spinster, Mary Lloyd of Ynys-hir, recorded that she was owed £500. She had been left a mill by her father. Mary, and others like her, such as Dyddgu of Llangrannog, who died in 1630 and was owed over £90, were in effect 'local bankers'. Less wealthy unmarried or widowed women also owned property, but could not carry out functions like Lloyd and Dyddgu. Yet any property, even a small number of livestock, did grant some independence. Only two cases before the Great Sessions, from the 1690s, hint at persecution for witchcraft in the county. And although the two women from the Nantcwnlle-Trefilan area were not punished, both were vulnerable, one a widow and the other the wife of a 'wandering crwth-player'. Many women accused of possessing powers which could harm others were the least powerful in economic terms. They dwelt in communities where superstition played an important part in social relationships, possibly as a means to explain and rationalize misfortune.

Records of fines demanded by the Council of Wales and the Marches, based at Ludlow, offer glimpses of the cultural activities engaged in by Cardiganshire people. In north Cardiganshire, for example, there lived a woman whose satirical abilities – she wrote, published and sang Welsh rhymes that contained some outrageous libels – cost her £3. This woman's comments which were woven into rhyme would be easily memorized and repeated by those who, unlike her, were illiterate. This case illustrates how the interest of the council in supervising justice in Wales and limiting the abuses of the gentry was supplemented by concerns with deference among the population at large. The libels of the lady of Llanfihangel-y-Creuddyn suggest a society alive with tales and rumours and offer an example of how the majority oral culture and that of the literate minority could combine.

There was also a reaction against traditional activities which, according to their opponents, were more harmful than many assumed. John Lewis of Glasgrug warned of the pernicious effects of the superstitious 'ceremonies that are among us, passing under the name of old harmless custom'. Yet this Cardiganshire critic did not dismiss all popular belief, merely those practices which could pose a theological challenge to his Puritan beliefs. For instance, despite Lewis's condemnation of activities such as 'peregrinations to wells', which were construed as Catholic, he did not deny the existence of that herald of death, the corpse candle. Rather, he incorporated it into his world-view when he explained that it must be a sign from God. Less judgmental, purely descriptive accounts of customs are provided in responses to Edward Lhuyd's *Parochialia*. These also show the part superstition played in the lives of people at the end of the seventeenth century. At Llangybi parish, the sick were placed under a standing stone, 'Lhech Gibi'; if the ill person slept they would recover, if they did not it was taken as proof that they would die. A letter from a minister, John Davis of Genau'r-glyn, written in 1656, described another common apparition – a dart of light travelling through the air and which continues to sparkle for some time after landing 'upon Free-Holders lands'. This phenomenon tells us something about the value placed on land in seventeenth-century Cardiganshire as it foretold the imminent death of one who owned the land it fell upon. Although not leaving a physical trace these must have had a social impact because they signified a change in the ownership of a precious resource. Seeing or hearing of this was said to encourage people to write their wills, an act which would clarify succession and remove doubt. Moving from beliefs to activities, a respondent to Lhuyd's enquires from Nantcwnlle reported that: 'Tennis and fives and football are their vocations.' It is a pity that more respondents did not note such features. Only two of the eighteen Cardiganshire parishes that are described in this compilation refer to the amusements of the inhabitants. The other, from Troed-yr-aur, refers to '*knap*', adding that it was played in part of the neighbouring parish of Penbryn. Perhaps these brief allusions reveal that the game was not as popular as it once had been.[16]

Although barely 5 per cent of the population made wills, these and other legal records provide insights into lives, possessions and conventions. They recorded cases of poverty, such as that of Griffith ab Evan of Caron who was called before the court of Great Sessions in 1629 for perambulating 'upp, and downe' with a drum and pipe. Concern about the parish poor is shown in the will of 'Meredith Llewellyne' of Henfynyw parish in southern Cardiganshire, composed around 1656. He left some corn and a 'stone of cheese' for the 'poores' of the parish to be distributed at Christmas following his death. The value placed on oxen, which were then more commonly used than horses for ploughing and transport, is also shown in this will. The grant of flannel to make a female relative of his 'a shurt or smoke yearly during her natural liefe' demonstrates the importance of this material for clothing, and perhaps reveals how often these garments would, ideally, be replaced. Moelwyn I. Williams refers to the 'interesting but unusual bequest' of 10 *s.* to his landlord and concluded that this indicates that landlord and tenant were 'on amicable terms'. Yet a collection of material gathered by Melville Richards, noted how in a nearby part of the county freeholders were expected to pay this amount to the manor 'ffor a Heriott or Mortuary upon death'.[17]

Differences between the lives of the rich and poor in the county struck Thomas Dineley who toured Wales with the duke of Beaufort, lord president of Wales, in 1684. 'The vulgar here are most miserable, as the rich are happy and high both to an extreme.' While the poor ate oaten cakes for bread and many drank water alone, the estate owners had plenty of French wine, 'clarets especially'. No mention was made of those who lived between these extremes, but this should not be taken as proof that none existed. Dineley was struck by the proximity of extremes. This contrast was evidently far greater than he was used to, or saw in neighbouring counties. Yet the wealthy, although supping French wine, also had distinguishing features worthy of note. A native wine made from 'resberryes' 'off the mountains' was made by the 'gentlewomen', and the area had a reputation for punch 'which they make to a miracle'. Despite poverty, widespread some parishes were noted for the longevity of their inhabitants by respondents to Lhuyd's queries. Parishioners of Llanwnnws had an average life expectancy of eighty years.[18]

The expansion and consolidation of European influence overseas encouraged some Cardiganshire people to travel across the Atlantic in the seventeenth century. Early indications of movement from Cardiganshire to North America can be discerned in the name of Cardigan given to a settlement which was part of a colony called Cambriol in Newfoundland established by the Carmarthenshire squire William Vaughan in 1617. There was increased migration in the later seventeenth century. Departure points were at Liverpool and Bristol. Some records from these ports survive, though not enough to provide even an approximate picture of the extent of this movement. Thirty people from Cardiganshire left Bristol in the latter part of the century, the majority of whom went to Barbados and Virginia. Many of these were what were called 'servants to foreign plantations'. These individuals were persuaded to migrate by labour recruiters who, among other things, spoke of increased marriage prospects for women who went abroad. Although the majority of these were in their twenties, some were younger. In Liverpool William Griffith, aged twelve years, was bound to Barbados for four years. For many, Barbados, whose white population declined in the latter half of the century, was a stepping stone to other new world destinations. Others who left Cardiganshire at this time included small numbers of

Quakers who contributed to the movement of this group to Pennsylvania from the 1680s.

Among those with means, formal education took a firmer hold during this period. John Lewis, though not a product of a university, was as certain of the Welsh gentry's intellectual capabilities as others were of its genealogical pedigrees. Lewis illustrated this point himself by demonstrating a broad knowledge of classical literature in his publications. Many Welshmen at this time used legal training, at one of the four Inns of Court, as a kind of university education. Of the 2,400 Welshmen who attended the Courts before 1850, half of them went in the seventeenth century. Legal training was seen as a requirement for those members of the leading landowning families who aspired to local office. Knowledge of the law also protected and furthered a family's socio-economic standing. A lack of large landed families meant that, compared to other counties, notably Denbighshire, Cardiganshire did not send a large proportion to the Inns. Even so, there was a long-standing tradition for the landed of Cardiganshire to go to the Inner Court; the afore-mentioned John Lewis and John Jones of Nanteos both trained there in the first half of the century.

Humbler individuals manifested educational aspirations too. Responses to enquiries made by the scholar Edward Lhuyd, whose mother, Bridget Pryse was from Glan-ffraid near Tal-y-bont, indicate some pockets of literacy. In Cellan the many small craftsmen – bookbinders, harpers and shoemakers – could evidently read, as some in the parish 'can give very good account of their faith'. Other proofs of literacy can be found in wills. David Hugh, who died in 1690, was a small farmer from Cellan who left £1 worth of books. Not all landholders left books in their wills. Thomas Lloyd of Bronwydd in Llangynllo parish, for example, may have owned a 'Silver Beere Bowle' worth £1,200 sheep and £600 in 'rady money', but this inventory from 1663 does not mention any literature. Wealth did not necessarily equal literary interests.[19] While some artisans and small farmers were literate, formal education was not in a flourishing condition. The Welsh Trust Schools were founded on the initiative of the Puritan Thomas Gouge in 1674. Two Trust Schools were founded in Cardiganshire. Like the earlier ones promoted by the Puritan administration they were located at Cardigan and Lampeter. It is unlikely that their efforts reaped significant rewards because the Bibles they used were in English, a language most could not speak let alone read.

Two descriptions of the county from the 1670s in the atlases by Blome and John Speed afford some idea of how the people of Cardiganshire were defined. Both provide very similar descriptions of the county's geography, but they differ in one important respect, that is the names given to the inhabitants. Speed's description mentions that in 'Welsh' Cardiganshire is called 'Sire Aber-Tiui'. Blome's account states the county is 'by the Britains called Aber-Tivi'. As descendants of pre-Saxon inhabitants, the Welsh were known as the British. The word had none of the connotations of the Saxon 'Welsh' – which meant foreigner. Although the county's official name was the English term Cardiganshire, as long as the majority of the population were monoglot Welsh-speakers the Welsh name, Sir Aberteifi, predominated. However, Dineley's comment that 'the vulgar' called Cardigan 'Abertivi' indicates how the Welsh language was, for many, a mark of lower rank, rather than a sign of descent from the ancient Britons. Although the superiority of English in many fields was unchallenged in the following century, there were religious and cultural changes which demonstrated that Welsh was not merely the language of the uneducated.[20]

VII

The Eighteenth Century

Elections in eighteenth-century Cardiganshire were either torpid or torrid affairs. Landed families monopolized the county seat, so incumbents were frequently unchallenged. Electoral law was often overlooked during these uncontested elections; in 1701 Lewis Pryse of Gogerddan was returned despite being under twenty-one, the minimum age for an MP. When the 1694 Triennial Act, stipulating that elections take place every three years, was introduced, rival families often agreed not to engage in expensive elections. Even after the Septennial Act (1716), when elections did not have to take place for seven years, costs were prohibitive. At the end of the century elections in England and Wales cost £5,000 on average, a fivefold increase from the average cost in 1700. A seat for up to seven instead of three years was eagerly fought for. Given the cost, however, large landowners were unlikely to be challenged by less wealthy rivals. Between 1754 and 1790 no elections were fought for the county seat. In this the county was typical. For example, only 17 per cent of seats in the House of Commons were contested during 1761. Of the two seats, the county was considered the more prestigious, though the borough seat was pivotal in the machinations of the county's elite. Differences in the type of person entitled to vote in the two seats reflected their relative importance. In the 1741 borough election few voters on the register were listed as esquires or gentlemen; indeed, one was a 'fiddler'. Whereas a burgess would often be created at the whim of a power hungry aspirant with influence in the borough, the freeholder, who was entitled to vote in the county election, had to posses land or tenements to the annual value of 40 s.; a list of freeholders compiled for the 1761 general election identified some 952 members of this enfranchised portion of Cardiganshire's populace.

Usually, the political dividing line was drawn between Tory Gogerddan on one side and Whig Trawsgoed on the other. For much of the century the Tories, associated with the exiled Stuart monarchy, performed poorly on the national stage. Party tags, although used at the time, were not the only influences that shaped Cardiganshire politics. Questions relating to the relative balance of parliamentary or mon-archical influence and the position of the Anglican Church, on which loose Whig and Tory definitions were based, were frequently over-shadowed by local concerns. In 1701, for example, Humphrey Mackworth decided to expand his influence beyond mining and take the county seat. Mackworth, a Tory, literally bought the support of the Whig and Tory houses of Trawsgoed and Nanteos with generous offers of Glamorganshire coal. Yet, at the end of the year, young Pryse took the seat.

Nonetheless, party politics was important. Pryse hoped that the reign of Queen Anne, who was more favourably disposed to the Tories, would benefit him. His hopes were soon deflated, however. Little was done to secure his interests primarily because the head of the county bench of magistrates, Lord Carbery, sympathized with the Whigs. In 1708, at a time when Whig fortunes had improved, Lord Lisburne of Trawsgoed supported fellow Whig Thomas Johnes, of Hafod and Llanfair Clydogau, in the contest for the county seat. Such a substantial challenge compelled Pryse himself to stand against the Whig interest; the county seat was currently held by one of his supporters. Of the enfranchised freeholders, 383 supported Pryse and 347 voted for Johnes. Johnes contested the result, but the Whig dominated House of Commons upheld the Tory victory. Two years later a coalition of squires tackled the Gogerddan leviathan. This challenge succeeded through a combination of bribery and Pryse's ideological inflexibility. Pryse originally wanted his nominee John Meyrick to take the seat. Mackworth, who was declared a fraud when his Company of Mine Adventurers became bankrupt, opposed him. Once again, Mackworth united men of differing political persuasions: William Powell of Nanteos – reputed to have joined Pryse in a toast for the exiled Stuarts – and the Whig Lord Lisburne. Walter Lloyd of Voelallt could have reinforced Pryse's defence, but the latter would not combine with a Whig. Consequently Pryse lost, though by only a slender margin. Later, Johnes took the county seat in 1713 after Pryse decided to stay out of the contest. Cardiganshire's Whigs, it seemed, had anticipated the national swing to the Whigs brought about by the Hanoverian succession of 1714.

Yet a gout-ridden Pryse fought back and defeated Johnes. After his victory suspicions about his lack of loyalty to the new royal house were aroused when he failed to attend Parliament and swear allegiance to the monarchy. In 1717 Stuart supporters had contacted Pryse and they mentioned a prospective Jacobite landing in Pembrokeshire. An indication of the tension at this time can be seen in Lisburne's request for troops during that year. Despite Pryse being removed from Parliament, Gogerddan's influence continued. Pryse's nominee was returned in the 1717 by-election, and another did not face opposition in the 1722 election. Such influence lends some credence to the hyperbole of English Jacobites who thought Pryse 'ruled all his shire'. However, another troubled period for the Tory interest commenced after Pryse died, leaving no effective head of Gogerddan, the heir Thomas Pryse being only four. This uncertainty led to a clash between the Nanteos and Gogerddan interests. Despite a temporary entente in 1727, Thomas Powell of Nanteos lost a contest for the county seat to the second Lord Lisburne by sixty-four votes.

Mobs often participated in British politics during the eighteenth century, so elections could become colourful and violent affairs. Supporters of Thomas Powell and the Gogerddan candidate, Richard Lloyd of Mabws, clashed during the 1729 by-election for Cardigan borough. As a result, one Lloyd supporter was killed. Powell had created voters in Tregaron, thus enabling him to secure a victory. Yet a parliamentary committee of elections ruled that Tregaron was not a valid contributory borough. Therefore, the town was disenfranchised, and Lloyd was awarded the seat in 1730. Although Powell's actions provoked one of the most violent scenes in eighteenth-century Cardiganshire, three years later at Drury Lane he calmed down a restive audience who disliked a lacklustre play and ensured that the manager reimbursed the audience.

Lloyd, who had exploited Gogerddan's weakness, was eventually ousted by Thomas Pryse in the 1741 borough election. In that year Lloyd's ally, Walter Lloyd of Peterwell, lost the county seat to Thomas Powell. A political environment that depended on the influence of powerful individuals meant that the untimely death of Pryse created problems, his heir John Pugh Pryse was aged seven. One of the trustees of the Gogerddan estate was John Philipps of Picton Castle, who expressed his intention to 'preserve' the 'family interest'. This mainly involved repressing the ambitions of Wilmot Vaughan, son of the third Lord Lisburne. When the Whig John Lloyd died, the county seat became available, thus arousing Vaughan's aspirations. Vaughan had obtained the support of the Duke of Newcastle, though he had to explain to this statesman how he came to have the support of a Tory, his friend Revd William Powell. Nanteos and Trawsgoed had cooperated on a different matter in 1753 when they challenged the Crown's right to lay claim to the lead discovered at Esgair-mwyn. This political alliance outmanoeuvered Philipps, one of the leading figures in Welsh politics, and Vaughan was returned in 1755.

Once again the coming of age of a Gogerddan scion transformed county politics. John Pugh Pryse was the county member from 1761–8. Unlike his recalcitrant predecessor John, but like many country gentlemen, he kept an independent position. He voted with the opposition on the John Wilkes affair. Evidence of interest in this champion of liberty in the area can be seen in the tavern named the Wilkes Head near Llandysul. Yet a distinctly local affair, the rise of Herbert Lloyd of Peterwell, left a greater impression upon the county's history than Pryse's parliamentary activities.

Lloyd gained the borough seat in 1761 after a contest against a fellow Whig, William Vaughan – political affiliations offered no protection against personal antipathy. His fierce disposition was such that Pryse allied with Nanteos and Trawsgoed. In order to combat him, Pryse used his influence to create burgesses at Aberystwyth and Cardigan. Likewise, Lloyd inflated Lampeter's burgesses and it appeared that a confrontation between the county's established elite and a challenging borough, as had happened some forty years before at Tregaron, would recur. Plans were made to contest Lampeter's status as a contributory borough. Preparations for the clash included securing a favourable mayor of Cardigan because, as returning officer, the mayor could disallow votes. Even when the pro-Lloyd mayor was removed, the alliance of squires knew they faced a significant contest. Lisburne secured the uncontested county seat which he held until 1796. Pryse, who took the Merioneth seat, selected a relative with ministerial experience, Pryse Campbell, to battle against Lloyd. After Lloyd gathered together the Lampeter burgesses, numbering some 2,000, they set off for Cardigan, but returned when their chosen mayor declined to resume his peculiar role.

This land-hungry and self-aggrandizing landlord had a second chance in 1769 after Campbell died. His second opponent was another outsider, Ralph Congreve from Berkshire, chosen purely because he had sufficient funds to finance his candidature. During the contest, which Lloyd lost by 1,704 votes to 1,950, Congreve did not appear. As a result, Lloyd ruled the streets and his supporters produced the sort of satirical street parades which often enlivened elections in this period. A 'tinker boy' was dressed up to mimic the alliance's candidate. Seven months later Lloyd had died while on a journey from the gaming tables of London to the health-giving waters of Bath.

Far more is known about the foibles and interests of the county's squires than other sections of society. Even a shipwreck can tell us something about their tastes. A Spanish ship sank near Aberaeron in 1701 and its cargo, thousands of oranges and lemons destined for Lord Lisburne, were washed ashore. Stories of dissipation reveal how an individual could harm an estate's fortunes. The tastes of John Vaughan of Trawsgoed – the second Lord Lisburne, 1721–41 – extended beyond fruit from Spain. Gambling and port soaked up his money. Strategic marriages could not repair the damage wrought by his lifestyle. Indeed, an extravagant second wife, Dorothy, drove a small carriage drawn by two mastiffs with a 'silver-mounted harness'. His election to the House of Commons, and consequent immersion in London society, took a hefty financial toll; he spent £800 on an aviary of mistresses. A decline from late seventeenth-century prosperity to the penurious condition of 1741 was the result for a man who was described by his brother as one 'indolent in the management of his affairs'. Betting took place at Llanfair Clydogau in Thomas Johnes's mansion. During the mid-1700s the gambling fests held there attracted politicians from London 'for weeks together'. Local squires such as Herbert Lloyd performed poorly against this metropolitan competition, so perhaps part of the attraction of gaming in this distant location were the winnings that a leading politician could pick up from a game with these 'country gentlemen'.[1] Cockfighting also drew money from the wealthy and the poor alike in the county during the eighteenth century.

Some of the county's important landowners were members of the Society of Sea Serjeants. The society met annually in one of the ports of south-west Wales. There was a gathering at Cardigan in June 1761 which was marked by a week of festivities. This society, pre-dominantly composed of High Tories, was suspected of being a Jacobite association. They were said to have concealed portraits of Prince Charles Edward in their snuff boxes. Yet this social event was steeped in sentimentality rather than potential rebellion. The cost of staging this event was significant as there were family members, servants and horses to keep. Activities included balls, trips to view the ruins of Cilgerran, fishing for salmon in the Teifi and a moonlight journey by yacht in Cardigan Bay. Emphasis was placed on how gatherings afforded opportunities to engage in civilized forms of pleasure. One of the society's objects was to participate 'in innocent mirth and recreation'.[2] Swearing was frowned upon. Evidently, these rules were written at a time when contrary behaviour among the better-off was common. Another mark of respectability was added from 1749 when a female patroness, young and unmarried, was chosen from the area in which the meeting was held. In 1761 Anne Louisa Lloyd of Bronwydd was patroness.

Other activities enjoyed by the gentry included foxhunting and collecting manuscripts. The former united various levels of landed society. During the mid-1730s the Tivyside Hunt Club was founded and the Cardigan Hunt was established later in the century. Some estates, notably Gogerddan, kept their own packs. Giving gifts to hunts was a useful means to curry favour. Thomas Powell of Nanteos donated £10.10 s. to Cardigan Hunt in 1785, and £7.14 s. to the Tivyside the following year. Status could also be raised through the pursuit of literary interests. The Edinburgh University-educated Thomas Johnes the younger possessed an impressive collection of manuscripts and was particularly interested in medieval French chronicles. Some Cardiganshire notables did not ignore Welsh heritage. The Lloyds of Alltyrodyn, who expressed sympathy towards Nonconformists, possessed a substantial collection of genealogical texts. Remnants of the patron–poet relationship persisted in south Cardiganshire too. The cobbler poet Ioan Siencyn from Cardigan was invited by the owners of Teifiside houses to read poetry at Christmas time.

Eminent landowners also assumed military roles in the local militia. The French threat prompted the Militia Act of 1757 by which men from each parish, aged between eighteen and fifty, were randomly selected by ballot to serve in the force. Major William Lewis, who chose John Nash to design a mansion at Llanerchaeron, commanded 103 Cardiganshire men who were among the force to whom the French invaders of 1797 surrendered on Goodwick Sands, Pembrokeshire. The following year he became colonel of the force. Maintaining order placed demands on the militia: in 1764 their duties included guarding a shipwreck from looters in Llanrhystud parish. Yet this group of men could cause disruption. For instance, at Trerhedyn in 1780 locals clashed with the county's ostensible guardians outside a tavern. This force, which usually numbered around 120, could be called to serve outside its home county. Parish ratepayers were annoyed when they were called upon to support the families of militiamen away in Cumberland during 1795.

Lewis Morris noted the pursuits of other classes in northern Cardiganshire. The Anglesey-born antiquarian was Steward of the Crown Manors in the county. Physical activities, notably wrestling and 'pitching a bar over arm', predominated. Some of the wrestling events, which took part in Anglican chapels at Ysbyty Cynfyn and Ysbyty Ystwyth were annual events held on New Year's Eve. Wrestling was watched by 'young women', and 'old champions' were enjoined 'to see fair play'. Another distinctive feature noted by Lewis was the little wedding (*priodas fach*). This amounted to a trial wedding and was popular among the lead-mining population. Unsurprisingly, the Anglican Morris thought this was a 'ludicrous' practice. In 1753 the Marriage Act was passed which declared that vows exchanged between two people did not constitute a marriage; the only legal marriage was one held in church and read from the Book of Common Prayer.

However, Morris thought that this area 'where an Act of Parliament is looked upon as no more than a Ballad' was unlikely to relinquish such a convenient, and cheap, custom.[3] The little wedding allowed either partner to leave after a month trial period, and this arrangement suited a transient mining population.

By contrast, conventional weddings were prolonged, communal affairs. A week or two before the wedding, a bidder (*gwahoddwr*) visited houses carrying a long stick decorated with ribbons. He advertised the wedding, the gifts expected and the entertainment. Wealthier free-holders sent invitations in English, an indication of the status accorded this language. These celebrations were energetic affairs. On the way to church the bride's party made mock attempts to flee and limbs were often broken in these dashes. After the ceremony, celebratory drink and food were consumed. Presents included cheese and butter, which were sold after the wedding, providing ready money for the couple. It was expected that the couple would repay these donations by giving gifts at future weddings. The prospect of gifts, whose return lay in the future, may have contributed to an increase in early marriages.

The physicality of wedding celebrations was just one aspect of a society where the public demonstration of emotions, such as vengeance, was common. Criminals, stripped to the waist, were punished in the county's towns and many assembled to witness these events. Stealing eleven pence worth of clothing resulted in Thomas Davies of Llangoedmor parish, near Cardigan, being whipped at both Cardigan and Aberystwyth. A woman, Margaret Davies, also of Llangoedmor, suffered the same fate for stealing cloth. Sometimes public opinion influenced the nature of the punishment. If sympathy was expressed the whip was coated with a blood-like substance, and the offender was not flogged. Whether this was a common commutation is not known, though there was one case involving an elderly man who had stolen peat for warmth. In addition, the Quarter Sessions records reveal that unsanctioned violence was common in comparison to later years. Part of the problem, identified at a Quarter Sessions in 1773, was an increase in unlicensed alehouses. In addition, landowners sometimes gathered together mobs to further their ambitions. On one occasion a female tenant for life leased out mines to the Company of Mine Adventurers and this commercial activity attracted Thomas Powell of Nanteos, who thought he had a claim to the lands. About a hundred of his tenants, servants and miners formed a mob and chased the miners away.

Poverty produced suffering, compelled people to steal clothing and placed demands on those who contributed to poor relief. Llanrhystud parish's poor rate rose from a mid-century sum of 4 *d*. in the pound to 4 *s*. fifty years later. This burden increased during the last two decades of the century. Population growth was at the root of this problem, which was then being experienced throughout England and Wales. Cardiganshire's population increased from an estimated 27,000 at the start of the century to 32,000 in 1750, and by 1801 it was 42,956. Various reasons have been suggested for this upward trend including the cultivation of the potato, fewer food crises and the demise of plague. Nonetheless, there were episodes of high mortality during 1729-31, and Lewis Morris recorded outbreaks of fever (possibly a mild form of typhus). Smallpox ravaged the county in the early 1760s and there was a shortage of food towards the end of the century. That the population, many of whom lived in hovels, increased in these circumstances underscores the extent of the demographic transformation.

Parishes were responsible for the poor, so a destitute and pregnant woman presented a problem as the parish could be responsible for the child. Thus attempts were made by the overseers of the poor at Tregaron in 1797 to remove a woman to her parish of origin. For the more fortunate, such as Evan the Lampeter 'parish ideot' who received clothing and lodging, aid was given in kind. In order to avoid confusing the native parish claimants with others from beyond the area, the letters 'LP' – signifying a Lampeter pauper – were to be worn by those receiving aid. Yet repeated decrees to ensure that paupers wore the identification testify that this demand was difficult to enforce. There were other, less stigmatizing, means of acquiring sustenance, such as temporary migration; some helped with the harvest in western England. And a new form of security, the benefit club, emerged in the county; the first recorded club was established in 1771 at Llanfihangel Ystrad.

Amidst this poverty there was an increased awareness of religious and educational matters. Perhaps notions of a better life and afterlife were sharpened by demographic and economic shifts. Methodism entered the county's history in the eighteenth century and continued to play a prominent role until the twentieth century. Its approach emphasized the importance of saving all soul by any means possible. This active interpretation of Christianity involved preaching in any parish, often under the sky rather than in buildings. Informal and impassioned, it attracted for the same reasons as it repelled. Taking spiritual inspiration from European sects like the Moravians, with their emphasis on faith as personal experience, the county's Methodists combined this with the force of open-air preaching which George Whitfield had practised in America. It would be difficult to overemphasize the influence of Methodism. True, not all people were Methodists (in 1745 there were at most 200 active members in southern Cardiganshire). But Methodist manners 'methodized' other religious groups – it imbued them with feeling and emotion. Furthermore, modern

Wales has been shaped as much by those who attempted to deny its influence as those who succumbed to its content and style.

Methodism was strongest in the south of the county. Here followers were often identified on the basis of their religious predilection. In 1745 Revd John Pugh, Llanarth, noted in his diary that he 'baptised Ann the daughter of a Methodist'.[4] One reason put forward for its belated arrival in the north has been the role played by the Anglican landlords who owned the large estates which predominated there. Cardiganshire mirrored the pattern of Wales as a whole, as the Methodist tide, like that of many other dissenting branches, spread northwards from southern bases. The first Methodist exhorter to visit Anglesey was Richard William Dafydd of Cardiganshire. Methodists from the county were immortalized in elegies composed by Carmarthenshire's William Williams of Pantycelyn. Pre-eminent among these was Daniel Rowland, whose statue, completed in 1883, can be seen in Llangeitho. His story reveals the interplay between styles of preaching and various denominations. Rowland learned from a popular pastor at the Independent church, Llwynpiod, Revd Phylip Pugh, that to gather large congregations he had to 'thunder'. Later, the Anglican educationalist Griffith Jones contributed to Rowland's style when he prayed for the young dramatic preacher. Rowland felt transformed, saying that, after experiencing a conversion through feeling not just thinking, he now thundered from the heart. His performances drew crowds, but his emphasis on punishment overshadowed the idea of Christ's mercy. Pugh convinced Rowland to balance his sermons. With this balance of darkness and light, Rowland evoked proclamations, such as *gogoniant* (glory), from the congregation. Though he visited other parts of Wales, Rowland, unlike the other leading Methodist Howell Harris, was not a great traveller. His published sermons spread his name and people travelled to see him from all over Wales, often experiencing harassment on the way. Their return from Llangeitho was as important as the journey there because they returned with even greater enthusiasm and told others about his spectacular oratory.

Memories of the religious extremes witnessed in the previous century might have spawned opposition to the Methodists. Other opponents saw their existence within the Anglican Church as a threat to that institution. Many looked down their noses at the demonstrations of joy elicited at meetings – they were nicknamed 'jumpers'. At Llanilar a mob assembled by the squire of Aber-mad hurled missiles at Rowland. Later the same landlord sent two servants, one Welsh and the other Irish, to assault him. In a tale which tells us something about the prevailing negative image of the Irish, the Welshman was moved by Rowland's words and tears, but the Irishman wanted to attack him. The

Welshman prevailed and Rowland was left unmolested. When told that the preacher was weeping at the meeting, the squire felt that his cronies had carried out their task. Varying receptions greeted the other leading Methodist, Breconshire-born Harris, who met Rowland in 1737. In 1741 Harris approached Cardigan town with caution. Some scoffed, but many gentlemen sympathized with him. Later that year he had a warmer welcome whilst preaching outside the Red Lion near the church. Harris noted that in general the towns were less receptive to religious messages than country areas, but on this occasion Cardigan provided 'more Civility ... than hardly any other Town in Wales'.[5]

The removal of Rowland from his church, possibly a result of the 1762 revival that he engendered, was a precursor of the future rupture between Methodists and Anglicans. This revival in support led to an increase of a distinguishing feature of Methodism, the societies (*seiadau*). Here members would gather, with or without the minister, to select or remove members and reflect on their experiences. Many young women attended these spiritual rumination societies where people gathered and recounted struggles with their passions. Though this was not done with the intention of fulfilling these temptations, it doubtless provided a release. The Wesleyan variety of Methodism, unlike the Calvinistic type espoused by Rowland, did not find fertile soil in Cardiganshire with its overwhelmingly Welsh-speaking population and rapidly expanding Calvinistic roots. Indeed, Wesley declared in 1747 that he did not want to vie with the Welsh Calvinistic Methodists in their strongholds. Other dissenting bodies adopted some of the style of worship displayed by the Methodists. Thomas Grey of Cilgwyn was an Independent whose congregations displayed a Methodist-like enthusiasm. Similarly, the Baptist preaching giant, the one-eyed Christmas Evans, evoked emotional responses when he returned to southern Cardiganshire where he was born. Evans, who lost his eye in an attack in Herefordshire where he had gone to work on the harvest, has been pronounced the first Baptist to become well known throughout Wales. He also advocated temperance and delivered sermons illustrated by aspects of his congregations' everyday lives.

A very different brand of faith also emerged in Cardiganshire. The 'rational Christians' were explicit in their condemnation of the emotional excesses demonstrated by the Calvinistic Methodists. Not inclined to accept the political status quo, or the idea of original sin, they held that people had free will and that their fate was not predestined – this was an echo of the debate between St David and adherents of Pelagianism. The Academy at Carmarthen turned out many of these rational dissenters who were more open to ideas of political liberty. These followers of the ideas of the seventeenth-century Dutchman James Arminius were named Arminians. Llwynrhydowen was the location of the first Arminian chapel in Wales and Jenkin Jones from Llanwenog was behind its growth. The area's religious radicalism increased when in 1742 Jones's nephew, David Lloyd, succeeded him. Lloyd had adopted Arianism, the belief that Jesus was not a divine being. A radical, Lloyd supported American independence and smote the Methodism that surrounded him thus: 'Calvinism, besides its being a heap of Absurdities, is generally attended with a great Deal of blind Fury, Bigotry, and Enthusiasm.' In fact, he doubted whether it was any better than paganism.[6]

Similarly, Dafydd Dafis, a corpulent schoolmaster, was a dissenter of national standing. He was reputedly so large that neighbours would not let him borrow their horses, and that he was beloved by his tailor. Educated at Carmarthen by the Arian Jenkin Jenkins, Dafis proclaimed his sympathy for the French revolutionaries. Yet this radical dissenter educated many prospective Anglican churchmen in his renowned school at Castellhywel – nicknamed the Athens of Cardiganshire. However, when Samuel Horsley, who was an eminent scientist, became bishop of St Davids, he refused to accept any man who had been educated at Castellhywel into the ministry. Horsley had clashed with fellow scientist Joseph Priestley over the divinity of Christ; Dafis, on the other hand, sang the praises of this Unitarian giant. The doctrines espoused by Lloyd and Dafis, and held by a significant number of radical artisans such as Evan Thomas, a cobbler from Llanarth, were moving towards Unitarianism, a creed which rejects the trinity and became legal only in 1813.

Some of the most pointed attacks on the Anglican Church in Cardiganshire came from within. An outspoken critic was Lledrod-born poet Evan Evans (Ieuan Brydydd Hir), one of the clerical men of letters who came from Cardiganshire; others included the *halsingod* composer Samuel Williams and his son Moses, who helped his father copy Dafydd ap Gwilym's poems. Evans condemned the Anglo-bishops, protesting that no Welsh-speaker was appointed to the bishopric of St Davids in the eighteenth century. Equally harmful was the fact that curates were often in charge of several parishes, and much of the money gathered from tithes went to secular owners. In a letter to Richard Morris, written in 1767, Evans stated that, although born here, he 'would be glad to leave to-morrow'. Methodists, those 'wild enthusiasts', unnerved him. Blame was attributed to the Reformation which had bled the church dry and allowed the 'fanatics' to gain ground. To counter these 'enthusiasts', a 'reputable set of clergy with good salaries' was required. Erasmus Saunders had remarked upon the poor condition of the Church in 1727. The church buildings in the diocese of St Davids were in such a state that it looked as if the 'Turks and Saracens' had recently torn through the land. Despite this the people of the diocese, 'owing to our Solitude, or our Poverty, or natural Disposition, or to the extraordinary Grace of God given us', were especially religious. Yet it was the 'poor Inhabitants of these Mountains', who travelled long distances in bad weather to church, who were to form the germ of the Methodist movement.[7]

Education and religion were bound together in this period. This relationship is demonstrated in the life of the churchman Edward Richards, who taught Evan Evans at his school in Ystradmeurig. Richards was said to have mocked Llangeitho-bound Methodists, thus demonstrating that tensions within the Church could be as prominent as those between it and the long-established dissenters. His friendship with the Nonconformist Dafydd Dafis, who wrote an elegy when Richards died, was based on their interest in Welsh literature; both also found Methodist display disconcerting. In another of those conversion tales, though in this case one of manners rather than faith, Richards altered his playful ways after his talented brother drowned in the Ystwyth. Reformed, he continued his brother's school in the mid-1730s. On deciding to teach older pupils, Edward spent some six years educating himself in mathematics, classics and theology. His poetry earned him the patronage of some of the county's leading houses – including Trawsgoed and Nanteos. It was due to this man, and his eminent successor Revd John William who ran the school from 1777–1818, that in later years there were stories about learned men meeting agricultural labourers fluent in Greek when they passed through Cardiganshire.

According to tradition, Edward Richards was a pupil of the afore-mentioned Revd Pugh who established a school where, for a fee, both male and female children were taught. Educational improvement was spread by less formal means via Pugh, who lent his books to people in the locality. From his records we can see how locals sampled his collection. Mrs Jenkins of Llanddewibrefi, for example, borrowed 'Keill's Physics'. One of his most popular titles was 'Whole duty of a woman'. It is likely that such works were read to others, thus circulating ideas and knowledge. Though it must also be remembered that local authorities on various subjects – like Siôn Britsh Coch of Lampeter whom farmers consulted about the weather – played an important part in the transfer of knowledge in eighteenth-century Cardiganshire. These sources of folk wisdom represented what Robert Redfield called a 'little tradition' that existed alongside the ideas of the literate elite that were beginning to permeate the county.[8] While short lived, the first printing press in the county, established at Atpar in 1718, both reflected and contributed to the latter tradition.

Formal educational movements gathered pace as literacy was increasingly seen as the only way to save souls. The Society for the Promotion of Christian Knowledge (SPCK) was more active in counties to the south of Cardiganshire. Only two schools were established in the county: the first a charity school founded by Mackworth to educate children attached to mines at Esgair-hir from 1700, and the second at Llandysul from 1727 where Dr Thomas Pardo taught ten boys. Instruction in SPCK schools was mainly in English, and education through this medium curtailed their benefits. Far more effective was the distribution of books, including Welsh-language Bibles, by the SPCK. Griffith Jones's circulating schools, which commenced in 1737, constituted a leap whereas previous educational efforts had been steps. These schools played a central role in spreading literacy until the scheme faded towards the end of the century after the deaths of its leading figures – Jones and Madam Bridget Bevan. Their mission was unambiguous. Jones stated that they were not seeking to make pupils, who were of all ages, 'gentlemen' but 'heirs to eternal life'. Therefore, schooling needed to be in the native language and shaped to fit into the lives of the rural poor. During the thirty-nine years when it was at its most active, an average of 1,243 children and adults in twenty-one schools and 250 locations were instructed in the county, mainly in the south. The clergy played an important part in this endeavour by providing places and suggesting teachers. For three or four months a year, at times when the demands for agricultural labour were least pressing, scholars were taught to read the word of God. Contemporary reports mentioned the poverty of these 'poor children'. One observed that 'their Garb is extraordinarily poor and mean'. The thirst for knowledge, whether to secure the afterlife or improve life on earth, is demonstrated by the actions of these poor attendees some of whom, at Brongwyn in 1771, were not examined at church 'for want of Clothes'.[9] This increased opportunity to read amounted to a shift in the county's culture, and prepared the way for the Sunday schools which mushroomed from the 1790s.

Towns expanded during the century. John Wesley, writing in 1777, observed that Cardigan was 'continually increasing both in buildings and in number of inhabitants'. One of the new buildings was a Guild Hall completed in 1764. A growing awareness of the town's civic role was demonstrated when there was a change in the location where the Quarter Sessions were sited. At the start of the century it was held in a dilapidated room in the castle, by 1765 the Cardigan session was held in the hall. Aberystwyth experienced even greater development. An increase in population brought some environmental problems, notably more waste being deposited in its streets. A number of residents were brought before the Court Leet for dumping rubbish. Those responsible for clearing it up, the town scavengers, did not always carry out the tasks assigned them. Daniel Defoe remarked upon the wealth and dirt of Aberystwyth in the 1720s. The coal he mistakenly thought was mined in the area was an indicator of the town's importance as it was the fuel for this place where the people 'look'd as if they liv'd continually in the coal or lead mines' but 'are rich'.[10] Trade in lead ore was a boon to the town. *Banc y Llong* (The Ship Bank), reputedly the first bank in Wales, was founded in 1762. In the following year the town's increased importance was substantiated when the customs house was moved there from Aberdyfi.

Later in the century many visitors frequented the town, whose sanitation, though not excellent, was better than it had been when Defoe passed through. Catherine Hutton's diary, which described the town in 1787, noted how locals complained that sea bathers and those taking the chalybeate waters had led to a rise in the price of provisions. Ten years later, the town was regarded as the 'Brighton of Wales'; though Swansea had also been given that title by the *Gloucester Journal* in 1786. Such designations demonstrate the importance of leisure and tourism in fashioning the town's identity. There were attractions outside the town. A 1796 guide depicted Hafod, Devil's Bridge and Strata Florida abbey 'and other scenery in that district of Cardiganshire'. This publication warned that locals hired as guides often took visitors to Devil's Bridge but not to all the desirable points of vantage because 'half the trouble will secure the expected fee'. One 'gentleman' dealt a local 'lazy clown' a few blows with his horsewhip for omitting some sights from the tour.[11] Evidently tourism could furnish locals with extra money. Yet, alongside the desire to enjoy the scenery, there was at times a struggle between guides and guests, the latter wanting to experience all the visual pleasures. This, together with Hutton's comments about inflation, serve as reminders that the arrival of visitors' money could bring pockets of conflict in its wake.

War spurred on the local economy because tours of the continent were impracticable and minerals were needed for the war effort. After Mackworth departed, mining activity lessened. It was not until the 1730s, when new silver and lead deposits were unearthed, that it resumed in earnest. Each discovery brought migrants from Yorkshire, north Wales and Cornwall. Thomas Bonsall, who worked many mines including Cwmystwyth for Nanteos, was from Derbyshire. Some Iberians worked in the mines after being shipwrecked on the Cardiganshire coast. Other smaller, less magnetic, mining enterprises took place at New Quay and Llanfair Clydogau.

Tensions between central authority and local interests erupted when the Crown claimed the buried fruits of Cardiganshire's unenclosed uplands. Indeed, this century was marked by struggles over rights to upland property. These disagreements stemmed from both overpopulation and commercial interests, squatters and gentry. Lewis Morris, upholding the royal interest in mines, took over the promising excavation at Esgair-mwyn. In 1753 two local landowners, Lord Lisburne and Revd William Powell, sent a force of miners, tenants and a pistol-wielding Herbert Lloyd to Esgair-mwyn. They took ore and incarcerated Morris. Although the Crown did ensure his release, and temporarily sent troops to work the mines, the local interest held out. Lord Lisburne gained rights over the mine which proved especially fruitful after 1765. From 1750–71 Cwmsymlog mine was revived and this benefited the Gogerddan estate. As well as male miners, women, who carried the ore from opencast mines, were employed. Additionally, local farmers used their carts to transport ore. Even so, agricultural work was prioritized; during harvests the mines were often idle. Extractive industry could harm agriculture. In 1731 at Eglwys-fach livestock that had drank from the lead-polluted river Einon died, and the miners were charged at the Great Sessions. Legal records also afford examples of human casualties, such as John Thomas who was trapped under rock at Cwmystwyth for an hour and died four days later.

Fishing was an important industry, providing valuable nutrients otherwise lacking in the protein-deficient diet of the poor and revenue for those who fished. In the 1740s Lewis Morris estimated that there were ninety-seven small sloops between Aberdyfi and New Quay. Some extraordinary catches were recorded. Morris mentioned that during one night in 1745 a total of some 1,386,500 herrings were brought to Aberystwyth. The gifts offered up by the sea also played an important part in the lives of the county's inhabitants. Cardiganshire's coves offered opportunities for clandestine operations and the coast earned a reputation for smuggling. Smuggled salt from Ireland, used as a preservative, was an especially valued commodity. Alcohol was another important item; there were tales that Herbert Lloyd received wine from the notorious Sion Cwilt, who lived in the upland area of southern Cardiganshire which was named Banc Sion Cwilt after him. Howell Harris preached against such activities when he visited Penbryn in 1743.

Increasing population and poor agricultural practice put pressure on the land. Enclosure had been taking place since 1763 in the south of county, yet the hilly east was mostly open – 47 per cent of the county was waste and common in 1795. Farmers were prone to harvest crops, mainly barley and oats, until the soil was exhausted; ameliorating crops like turnips were not common, neither were fallow periods. In the 1720s Defoe wrote that despite what was said about the county being the source of cattle for much of southern England, the rearing, unlike the fattening, of cattle did not need good soil. Lime was used as a fertilizer, but the cost of carting it was prohibitive. Enclosure during the late eighteenth century increased the number of farms and provided more employment. At the same time, population pressure meant more people moved to the hilly areas and cottages were established on common land. Many of these encroaching cottages, such as those near the Trawsgoed estate, were destroyed. Tenants, keen to protect their grazing rights, opposed them as well.

The efforts of the Cardiganshire Agricultural Society, established in 1784, ensured that some innovations percolated through the county. Nonetheless, there were earlier innovators such as Thomas Pryse of Gogerddan who, in the 1740s, grew turnips on his farm. Developments were recounted by an elderly man from Penbryn who, towards the end of the century, recalled a time when there were only two wheeled carts in the parish. But in 1794 he thought there were about sixty. An indication of the diffusion of knowledge from south to north was also given by this man when he reflected on the fact that the scythe and cradle was first heard of in northern Cardiganshire from descriptions provided by members of the Carmarthenshire militia who were lodging in Aberystwyth.

Thomas Johnes of Croft Castle in Herefordshire, who inherited Hafod, was a key figure in the county's agricultural as well as political history – Johnes represented the borough seat between 1775–80 and, like his father before him, later held the shire seat. He was admired for his philanthropy; during the cold winter of 1799 he employed all the poor who asked for work. As a farmer, he had vision and an avid interest in innovations. Unlike many other men of property, who abandoned their land for urban living, Johnes dedicated much of his life to running his estate. In 1800 he published *A Cardiganshire Landlord's Advice to his Tenants*. That there was also a Welsh-language version of this text reveals his desire to disseminate ideas. Drainage, crop rotation, turnips, yarrow, the Rotherham plough and Scottish threshing machines were all components of this pioneering farmer's arsenal. There was, however, a struggle between traditional ways and Johnes's ideas. Local farmers were proven wrong when he managed to grow wheat on unpromising land. His experiments with sheep were less successful. In 1799 he had some three thousand, several of which were a cross between the durable Cheviot and the meatier Ryeland. Many were lost during the cold winter, and the Merino sheep, originally gifts from Spain to George III, perished. The 20,000 sheep owned by Mr Williams near Tregaron, who was nicknamed the 'Job of the West' such was the size of his flock, were probably hardier, established breeds. Yet the cultivation of better grass by Johnes meant that weightier cattle could be maintained. And his afforestation project – the estate cultivated over two million trees between 1795 and 1801 – was a success. Most were larch, but alder (well suited for making clogs as it is easy to shape and does not split easily) and broadband elms were also grown. This compensated somewhat for the wanton removal of timber carried out in previous centuries.

Less notable figures than Johnes introduced improved agricultural practices. Anne Evans of Highmead, in the south of the county, was praised as being 'a lady' whose 'agricultural knowledge and practice far exceeded that of any man in the county'.[12] After the death of her husband, Herbert Evans who had built a grand mansion in 1777, she assumed responsibility for the estate. Her records of the dairy farm cover the last twenty years of the century and contain many observations on agriculture. Evans's discovery that feeding turnips to cows when in milk made the butter taste unpleasant offered a rare negative slant to the current near-universal promotion of the vegetable. These accounts also offer an insight into the work lives of dairymaids who tended the cows and made cheese and butter. Cows were milked in the morning and evening, so the maid's work began early and ended late. Yet only the men were allowed butter at breakfast. Butter was valuable and servants had salty preserved butter while the best was sent to Bristol and London. During the eighteenth century, however, Welsh butter acquired a bad name because of the fraudulent activities of some butter makers who misled buyers about the weight of their produce; they also allegedly mixed fresh and old butter.

The eighteenth century was a time of heightened economic activity. An indication of the buoyancy of trade can be seen in worries, expressed in 1763, about the proliferation of unlicensed drovers. Notices were placed on the doors of parish churches warning people about this phenomenon. More respectable traders could find their activities recorded in poetry. Ioan Siencyn wrote an elegy to Thomas Makeig of Llandygwydd parish. There were rumours that this mercer and yeoman had fled his native Scotland after the Jacobite rising. Siencyn praised him as 'a keen agriculturist' whose 'acres' 'were highly productive'. Moreover, 'he built houses and made good use of the produce of the soil'.[13] Other small-scale entrepreneurs at this time included the many female knitters and hat makers of Mynydd Bach and Banc Sion Cwilt. The fleece in the south of the county was well suited for felt making. This diversification offered a source of cash which supplemented the relatively poor pickings in these upland areas.

Towards the end of the century greater efforts were made to improve Cardiganshire's roads. When travelling considerable distances some would keep moving all night; in 1784 John Pugh left Brecon at 1 p.m. and reached Llanarth at 'the dawn of the morning'.[14] During 1770 an act was passed that entitled turnpike trusts to be set up in the county; this attracted capital from those who thought that investing in road building would reap rewards. For this purpose the county was divided in two – the Aeron being the boundary. Tolls were not exacted from all who passed through the gates, which began to appear on approaches to Aberystwyth and Lampeter. Those on the way to chapel, for example, were exempted. Yet the evasion of tolls was a problem, and as early as 1773 trustees discussed methods to lessen avoidance. Some chose to pay a lump sum; Revd Powell of Nanteos gave two guineas for his family and servants to pass without having to pay. Mine owners entered into similar agreements regarding the transportation of ore. Resentment towards tolls erupted in the following century. But the Rebecca Riots, as they came to be known, were just one episode in the first half of the nineteenth century, a period marked by sporadic popular disturbances.

VIII

The Nineteenth Century

William Pitt the younger remarked that the question of peace or war was not as 'formidable as that of the scarcity with which it is combined'. Want overshadowed Cardiganshire during and after the conflict with France. Agricultural prices fell in 1813, rents increased – those on the Trawsgoed estate rose threefold from 1801 to 1814 – the end of the war brought unemployment, there was a poor harvest in 1816 and there were food shortages the following year. Beggars beseeched the gentry at their houses and debtors filled Cardigan jail. By 1819 the amount parishes contributed to the Poor Law was double that of 1816. Perhaps this context of deprivation explains the behaviour of those Aber-porth people who gulped down wine washed up by a French shipwreck in 1817, eleven of whom died from exposure to the elements as they lay inebriated on the beach. Smuggling and the looting of lost vessels was endemic on the coast of early nineteenth-century Cardiganshire; in June 1832, for example, smuggled French brandy was on sale for 12 *s.* per gallon. Desperation and the centrality of Carmarthen as a market town can be seen in the actions of some unfortunates from Cardiganshire. Many from the northern, or 'upper' as contemporaries called it, portion of the county walked some 40 to 50 miles to Carmarthen and begged for bread there in 1817. Letters to the press called on the county's gentlemen to help, and charitable endeavours, local and central, brought forth clothes and money which were then dispensed to these 'pitiable objects'.[1]

Poverty led to popular disturbances and confrontation with the authorities. Eventually, regular troops were called upon and the 55th Regiment moved from Cardigan to Aberystwyth in 1816. A mob that attacked officials who were collecting a debtor's goods in lieu of payment did not disperse after the Riot Act was read. Shots were fired by the 55th Regiment; however, the only damage was that done to the hat of the leading rioter. Opposition to writs also occurred among lead miners, and there were attacks on officials in 1818. Such disturbances were common until 1822. Discordance was not confined to urban areas. In the countryside the struggles over land, involving squatters or protests generated by enclosures rather than debts, aroused the most passion. From 1793 to 1815 some 10,000 acres in the county were enclosed. Upland commons enabled poorer people to harvest peat for fuel. On Mynydd Bach in 1815 enclosure commissioners were threatened and their equipment taken. To call their force together these defenders of traditional rights blew horns. Their night meetings, secret oaths and anonymous letters indicate that there was no small amount of organization behind the disturbances. Women, sometimes armed with cooking utensils, also confronted enclosure commissioners. When the commissioners sold land on Mynydd Bach the slightly built Augustus Brackenbury from Lincolnshire bought 850 acres, possibly as a sporting ground. The struggles for land between this newcomer and the locals during the 1820s were christened *Rhyfel y Sais Bach* (War of the Small Englishman), although some sources hint that he may have been Jewish or Irish. Incidents during this conflict involved the burning down of the first property he erected there – he built a moat around his second dwelling – and Brackenbury's destruction of turf which had been collected by the native population; worse still, this was done on the Sabbath, proof of this diminutive impostor's malevolence. His second house was raided and the moat filled up – a symbolic gesture as the aim of this struggle was the removal of barriers. Attempts to bring locals to justice were frustrated. In the end, after building a third house, Brackenbury left.

Similar techniques to those employed by the enclosure protestors were used during the anti-toll-gate disturbances of the 1840s known as the Rebecca Riots. Unlike the Swing Riots in southern England in the previous decade, these upheavals involved farmers rather than agricultural labourers. The cost of transporting goods and supplies, especially lime which was an important fertilizer, added another burden after the bad harvests of 1837–41. When the agricultural situation improved, in 1842, an industrial depression had an adverse effect on farmers' fortunes. Lime was often transported by sea; there were twelve kilns between New Quay and Aberarth. However, inland farmers relied on road transport, and they collected the substance from Carmarthenshire. Many Cardiganshire cart drivers who transported lime were renowned for their recklessness, some were drunk and, according to many contemporaries, they displayed 'extreme insolence' when driving along Carmarthenshire's roads.[2]

Chronologies of the riots trace their origins to a brief spark in Pembrokeshire during 1839. This occurred just before the lime was laid and led to the removal of the gates. Most accounts note how the anti-toll-gate agitation then remained dormant until late in 1842. Nonetheless, according to Morgan Ebenezer Morgan in his brief history of Tregaron, in 1841 the town's toll gate was torn down and tossed in the Teifi.[3] In response, the authorities sent troops from Shrewsbury to maintain discipline. This attack on a gate next to the bridge on the Lampeter road was thought to be the work of men from the Vale of Aeron. Those travelling from Llangeitho to Tregaron had to pay the toll even though they did not use the road because the Llangeitho road joined just before the gate.

Although the riots were, as David Williams argued, acts of 'recklessness' brought about by 'poverty and suffering', these actions had foundations in established beliefs about what was fair which assumed violent form in times of stress.[4] Attacks on gates were selective; there was reason in recklessness. At Cardigan in June 1843 rioters destroyed gates on the Aberaeron and Llangoedmor roads but desisted from doing the same to one on the Newcastle Emlyn road. Moreover, before the Llangoedmor gate was attacked, a widow, who was the toll collector, asked that her property be left unmolested and the leader assured her that only the gate would be damaged; though the wife of a gatekeeper at Capel Gwndwn, who was blinded by gunpowder during an attack two months later, was not so fortunate. Rumours and misinformation, such as reports that thousands of rioters had tossed dragoons into the Teifi at Newcastle Emlyn, contributed to the fervid atmosphere. To limit tension, Cardigan Trust, the major toll-road trust in the south, reduced tolls in July. Yet on 1 August the gates around Lampeter were removed in what was the rioters' most active night in the county. On the following night, the Aberaeron gates were destroyed, and there were rumours that its workhouse, the county's first (established in 1839), would be assailed. A Lampeter surgeon reported speaking to a wealthy English monoglot who was part of the mob. Clearly, many types of farmer and landowner felt aggrieved. Attacks declined after the summer, though a gate near Cardigan was removed in March 1844, despite there being Royal Marines in the town. Twenty days before this incident the report of the commissioners investigating the disturbances was made public. Their recommendations, notably the consolidation of trusts into one county organization and uniform tolls, were included in an Act passed by Peel's second government.

Wider issues emerged during the disturbances which revealed fissures in a society undergoing economic distress. There were tensions between tenants and landlords, and between Anglicans and Nonconformists. Corn belonging to landlords in southern Cardiganshire was burnt in 1842. An increase in the rate of tithe in Penbryn parish led to one man who refused to pay having his family Bible taken by the bailiffs. Before 1836 tithes were paid in kind, but from that year they were paid in cash, and in some places like Penbryn the revised totals were far higher than their previous equivalents. The Anglican vicar who pursued this legal action was threatened with a broken arm and leg by Rebecca unless the Bible and the cash difference between the old and new tithe was returned to all parishioners. Marines from Cardigan were sent to guard the vicarage. In the neighbouring parish of Llangrannog, another vicar was threatened because he used a school house, paid for in part by Nonconformists, to hold Anglican services – his curate later had his ribs broken for providing evidence to magistrates. Conversely, a Unitarian minister, Thomas Emlyn Thomas of Cribyn, defended Rebecca, prepared petitions to the queen, and orchestrated mass meetings at Pen Das Eithin and Llanarth. At a rather different gathering, a ball for the gentry at Aberystwyth in 1843, the reports of *The Times*'s correspondent, Thomas Campbell Foster, whose accounts were sympathetic towards the protesters, were condemned. However, a number of the issues raised by the rioters were addressed by the end of that year. Concessions on the part of lay impropriators at Penbryn alleviated tensions, and Abel Lewes Gower of Castell Malgwyn agreed to remove a salmon weir at Llechryd, which had been attacked by some three hundred Rebeccaites earlier that year.

There was a strong moral component to some of these disturbances which drew on traditions which predated Rebecca and continued after the riots faded. In Llandysul parish, during 1843, men assaulted a farmer who had acquired a farm to which many in the community thought he was not entitled. There were more public demonstrations of community disapproval, called the *ceffyl pren* (the wooden horse), which involved carrying the transgressor (often a wife beater, as at Llanarth in 1861) or an effigy on a wooden pole for all to ridicule. Mock auctions, as happened in Llangrannog during the anti-tithe agitation of 1843, involved a transgressor being sold to the devil. Indeed, as late as 1872, when the county was renowned for its lawfulness, the *ceffyl pren*, together with a case of petty larceny, were the only cases brought before the Cardiganshire Spring Assizes in that year.

Cardiganshire's political landscape was transformed during this century, by changes in the structures of both representation and consciousness. After the 1830 election the potential political impact of Nonconformity was demonstrated by the numerous petitions from the county's towns and chapel congregations calling for the abolition of slavery. There was also substantial support for parliamentary reform; both the county's MPs, Pryse Pryse for the borough and William Edward Powell for the county, backed it. When the Reform Bill was passed, householders of properties worth £10 per annum and above, together with freemen living within 7 miles of the borough, were entitled to vote; these numbered 1,030. The Atpar contributory borough was expanded over the Teifi to include Newcastle Emlyn. There were 1,184 voters in the county (mainly 40 *s*. freeholders). Yet these reforms did not result in a fluid political environment. The borough seat was uncontested from 1812 to 1841 and from 1855 to 1885; the county did not poll from 1741 to 1859. Still, all was not static as rumours about challengers often kept incumbents on their toes.

Changes in political consciousness are often first observed at the local level. Some of the earliest signs of change can be detected in Aberystwyth during the 1830s. The Municipal Corporations Act (1835) reformed the governance of the town as it enabled all males over twenty-one and occupied, either as owner or tenant, a house that paid rates were to partake in the election of the corporation. As a result, the lower middle class – shopkeepers, hotel owners and craftsmen – became politically active. Religion spurred on this awareness. When Nonconformists were required to pay Church rates towards the building of a wall to protect St Michael's church from the sea some chapelgoers resisted. Those who refused to pay had their property impounded. A similar independent spirit could also be found in rural Cardiganshire. In the 1850s the radical Independent minister, David Rees, praised '*pobl Penuwch*' (the people of Penuwch), almost all of whom were freeholders.[5] Deferential bonds did not therefore compel them to support large landowners. Rees thought they were very pious and the ideal antidote to the Tories.

As in previous centuries, the Whig Pryse family overshadowed Cardiganshire politics. Pryse Pryse, who supported the abolition of slavery, held the borough seat when a challenge was mounted by J. S. Harford of Blaize Castle near Bristol and Falcondale, Lampeter, in 1841. Although much was made of Harford being an outsider – Pryse's supporters stressed that, unlike his opponent, Pryse spent the money gleaned from his estates in Wales – the result was close, Pryse winning by twenty votes. The results reveal a geographical divide, a reflection of the contestants' respective spheres of influence; Harford led in the south, but Aberystwyth supported Pryse. Harford launched what Francis Jones has called 'his second assault on this bastion of Gogerddan Whiggery' in 1849. His former opponent died that year, so in this contest he faced Pryse's eldest son, and namesake. The result, 299 to Pryse and 291 to Harford, was even closer than the 1841 election. Songs penned at the time shed some light on the county's political culture. Pryse's fox hunting activities were drawn on – 'Tally ho! tally ho! Let us cry as we go / To the sports or the hustings his

worth to proclaim'. Such songs illustrate how leisure, and the connections wrought during it, went hand in hand with politics during this
period. A second song lambasting the 'Bristol town Tori' and the Tories
of Lampeter and Cardigan, illustrates the north/south divide in the
county and the theme of native and outsider, both of which were to
recur in the county's political history.[6] The 1852 election, when Pryse
(who had by then changed his surname to Loveden) faced John Inglis
Jones of Derry Ormond, was another north-versus-south battle.
Geographical divides like this demonstrate that although the county's
natural boundaries meant that it was, in John Edward Lloyd's words,
'destined by nature to be a single area', humans were more than
capable of drawing lines within the region.[7] Jones polled a majority in
Cardigan, but the Loveden stronghold of Aberystwyth had more voters
and this weight advantage secured his victory. Later eviction scandals
were foreshadowed when fourteen tenants were removed after having
gone against the wishes of Conservative landlords.

During the later 1860s grander issues drove political struggles.
Ieuan Gwynedd Jones identified a conflict between two different
views: deference for social superiors against the rule of the majority.[8]
However, the 1865 county election was between two kinds of wealth,
old and new, landed and entrepreneurial, rather than clearly delineated
opposing sets of beliefs; both candidates were Liberals of a
conservative hue. In 1865 the coal and railway owner David Davies
stood against Thomas Lloyd of Bronwydd; the latter was supported by
Gogerddan. The former lost by 361 votes. Lloyd had gentry support,
and Nonconformists did not fall into line behind the Calvinistic
Methodist Davies. Nonconformity was not yet the political force it
would become. Revealingly, around this time an attempt to establish a
Liberal paper to oppose the Conservative *Aberystwyth Observer* failed.
A new geopolitical fault-line was carved by Davies, a native of
Merionethshire. The entrepreneur did not win a majority of votes in
Cardigan or Aberystwyth, but the eastern part (Lampeter and Tregaron)
– where his proposed railway would run – supported him. After this
election, the 1867 Reform Act increased the county electorate from
3,520 to 5,115, as £12 occupiers entered the political nation, and the
borough electorate rose from 685 to 1,561 due to the householder
ratepayer franchise.

In 1868 Evan Matthew Richards of Swansea, another man who
made his wealth through industry – namely, shipbuilding, lead and
silver – stood for the county. On this occasion new money had
Gogerddan backing. His contest against the Conservative Edmund
Malet Vaughan polarized the county more than any previous competition; it led to the birth of an exceedingly Liberal county. The Irish

Church issue made it hard for tenants to vote with their landlords; they empathized with the Irish who, like them, lived under an alien Established Church. Richards won by 156 votes, although he was in a minority at Lampeter and Tregaron. David Davies sent some of his railway navvies to serve as a bodyguard for those Liberals who might have felt intimidated while voting at Tregaron, a town some contemporaries considered a Tory stronghold. Indeed, the election was marred by pressure on tenants to mimic their landlord's political persuasions. The families of Nanteos, Llanina and Derry Ormond were condemned for pressurizing their tenants. A select committee investigation into the conduct of the election discovered forty-three evictions. The 1868 elections provided martyrs and an inspirational foundation for later manifestations of Cardiganshire Liberalism.

Whilst tensions between landlords and tenants were not universal, the election of 1868 underlined significant, previously latent, divides about tenants' political and religious independence. The Tregaron-born peace campaigner, and Liberal MP for Merthyr Tydfil, Henry Richard, used the unpleasant consequences of this election to support arguments for the secret ballot, which was introduced in 1872. Other issues, such as the right to hunt game, remained contentious. Tenants were evicted from Trawsgoed for shooting rabbits in 1875 and 1893. Temptations to poach must have been all the greater in the parishes of Llangeitho and Blaenpennal because in 1866 they had 'been esteemed as one of the finest partridge countries on the island of Great Britain'.[9] Although concerns about security of tenure and other aspects of what was then called the land question may have been exaggerated – as the Welsh Land Commission discovered in the 1890s – MPs would have to pay attention to the interests of an increased electorate.

David Davies, who was returned for the borough in 1874 and was unopposed in 1880, understood how to strike a chord with the voters on day-to-day issues. He did not advocate the disestablishment of the Anglican Church in Wales, yet he supported the abolition of the tax on farmers' dogs and championed temperance. Moreover, he wanted rabbits to be taken off the game list. The fact that Thomas Edward Lloyd of Coedmor defined himself as a 'Liberal Conservative' demonstrated how far the political axis had shifted in the Liberal's favour. Lloyd defeated Richards for the county seat by 215 votes. Throughout this election, Lloyd made much of being a local man, and Richards did not have Gogerddan support on this occasion. Lloyd, who was beaten by over 800 votes in 1880 by the Liberal barrister Lewis Pugh Pugh, was the last Tory to stand for Cardiganshire. What the *Cambrian News* pre-emptively called the 'broken reed of Conservatism' in 1872 had eventually fallen to the ground.[10] Nevertheless, the

Conservative *Aberystwyth Observer* continued until 1914. John Gibson, editor of its print adversary the Liberal *Cambrian News*, established in 1867, was a Liberal lodestar, despite being a critic of claustrophobic rural society.

From 1885 the Liberal position was consolidated. Redistribution in 1885 abolished the borough. There was much opposition to this locally; it even united the parties and there was a feeling that the county was losing out to Glamorgan which had acquired more seats. With the extension of the franchise of 1884 (all men who paid a rental of £10 per annum or held land worth that amount could now vote), and the addition of the borough voters, the electorate increased from 5,026 in 1883 to 12,308 in 1886. Conflicts within the Liberal Party marred their victory, however. In 1886 David Davies, a Liberal Unionist, lost by 9 votes to W. Bowen Rowlands an Anglican from Haverfordwest who, significantly, supported Home Rule for Ireland. Although Cardiganshire was Protestant to the core, the plight of Ireland was wedded to Welsh aspirations in the county. Joseph Chamberlain's attempts to win over Welsh voters failed, even when in 1892 a Welsh-speaking Liberal Unionist draper from Birmingham employed a farmer who had been evicted in 1868 on his platform. This symbol of past wrongs could not counter the clamour against current injustices, the draper lost to Rowlands by 1,963 votes.

After Rowlands retired, the leadership of the Liberals in the county passed to Matthew Vaughan Davies of Tan-y-bwlch, he stood as a Conservative in 1885. Despite criticism from within the Liberal Party, this Anglican landlord won substantial support. He was local, appealed to the less sophisticated voter and stood for the county beyond the partisan Liberals of the Aberystwyth shopocracy. The latter group deemed him an eminently inactive MP – the *Cambrian News* opined that the extension of the franchise was a pyrrhic victory as Liberal votes ended up in the hands of a former Conservative and that at least his opponent, J. C. Harford was 'an honest Tory'.[11] Even so, he fended off two challenges from Harford in 1895 and 1900. But, beyond this peculiar figurehead, the county maintained its sound Liberal credentials. The first county council in 1889 represented a Liberal high tide (there were thirty-six Liberals to ten Conservatives); indeed, there were more Nonconformist ministers in this body, which replaced the JPs, than landowners (four to three). Many councillors were tenant farmers and small businessmen. In addition, there were stirrings which evoked the disturbances of the early nineteenth century. Anti-tithe activities flared up at a time of agricultural depression in the late 1880s and early 1890s. Penbryn, Llangeitho and Cellan were among the parishes affected, and the tithe issue added volume to the call for the disestablishment of the Anglican Church in Wales.

Indeed, pastoral farmers experienced trying times from the mid-1880s to the end of the century. Wages rose slightly while livestock prices were low. More labourers and servants moved to south-east Wales in these decades, and arable land was turned over to rearing stock. Foreign imports contributed to the malaise. From the 1880s imported bacon took some of Cardiganshire's market. Many tenants also moved to larger farms without sufficient financial reserves or skills. These unfavourable economic conditions that contributed to the tithe unrest were just one of the challenges faced by farmers in this century. Widespread enclosure, discussed above in the context of popular disturbances, did not herald the economic transformation that many had envisioned. Although the partitioning of commons provided property, the consequent restriction of grazing rights limited the amount of animals the farmer could maintain. Additionally, few could afford to buy land because the cost of fencing was prohibitive. Enclosures brought wealth to wealth, enabled some squatters to gain legal status, removed common rights and led to little improvement in upland areas generally.

One reason put forward for this lack of improvement was the innate conservatism of the farmers in this part of Wales. Thomas Johnes felt the need to inject some entrepreneurial spirit into central Cardiganshire in the form of 100 Swiss families. In 1815 he asked the government for funds in order to do this, but the Home Secretary, Viscount Sidmouth, refused. Later, the local press took on the role of championing innovation, applauding ploughing matches and agricultural societies. During times when agricultural products fetched low prices, landlords often granted rent abatements or sometimes reduced rents in order to ensure that farms remained occupied. At the rent audits of the Blaenpant estate in January 1850, for instance, they were reduced by 10–15 per cent. Suggestions that the answer to west Welsh woes was to 'farm higher', that is to invest in new techniques, were countered in one case by the comment 'God knows the poor Welsh farmer has to farm high enough, his mountains will testify it'.[12] Similar debates resumed after a period of relative prosperity in the middle of the century. One commentator, in 1877, expressed frustration that farmers seldom fattened animals, that hills needed to be planted, bogs drained, and that people should hear less of 'poor Wales' and more of 'prosperous agriculture'.[13] The fact that land in Cardiganshire was, according to the 1873 *Return of Owners of Land* (also called the New Doomsday report), worth only 10 *s.* rental per acre, lower than any other Welsh county, made these demands all the more strident and frustrating.

General anxieties about the state of agriculture towards the end of the century found particular expression in worries about the decline in the standard of horses. The county was once famous for strong short-legged equines, but contemporaries felt that this strain had been diluted. They recalled the great demand for Cardiganshire cobs during the Crimean War when they were used as artillery horses. Efforts to improve this breed commenced in earnest during the 1870s; part of this drive was the introduction of the stud, 'Glasgow Laddie', in 1877. Throughout this period tenant farmers and larger landowners were being urged to refine their stock, and much emphasis was placed on the need to maintain the county's reputation. In a rapidly changing world this mark of distinction was to be cherished and nurtured. By 1890 a concerned observer reminisced about the horse shows which had flourished some twelve to fourteen years earlier, bemoaned the loss of stock and the rage for cheap sires and was perturbed at the prospect of the cobs 'losing its distinctive features'.[14] Perhaps this worry was justified given the fashion for Cardiganshire cobs which drew many English dealers to Ffair Dalis at Lampeter.

The arrival of the railway doubtlessly encouraged many to buy horses from Cardiganshire fairs. It also enabled celebrated Cardiganshire horses, like the pony owned by Dr T. D. Harries of Aberystwyth which won a jumping competition at Olympia in 1887, to move around the country swiftly. Aberystwyth was first reached from the north by the Cambrian Railway in 1864. Then, in 1867, the route from Lampeter, via Tregaron, came to the town. At first it was intended for the Manchester and Milford line, built by David Davies, to terminate at Llanidloes not Aberystwyth, and this may explain its name as termination there would have opened a connection to northern England. Other towns connected to the rail network included Llandysul (1864), Cardigan from Whitland (1886) and Newcastle Emlyn (1895). A plan to connect New Quay to Llandysul was mooted in the 1880s but did not materialize. It took around two and a half hours for the train to travel from Pencader to Aberystwyth in 1872. Three to four trains ran each day in both directions and stopped at all stations except Llangybi, where locomotives only halted on market and fair days. The gentry made use of this train when the Gogerddan hounds travelled to Strata Florida on it.

These railways, however, did not join the eastern and western portions of the county and, as a speaker at a meeting of the Cardiganshire Liberal Association at Lampeter said, it was easier to go by train to Aberystwyth from Lampeter than to travel to Cardigan. In terms of rail travel, the south-west was effectively cut off from the rest of the county. There had been excitement in Cardiganshire in 1839 when the Birmingham railway was constructed as it enabled travellers to reach London more quickly than before. But by 1885, when the county itself had the iron horse, some criticism was being voiced. Rail had contributed to the decline of the ports, it led to the depopulation of rural areas, and the rates charged by railways hastened the demise of local industries and crafts. The *Cambrian News* suggested national ownership of the railways in order to protect against exorbitant rates. However, according to an entry in the National Eisteddfod of 1884 about Welsh rivers, the arrival of the railway led to an expansion in the salmon trade. In the summer of 1883, half a ton of this fish was caught in the lower Teifi and sent to London and other cities in a single day.[15]

Crafts were probably fading from Cardiganshire society because the rate of migration out of the county increased during the later nineteenth century. Up until the 1870s the county's population had risen decade after decade, particularly in the first half of the century when it rose 59.3 per cent from 42,956 in 1801 to 70,796 in 1851. This growth was despite what contemporaries called the 'rage for emigration' to North America that took people to places such as New Brunswick and, later, Ohio.[16] From mid-century the migratory stream flowed more strongly in the direction of south-east Wales than abroad. After two decades of steadier growth, and a peak of 73,441 in 1871, the population fell. There was a drop of 10.87 per cent between 1881–91, and by 1901 the census recorded 61,078 people living in the county. Migration led to demographic imbalances; Cardiganshire had an aging and lonely population. There was a significant imbalance of the sexes, in 1891 there were 1,274 women for every 1,000 men, the highest proportion of females to males in England and Wales. Moreover, the report on the census noted that 'the female predominance has for five successive censuses been far greater than in any other county'. The census commissioners thought that females were trapped in the county because monoglot Welsh-speaking women could not enter service outside the area.[17]

In part, the decline in Cardiganshire's lead mines contributed to this fall in population. They had revived from the mid-1830s when, in 1834, the capable Cornish troubleshooter John Taylor, whose rationalization in Flintshire provoked disturbances but did not sacrifice workers' wages, became manager of Trawsgoed's mines. Taylor's talents improved the infrastructure of the estate's main mine, Frongoch, and it produced lead and zinc ore from 1834 to 1893. Other county landowners, Pryse and Powell, employed him too. Activity peaked in the 1870s. There were 1,824 lead miners in 1881; ten years later this had fallen to 781. Foreign competition and a decline in domestic demand took its toll. Conversely, domestic demand for flannel shirts and underwear for workers in the expanding coal mines of south-east Wales led to the Teifi area's becoming a centre of woollen manufacture, and the power loom propelled this development. Mills were closing elsewhere in Wales but by the 1890s they were located wherever possible in the Teifi valley. During this period weaving mainly took place in factories. There was still a domestic element, however, as women were often expected to take home blankets to hem and fringe during the weekend. Factories which exported textiles in the latter part of the century were located at many places, including Cribyn, Cellan and Llanwenog.

For many, prospects in south-east Wales, or with the milk trade in London, were better than those available in the county – in 1891, 6,000 men in the Rhondda valleys were from Cardiganshire, and unlike earlier migrants many settled there. These migrants brought their habits, and differences between them and the host society came to the fore. Some Cardis (as people from Cardiganshire were called) thought Glamorgan people were too liberal with coal. The regular use of coal came as something of a shock for those who came from an area where this fuel was expensive and alternatives like peat and culm (a mixture of anthracite coal dust, clay and water) were more commonly used. Such reputations could lead to the Cardis being seen as a miserly tribe, while others saw it as economy born of scarcity. Whether it was a virtue or vice depended on where one stood. Of course, a cautious mentality would be well suited to the ethos of the friendly societies which became more common in the county during this period. These included the Bee Hive club, established at Tregaron in 1827, and the Ivorites at Llanfihangel Genau'r-glyn founded in 1841. The latter conducted all business in Welsh. Other ways of 'making do' included the seasonal migration of women who walked to London – this took them five days – to weed public parks; these temporary migrants were described by the poet Daniel Ddu of Ceredigion. Another economizing activity carried out by females involved collecting wool left by sheep in upland areas which they later used to make clothes.

As the century progressed, Cardiganshire's towns were transformed – some lost functions, others gained new roles. The mid-century golden age of ship building and sea trade faded with the development of steam and rail; the last large ship built at Cardigan was launched in 1865. Trades that supplied the ship industry, such as rope making and carpentry, dwindled with it. Previous to its decline, shipbuilding attracted many from rural areas to learn these trades. When shipbuilding was at its peak in New Quay, the 1851 census revealed that most sailors were natives whilst many tradesmen came from outside. Tourism provided longer lasting benefits. Aberystwyth, for example, attracted a wealthier type of visitor in the days before the train, but had to defend its trade against cholera scares in 1832 and 1849. It was said in 1841 that the 'prosperity of the place depended on the strangers that visited it'.[18] Inland, Lampeter, Llandysul and Tregaron were service centres for the agricultural areas around them, though the number of inhabitants did fall during 1881–91, the decade of greatest population loss. Aberaeron, one of the few planned towns in south Wales, was developed in the decades after an act to improve the harbour was passed in 1807. Moral concerns about this town were voiced in some Nonconformist publications. In 1847, Aberaeron was seen as a place where the devil's hold tightened as the town grew. Evidently, the devil followed commercial activity, centres of population, and the circus. When a circus, including an elephant which later died after drinking lead-polluted water, arrived at Tregaron one Sunday in 1848, the religious fraternity was distressed to see so many prefer to peruse the exotic wonders than attend religious services.

Even when the county's population was falling, places of worship were being built and improved. The architectural landscape was transformed as chapels and churches were added to, repaired, rebuilt or built anew; many of the most impressive, like Mount Zion in Cardigan and Bethel in Aberystwyth, were in towns. Llanrhystud church was rebuilt in early 1850s. Its capacity was doubled, and a spire replaced the square tower. In 1821 the county had been identified by its lack of churches with spires. A thief reportedly came to the area to steal because a fortune-teller's crystal ball had shown that he would be buried in church which had a spire, and he believed there were none like that in Cardiganshire at the time. Smaller internal alterations could also transform places of worship. At Holy Cross Mount (Mwnt) pews were first introduced in 1853. Whereas there had been some seating for the wealthier portion of the congregation before this, others had to bring their own seats or sit on a bench across the wall. This period of church alteration transformed the Anglican Church and is in stark contrast to the situation in the early nineteenth century when the legacy of neglect persisted. A petition from Cilcennin in 1821 reported that the church had fallen down and that the poor but devout cottagers in this overpopulated parish could not afford to raise a new one. Dilapidated churches joined other items, like *cawl caws y tlawd* (cheese broth of the poor who could not afford meat), to epitomize Cardiganshire's poverty.

The 1851 census of religion provides information about the religious make-up of the county. This census led to an arithmetic war, as different groups claimed to be the largest, or attempted to explain why they did not have many attending that day, Sunday 30 March. Some, like the vicar of Gwnnws, blamed the weather. But the honest Calvinistic Methodist minister at Swyddffynnon stated that the young had gone to see an open-air baptism. Testimonies like this remind us that there were floating worshippers and of the power of spectacle, which was captured by the anonymous Cardiganshire artist called the Welsh Primitive in 'Baptism at Llanbadarn'. The Nonconformists, if taken as a whole, won the arithmetic war in the county as they comprised 77.5 per cent of worshippers. All the remaining 22.5 per cent were Anglicans. This exercise demonstrated how Nonconformity had expanded during the early nineteenth century. When the different denominations' figures are examined some distinctive features within the county emerge. The Wesleyan Methodists (6 per cent of worshippers) were reinforced by English miners, some 343 from Cornwall and Devon were in the mining areas during 1851, and they had a brass band at Goginan. Calvinistic Methodists, who had broken from the Anglicans in 1811, were the largest with 38 per cent. They were spread over the county, but concentrated in the east and north. As one of the most conservative denominations their predominance in these areas has been used to explain the relative lack of Rebeccaite activity there. Two of their leading figures were Ebenezer Richard (father of Henry Richard) and Ebenezer Morris. Unitarians made up 3 per cent of worshippers, but this small number packed into the mid-Teifi region constituted a thorn in the Methodist lion's paw, and was known as the 'black spot'. They maintained their outspokenness on political matters. Their journal, *Yr Ymofynnydd* (The Inquirer), described how, after Richards's election victory in 1868, freedom had lit up the county.[19] Of the other denominations, the Baptists constituted 8 per cent and the Independents accounted for 22 per cent, both were mainly located in southern Cardiganshire.

Between 1811 and 1851 the number of places of worship in the county increased from 140 to 240, and there were seats for 89 per cent of the population if they wished to attend. This provides some idea of the role played by religion in the county. We must remember, however, that not all seats were filled. For example, at Tregaron during the most popular morning service 3,325 of the area's population of 10,404 attended. Even so, enough people went to a Methodist meeting at Llangeitho in 1817 for robbers to take advantage of their absence from their homes. Attendance was common not universal, yet the seating and attendance figures meant that Cardiganshire stood in stark contrast with other parts, for example in Liverpool there were enough seats for only 31.1 per cent of the population. Cardiganshire was also an overwhelmingly Protestant county; an attempt to convert residents in Aberystwyth by Catholic Breton missionaries came to an end in 1849 with only one reported convert. Some missionaries from the county went overseas from the county. These included D. C. Davies of Llanddewibrefi, who was appointed by the archbishop of Canterbury to go to Kurdistan and lead the instruction of the Nestorian Church, and the Independent Thomas Bevan was one of the first Protestant missionaries in Madagascar.

Yet there were conversions to be made nearer to home too. The religious revival of 1859 landed as a spark in northern Cardiganshire delivered by Humphrey Jones who had been inspired by what he had seen in New York State. The other leading figure in this revival was the Calvinistic Methodist preacher Revd Dafydd Morgan. The revival was credited with emptying the taverns in Ysbyty Ystwyth. A resurgence of piety had consequences for the drinks trade. Eight publicans at Aberystwyth became teetotal, and a brewer emptied his stock into the Teifi. Some idea of the drinks trade at the time can be gleaned from *Pigot's Directory* of 1844 which counted sixty-eight taverns and inns in Cardigan, most on the waterfront. The drink issue enabled Non-conformity to demonstrate its moral superiority. Yet temperance was a two-edged sword, as the radical Independent minister William Rees discovered at Llechryd in 1880 when he was locked out of the chapel by leading members of his congregation who cultivated barley. Such incidents reveal the complicated nature of temperance and how economic concerns could override religious affiliations. However, even during the revival, *Y Drysorfa* (The Treasury), a Calvinistic Methodist journal, was not complacent and noted that there was much more of the Lord's work to be carried out in the county, especially to reduce rates of illegitimacy resulting from *caru yn y gwely* (the practice of unmarried couples' spending a night together in the female's bed).[20] This was thought to have declined after 1870, and contemporaries speculated that the 1870 Education Act contributed to its demise.

In 1860 *Yr Ymofynnydd* poured cold water on the revival in what it called the northern parts of the county. It suggested that prayer meetings were being held in taverns, and expressed shock about a prayer, reputedly given by Morgan at Swyddffynnon, which asked God to aid the efforts of those digging for mineral riches.[21] There were also secular currents which dampened the religious fire. Revd Rhys Morgan, minister of Llanddewibrefi, pointed the finger at the writings of Herbert Spencer, Charles Darwin and T. H. Huxley. It was a case of the origin of species supplanting the origin of sin. Indeed, the pull of the world, whether cerebral challenge or the conviviality of the tavern, could undermine religious efforts. Nonetheless, the county was seen as one of the most religious in Britain, and its culture was to a large extent shaped by churches and chapels.

Religion exerted a powerful influence over education. The changes in education during this century were significant and some of the county's leading names were associated with this endeavour; moreover, the county itself acquired a reputation in this field. Earlier in the century the schools at Castellhywel and Neuadd-lwyd, established in 1820 by Dr Thomas Phillips, trained many men for religious positions. Other notable institutions included Revd David Evans's at Llandysul and the Rhydowen Grammar School. Ystradmeurig's reputation, however, decreased during the century, perhaps because its curriculum, which avoided the sciences, failed to move with the times. From 1833 government grants were given to National Schools Society (Anglican) and British and Foreign School Society (non-sectarian) schools. Many Nonconformists went to National schools in the first half of the century; sectarian divisions over education were less marked in this period.

Evidence submitted to the Commission of Inquiry into the State of Education in Wales (1847) offers an insight into the culture and educational condition of Cardiganshire. The investigators visited schools and conducted question-and-answer sessions with children. From answers given by children at Ystradmeurig it was as if the Copernican revolution had never happened as they all thought the sun went round the earth. Their findings indicated that the poor were eager to acquire education but that an absence of schools – twenty-two parishes had no day schools – meant that opportunities to acquire an education were limited. Even where schools existed, however, the quality of teaching and the school environment were often unsatis-factory– at the Lampeter Church School 'neighbouring fields serve the children for the purpose of a privy'.[22] These reports judged that being a monoglot Welsh-speaker limited an individual's opportunities. Moreover, it appears that the poor agreed; they believed that a lack of English prevented placing their children out at service.

Despite advances in voluntary provision from the 1840s, the educational situation remained unsatisfactory. From 1870 the government supported the establishment of board schools where there was inadequate voluntary provision. By 1878 fifty-four of these schools had been established in the county. It could be argued, however, that Cardiganshire's educational 'take-off' came with the 1889 Welsh Intermediate and Technical Education Act. The first of these secondary schools was established at Llandysul in 1895. Drawing on the first generation of Welsh university graduates, 75 per cent of teachers had degrees, the county had more graduate teachers than any other in Wales in 1900. Furthermore, by the end of the century there were more children aged over sixteen being educated in Cardiganshire than there were in than any other county in Wales, with the exception of Glamorganshire.

Educational developments marked the pinnacle of the age of the *gwerin* (respectable, cultured, non-gentry). Hugh Owen led the campaign for a Welsh College from the 1840s and the MP David Davies contributed funds, as did many workmen. By chance a failed hotel became available in Aberystwyth. The *Illustrated Review* stated that the town was not a good location for the college. To avoid what it called 'educational provincialism' a site closer to the English border was suggested. The *Cambrian News* responded that 'the wonderful ignorance of the English mind' overlooks that it was in a central *Welsh* location.[23] Thomas Charles Edwards, Principal of Aberystwyth College 1872–91, declared that a university would, by helping to create, preserve and value intellectual life, make Wales a nation. There were plans to close the college, to which female students were admitted in 1884, during the 1880s. But along with Bangor and Cardiff it became part of the University of Wales, founded in 1893. By 1900 there were 474 students (in 1872 there had been twenty-six) and, together with tourism, the institution contributed to the growth of the town.

The county's other fount of higher education, St David's College, Lampeter, founded by Bishop Burgess in 1822, could have been established at Llanddewibrefi were it not for some reflection about accessibility and J. S. Harford's offer to provide land for the institution. Later, in 1855, an attempt to move it to Brecon was defeated. Its establishment was prompted by concern about the quality of education received by trainee ministers. Moreover, it helped Anglicanism maintain more than superficial roots in Wales. Students first resided there in 1827, and many of these – thirty-six of the college's first sixty-four entrants – were farmers' sons.

To counter what an 1850 college instruction called 'clownish lounging about the shops or market places', students at Lampeter were encouraged to exercise.[24] Accordingly, cricket matches commenced during this decade. Furthermore, rugby union established its first foothold in Wales at Lampeter in the 1860s. Association football arrived later in 1887. Indeed, the county as a whole was experiencing an influx of organized sport in the latter half of the century. Older violent community games, such as the *Bêl Ddu* (Black Ball) played between Llandysul and Llanwenog, had been disbanded in the first half of the nineteenth century. In 1861 there was a county cricket club called 'Ceredigion' which played visitors in Aberystwyth. And Cardigan's rugby union club, founded in the 1870s, drew with Llanelli in 1895. Yet some Nonconformists found sport distasteful. Principal Edwards of Aberystwyth was condemned for attending athletic events, and many thought it was unseemly for ministers to watch team sports; perhaps the memory of earlier communal games cast a shadow over later, more disciplined, events.

The county produced notables in the fields of religion and education who pepper the *Dictionary of Welsh Biography*. Some rose from humble beginnings and their lives consequently became examples of what could be achieved through diligence. To take one example, John Rhys, the son of a small farmer near Ponterwyd, became a leading Celtic scholar at late Victorian/Edwardian Oxford. Another giant raised in the north of the county was Lewis Edwards, born at Pen-llwyn, who established the Calvinistic Methodist College at Y Bala in the late 1830s. Sarah Jane Rees (Cranogwen) from Llangrannog was a distinguished female cultural figure in this century. She taught navigation at her school in this village, was a famous poet, and from 1878 to 1891 edited a journal for Welsh-speaking women, *Y Frythones* (The British Woman), which included articles in support of enfranchising women.

The life of the poet Thomas Evans (Telynog), encapsulates many of the characteristics of nineteenth-century Cardiganshire. Born in 1840, the son of a Cardigan boat maker, Evans did not receive an education, but desired to learn. At eleven he started working on ships sailing between Welsh ports but was ill-treated. Like many young men he chose to leave the county and became a miner near Aberdare. The first expression of his poetic talent was in a letter to his mother which contained a song describing his new home. Thereafter, he flourished as a poet, winning awards at eisteddfodau, while working as a miner and being an active member of his Baptist chapel. A collection describing notable people from the county, published three years after his death by consumption in 1865 aged twenty-five, stressed how much he achieved despite the disadvantages of his youth and the nature of his employment with which he supported his mother.[25] Migration, religiosity, hardship and culture, were themes which shaped the county's history in the nineteenth century. All altered in the following era of technological and social change.

The Twentieth Century

Discussions about organized religion in the twentieth century are usually framed by the theme of decline; its demise is typified by abandoned or converted chapels. Some of these transformations happened in the first half of the century; a Wesleyan chapel in Cardigan was replaced by the Priory Street Cooperative stores in 1939. Yet, as attendance at places of worship fell rapidly from mid-century, the rate at which these structures transformed accelerated. To take another example from Cardigan, in 1976 the Hope English Congregational chapel was sold to the Welsh Office which demolished it in order to provide a wider entrance to Bath House Road. Behind these architectural alterations there were changes in people's thoughts and actions. The 2001 census figures indicate how the county, once renowned as one of the most religious, could hardly lay claim to that title at the turn of the twenty-first century. Although 70.8 per cent of respondents from the county declared that they were Christian, the average for England and Wales was 71.8 per cent. Moreover, those stating that they had 'no religion' were 19.7 and 14.8 per cent respectively. Students at the county's two university colleges may have skewed the figure, but this does not detract from the enormous changes in the social role of organized religion which occurred in the twentieth century.

Religion played a far more prominent role during the first decades of the century. A Royal Commission set up in 1906 to investigate Welsh religious life found that 74 per cent of those who were actively involved in organized religion were chapelgoers. Figures like these fuelled the campaign to disestablish the Church of England in Wales, the legislation passed into law in 1920. A Church Defence League was formed in response to this campaign. In 1913, 3,000 of its members marched through Cardigan. Congregations in towns declined less rapidly than those in rural areas where out migration removed many worshippers. Urban areas could maintain substantial congregations into the 1960s and beyond. There were an estimated 2,620 chapelgoers in Aberystwyth during the 1980s. The temperance cause was closely linked to religion at the start of this period. A branch of *Merched y De*, a south Wales female temperance group founded by Cranogwen, was formed at Cardigan in 1904. Temperance hostels, for those wishing to stay in an alcohol-free environment, meant that the movement offered commercial opportunities; one was established in 1905 at Bryn Square, Lampeter. Struggles over religious expression took place in towns too. The Salvation Army upset local authorities when they held noisy meetings at the castle grounds, Aberystwyth. From 1909 these gatherings were outlawed. However, as a result of this prohibition, chapel congregations who had held less audible meetings there were also prevented from using this space.

The 1904–5 religious revival, spread by Evan Roberts of Loughor and the media of the day, illustrates both the importance of organized religion in the early twentieth century and some of its weaknesses. Its starting point is claimed by several places, but for many it began at Blaenannerch in southern Cardiganshire. The county fostered and embraced the revial; Joseph Jenkins of New Quay and John Thickens of Aberaeron were pivotal figures. Jenkins, through initiating prayer meetings for young people and encouraging young women – notably Florrie Evans – to express their religious experiences, paved the way for the revival and contributed to its character. Nevertheless, a simple contrast between present-day religious quietude and Edwardian excitement can overshadow some of the problems that existed at that time. After all, it was anxiety over religious observance that prompted the invitation to the area of an English evangelical, the Calvinistic Methodist Seth Joshua, who contributed to the kindling of the revival. Moreover, Ieuan Gwynedd Jones has detected that the revival drew back former members instead of bringing in those with no previous connections with the chapels. Figures for the strongest denomination in the county, the Calvinistic Methodists, reveal how attendance peaked during the revival. The number of adherents, members who regularly attended religious services, was highest in 1906 but there was a steep decline afterwards, from a high of 20,353 to 10,619 in 1968. Sunday school attendance also dropped from 12,194 in 1905 to 2,371 in 1973. Those classified as communicants, people entitled to receive communion, fell from 13,272 in 1906 to 8,055 in 1973.

Nonetheless, for a time the revival reverberated throughout Cardiganshire in both print and deed. Allen Raine, the Newcastle Emlyn-born author and granddaughter of Dafydd Dafis of Castellhywel, who spent many years living on the Cardiganshire coast at Tresaith, wrote *Queen of the Rushes: A Tale of the Welsh Revival* (1906). Like earlier revivals, contemporaries reported changes in habits. W. Jones-Edwards related how the fair held on 25 September at Pontrhydfendigaid, which was usually the occasion when Cwmystwyth and Tregaron contingents came to blows, was transformed by crowds gathering to sing hymns.[1] Yet court records reveal that tensions could boil over in this heady atmosphere. During August 1905 two miners from Glamorganshire were arrested for being drunk and disorderly in Llanddewibrefi. They were 'cursing and swearing at the revivalists' while they were holding an open-air meeting. One asked the crowd to clear because they had prayed for long enough. Eventually, a policeman was compelled to wrestle him to the ground.

Other defining features of the revival included its popularity among the young and the role played by women. In November 1904 the Cardigan area correspondent for the *Cardiff Times* related how the 'religious awakening' was gathering momentum in Cardigan and the surrounding area 'particularly among the young' and in the Calvinistic Methodist chapels. There were expressions of 'deep and sincere feelings' at public prayer meetings. At that time there were many who volunteered to teach in Sunday schools, whereas in the past the young had been reluctant to take part in classes. Indeed, the young carried the revival torch well into the night and aroused some parental concern. At one chapel an elder had come to 'see what had become of his daughter' and found it difficult to separate a religious gathering held by youths which eventually dispersed at 11.15 p.m. Many meetings ran into the early hours. In *Tarian y Gweithiwr* (The Workers' Shield) there were reports of nightly meetings at Llangrannog in February 1905 where mariners, enthused by the Holy Spirit, gathered until 1 a.m. At Llanddewibrefi in 1906 Mrs Jones, Egryn, 'conducted revival meetings'. She also organized gatherings at New Quay that year, but the revival spirit was beginning to fade. Although the *Cambrian News* thought they were 'good meetings', it observed that 'the lack of the late religious fervour was visible'.[2]

There is a tendency to overemphasize recent changes in manners. Yet in Daniel Thomas's memoirs, published in 1916, this native of Dôl-y-bont was struck by a decline in the external manifestation of religious observance in the village. He contrasted contemporary Sabbath observance with that in the middle of the previous century. Especially noticeable was the current acceptance of whistling: sixty-five years earlier this had been unheard of. Other examples of leisurely activities impinging on the sabbath included golf and motor cars. During the interwar years some older people would not knit on a Sunday. Kate Davies noted how people walked more slowly during the 'day of rest', and how Unitarians and Independents would ignore each other on a Sunday while having cordial relationships all week. The appearance of a car on a Sunday caused a stir in 1902 at Pren-gwyn; the Independents were relieved when they saw that it was going to the Unitarian chapel.[3]

Changes in behaviour after the Second World War were noted by an alarmed resident of Llechryd in 1949 who wrote: 'Instead of full churches and chapels today we have full pubs, with women and young girls claiming preponderance.'[4] Comments like these also reveal anxieties about changes in the position of women in society after they had assumed many male tasks during the war. The polarization of alcohol and religion, in the form of debates over whether public houses should open on Sundays, continued into the final quarter of the century. This dispute demonstrated the gulf between notions of sabbath observance and the growing socio-economic role of leisure. From 1961, as long as 500 local-government electors wanted a poll, there were referenda held on Sunday opening. In 1989 the district of Ceredigion, then part of the county of Dyfed (1974–96), went 'wet'. Carmarthen had opened its doors to Sunday drinking in 1982. Only one other district, Dwyfor in what was then Gwynedd, held out until 1996. Forty per cent of the electorate voted on this issue in Ceredigion, far more than those long 'wet' areas like Cardiff where only 8.7 per cent turned out. A majority of 820 were in favour of opening the pubs in Ceredigion. Of course, drinking had gone on in clubs on Sundays ever since the legislation was passed in 1881. But the symbolic aspect was important. Those wanting to preserve the ban were defending one of the defining principles of Nonconformity. Moreover, the Welsh Tourist Board, concerned about visitors being put off by what some saw as archaic laws, supported the 'wets'. The area had played an important part in the clash between booze and the Bible, but eventually modern economic pressures supplanted older religious ones.

Other beliefs and customs were restricted, perpetuated or emerged in the twentieth century. The practice of shooting to celebrate weddings was condemned by the county's police force in 1916. In support, the *Welsh Gazette*, a paper founded in 1899 partly in response to feelings that the *Cambrian News* prioritized news from northern Cardiganshire, applauded their attempt to eradicate this dangerous tradition which had led to the death of a young woman in the south of the county. Less dangerous traditions like bowing to the moon were still practised in the early years of the century. This was no doubt a remnant of a belief in the moon's influence on agricultural endeavours. Even the technological and cultural transformations of the post-1945 era did not erase superstition. When the Penybont East housing estate was built in Aberystwyth during the late 1960s, the architects left out the number thirteen when they numbered the houses. They said that many would not live in a house bearing these reputedly unlucky digits. Increased technological activity led to new beliefs in powerful non-human forces. UFO sightings loomed large in the popular consciousness during the second half of the century, and in the mid-1950s witnesses from Capel Bangor and Llan-non reported this phenomenon. Some thought the strange flying objects came from the Aber-porth military base.

Increased leisure time, educational institutions and greater disposable income contributed to the growth of organized sport in twentieth-century Cardiganshire. The college at Aberystwyth promoted female sporting activity such as hockey, tennis and rowing. By 1914, the idea of women engaging in sport had been established and was not seen as something unusual. Schools also fostered sport, as a glance at sporting activity in Cardiganshire throughout 1906 reveals. Tregaron County School's hockey team played matches against Aberaeron County School. There were town teams too; Lampeter town's ladies beat Tregaron School. Boys from Tregaron played Lampeter town's football team. Descriptions of football matches in the early 1900s stress the sturdiness of players – evidently games could be quite physical. This told against the Tregaron boys when they lost to the stronger Lampeter town 2–1, but their superior team play was praised.

According to Donald Davies, team sports in Cardigan town benefited from the First World War because men gained experience in both rugby and football while serving in the forces. In the late 1920s a county football league was formed. Between the wars Cardiganshire teams also played in the Mid-Wales and Cambrian Coast Leagues. Football captured the imaginations of the inhabitants of more rural areas as well. In his history of Llanddewibrefi, D. Ben Rees noted how rugby never matched football's popularity in the parish.[5] There was a revival ('*adfywiad*') of Welsh football in the 1920s, a time when the national team, and those of Cardiff and Swansea, were doing well. Presumably, successes at this level inspired local efforts. Men from Llanddewibrefi went from house to house to collect money for a ball, and the team became known as the Dewi Stars. Motor transport enabled longer journeys to be taken and competitions with places from further afield. In January 1927, for instance, Cardigan's hockey team visited St Clears and Aberystwyth's college team played Caersws at home.

T. Llew Jones recounted the foundation of a cricket team at Pentre-cwrt, near the Carmarthenshire/Cardiganshire border, in the 1930s. Like the Dewi Stars, players eventually collected enough money to pay for their equipment, in this case three bats, two wickets, two leather balls and large gloves. In the days before lawnmowers, they used sickles to cut the grass in a field lent by a farmer. Often the only spectators were the cows, whose pats added to the perils of the game. Despite their rustic setting the team performed well against opposition.[6] Other cricket teams active in the 1930s included Borth and Waun Athletic, and there was a county cricket team called 'Ceredigion' which competed in the 1950s. In this decade, the local press had a sports page with photographs and lengthy reports of both local and national games. Gradually more activities were included and additional pages were dedicated to sport. By the 1970s darts and snooker leagues were reported. After the Second World War, there was increased interest in rugby union in Aberystwyth. Men from south Wales founded a club in the town during 1947. One of the most noted players from the area was Borth-born W. J. Morris – the cousin of John Morris MP for Aberavon and Secretary of State for Wales, 1974–9 – who won two caps when he played on the Welsh wing in 1963. Aberystwyth was abuzz when the 'All whites', Swansea, paid their first visit to the town in 1968, where they beat the home team 15–9.

Changes in cultural activities during the century, and the relative decline of religious meetings as social occasions, were noted in the reminiscences of John Williams, published in 1958. Dances, whist meetings and the Young Farmers' Clubs are fine, he reflected, but he did not think they should take the place of religious activities. However, groups like the Young Farmers were bound to overshadow chapels and churches as they contributed to the diffusion of youth culture in Cardiganshire when they put on rock-and-roll nights during the 1950s. By the 1960s Cardiganshire's contributions to pop culture were a source of pride. In 1968 the *Cambrian News* reported how Barrie Edwards, drummer in the London band Kate, was to appear on *Top of the Pops*. Another defining feature of the 1960s, an increased openness regarding sexual images and topics, also touched Cardiganshire when the Tal-y-bont publishers, *Y Lolfa*, published the first topless photograph in a Welsh-language magazine in 1965. However, thirteen years later magistrates in Aberaeron, acting in accordance with the Obscene Publications Act, confiscated and burnt 100 magazines, including *Playboy*, *Men Only* and the naturalist publication *Health and Efficiency*, which had been seized from a newsagent in the town. Another indicator that openness about sexuality had not percolated through the county's social fabric was provided by a study into the number of abortions between 1969 and 1972. A Welsh Office report by Dr Gareth Jones and Adam Jones demonstrated that Cardiganshire had the highest rate in Wales – 9 per 1,000 women compared to Anglesey's 2.8 and Glamorganshire's 7.8. One of the county's medical practitioners called for more sex education, increased availability of contraception, 'less pontification' and 'more awareness of the problems of young people'.[7]

Many of the categories used to define people in the middle of the century later lost their pertinence in a different social environment. Indeed, the groups reflect how communities – though tight-knit by today's standards – were more clearly defined by how they spent their leisure time. Studies of Tregaron and Aber-porth, conducted in the five years following the Second World War by Emrys Jones and David Jenkins respectively, were especially valued by social scientists because they were executed by Welsh-speakers whose academic training enabled them to see familiar sights with fresh eyes. Jenkins identified a divide between those people whose social epicentre was the tavern, '*pobl y dafarn*' (people of the tavern), and those whose social lives revolved around chapel or church gatherings, '*pobl y cwrdd*' (people of the meeting-house). Moreover, those who lived just some two to three miles inland were described as being 'from the country'. Jones's study of Tregaron emphasized the slow pace of life in the market town; people complained if they were served too quickly in a shop because one of the social functions of the shopkeeper, to talk about local affairs, was being neglected. His investigation also revealed how divisions in status within chapel congregations reflected their occupations and status in the secular realm. Evidently not all '*pobl y cwrdd*' were equal.[8]

Inequalities in rural Cardiganshire were stressed by Caradoc Evans in his 1915 collection of short stories, *My People*. Evans, who worked as a draper's assistant in Carmarthen and London before becoming a journalist and writer, was criticized for blackening the name of rural, Nonconformist Wales. His upbringing in Rhydlewis during the late nineteenth century, where unpleasant experiences at school and impressions of a community dominated by the chapel had been imprinted on his psyche, provided much of the material for his work. Highlighting both the distinctions in what was assumed by many to be a community free of class division and the inferior status of women won him few friends. While identifying some real unpleasantness in rural society, his focus on the dark side left him open to criticisms that he had selected only a narrow slice of the whole. Despite being accused of assaulting the Welsh character – the Lampeter dramatist Idwal Jones wrote an unpublished satire titled *My Piffle* – Evans retired to Cardiganshire. Yet Evans was only the most vocal and well-known critic of chapel life. As early as 1906 the *Cambrian News* remarked that Nonconformity was 'not keeping pace with the young life of the nation'. Sports, shorter hours of work and travel were encouraging people to expand their horizons beyond the chapel.[9]

At the turn of the twenty-first century the county was still pre-dominantly Welsh-speaking. The 2001 census, despite including many students from outside the area, revealed that 52 per cent spoke the language, the highest percentage in south Wales. Yet compared to 1991 there had been a decline of 7 per cent points. The number of Welsh monoglots in Cardiganshire declined rapidly during the century; in 1901 they constituted 50.4 per cent of the county's population. Even most of the towns had over 20 per cent who declared that they could speak only Welsh. A substantial drop in numbers of Welsh monoglots occurred in the twenty years between 1931 and 1951, when the proportion fell from 20.6 to 7.4 per cent. There was a 7.3 per cent point decline in the number of Welsh-speakers in the 1960s. By the 1990s many had been born outside the county; according to the 1991 census 35.6 per cent of the county's population had been born in England. Student numbers influenced the 1991 and 2001 figures (which recorded that 41.4 per cent had been born outside Wales), but just because an element of an area's population is transitory does not mean that it has no social impact. If it is less possible to use the language in everyday situations then it will cease to be the language of the community and will fade no matter how many learn it.

Attempts to bolster the language in the face of cultural and population movements were aided by the demise in the social status accorded to English after 1945. Some hundred years before teachers had urged their pupils to acquire English in order to climb the social ladder. Now, in a world where English was all around, those in similar positions sought to restore some balance. On the 5 October 1979, under the heading 'The English are Taking Over!', the *Cardigan and Tivyside Advertiser* reported the observations of Cynog Dafis, an English teacher at Newcastle Emlyn who later became the area's MP. Dafis noted that in 1976 nearly half of the primary school children in the Teifi valley were from English backgrounds. Figures for the Tregaron district indicate how this influx during the 1970s reshaped the county's linguistic contours. In 1967, 80 per cent of primary school children spoke Welsh as their first language; by 1983 the total was 45 per cent. Whilst many learnt Welsh, the change was phenomenal. Two of the organizations established in order to counteract this decline in the use and prominence of Welsh were founded in the county. During the interwar years Urdd Gobaith Cymru (the Welsh league of youth), which promoted Welsh among the young, was established. A camp at Llangrannog was opened in 1932. Cymdeithas yr Iaith Gymraeg (the Welsh Language Society) was set up in Aberystwyth during 1962 and members, most of whom were students, protested in the town during that decade. In 1977 they were condemned as 'vandals and layabouts' by the then Ceredigion District Council after they had daubed '*Tai i´r Cardis*' ('Houses for the Cardis') on their offices at Aberaeron. This was in protest at this authority's perceived reluctance to buy houses to prevent them becoming second homes for English people and the lack of council houses being built for locals.[10]

In addition to changes in the make-up of the area's population, there was the influence of a predominantly English media. Towards the end of the century, however, Welsh-medium television programmes, websites and radio stations, such as the bilingual Radio Ceredigion which first went on air in 1992, redressed the linguistic balance somewhat. Before these developments many feared that the Welsh language would be rendered inaudible amidst the deafening volume of an English-dominated media. Some, like Emyr Hywel a teacher from Penparc, refused to pay their television licence fees in protest. In 1972 Hywel was fined £10, but the case enabled him to publicize the argument that the dearth of Welsh programmes was killing the Welsh language and corrupting the nation's values. Such reactions meant that Welsh acquired a greater official or public presence as the century wore on. An effort was made to promote the Welsh equivalents for commonly used English names. Gwilym Jenkins, who was born in northern Cardiganshire in 1929, recalled how *Siôn Corn* was not heard of in his childhood and that it was all Father Christmas back then.[11] The county played a part in the battle for bilingual signs. Together with Merionethshire it argued against the then secretary of state for Wales, George Thomas, who held that bilingual signs would be costly and distract motorists. E. Roderic Bowen, the county's Liberal MP, chaired the 1971 investigation into road-sign policy. Whereas Glamorgan County Council opposed the introduction of bilingual signs, Cardiganshire's representatives argued that other countries like Belgium and Ireland did not deem them a threat to safety. In 1972 the Bowen commission's report supported the introduction of bilingual signs. During the latter half of the century Welsh became one of many 'minority' causes to acquire a louder voice in society. Its resonance is demonstrated by the fact that it both influenced road-sign design and inspired the art of Mary Lloyd Jones who has drawn many Ceredigion scenes which were influenced not only by the shape of the land but by the Welsh language.

Many natives of the county have expressed pride in the cultural and educational achievements which have taken place within its borders throughout the century. These cultural endeavours have contributed to the well-being of the Welsh language. Two of Cardiganshire's finest cultural pillars are the Llandysul publishers Gwasg Gomer, established by the Unitarian John David Lewis in 1893, and the National Library of Wales. Debates about where this institution and the National Museum should be located echoed throughout Edwardian Wales. In a comment which revealed some class prejudice, Lewis Morris, Penbryn, thought the museum should be in Cardiff because 'those people who would visit the museum would be a very different class of people from those who would go to the library'. John Williams, who had been Queen Victoria's physician, agreed, stressing the need to have it near 'the districts in which the Welsh feeling is alive now'. Eight of the thirteen Welsh counties concurred, as did the Privy Council in 1905, and it opened during 1909.[12]

Llanio-born Alun R. Edwards was county librarian from 1950, and his labours added to the county's cultural eminence in the second half of the century. Among other achievements, he was behind *Cymdeithas Lyfrau Ceredigion* (the Ceredigion Books Society), the Welsh Books Council established in 1961, and the introduction of library vans from 1962. In part, these endeavours were spurred on by the arrival of television in the 1950s. Like cinema, television did not receive a warm reception, though there was little of the Nonconformist outrage towards the small screen, as there had been towards the screening of religious films depicting Christ at Cardigan cinema in the first half of the century. In 1958 Edwards, in an annual report to the Cardiganshire Joint Library Committee, thought that the recent drop in book borrowing was due to an increase in what he called 'television fans'.[13] By 1965 some of these 'fans' were getting a rude shock as they discovered that, contrary to their assumptions, an indoor aerial did not prevent television detector equipment picking up signals from the set. Yet the educational use of the 'box' was recognized in 1958 when the headmistress of Ysbyty Ystwyth Primary School asked the Cardiganshire Education Committee if they would bear the cost of installation and maintenance. The director of education, Dr J. Henry Jones, agreed to pay for this, though he said that the Ministry of Education had ruled that local education authorities could buy only one set per 100,000 people and the county already had theirs at Highmead School, established in 1956 for children with special needs.

Education was a controversial topic at the start of the century when the Tory government's 1902 Education Act ended school boards and the county councils assumed their responsibilities. There was opposition to this change because it entailed rate support for denominational schools. At a Liberal meeting in Llangeitho that year it was said that the Conservative premier Arthur Balfour was against the boards because the people ran them. The county's MP Vaughan Davies opposed the bill. There was also opposition towards moves to close small elementary schools. Locals ensured that Strata Florida Abbey

School remained open in 1906; yet rural depopulation eventually forced its closure in 1952. Ystradmeurig School also closed in that decade. Considerable improvements were made to the infrastructure of schools during the Edwardian period. By 1914 some £40,000 had been spent on school facilities in the county. Nevertheless, forty-one of the county's 106 elementary schools were without water for washing and fifty-seven had no drinking water. Yet there was much concern about the children spending their time constructively when schools closed as a result of the 'Spanish Flu' that struck the county in 1918.

By 1913 there were five intermediate schools which catered for 339 boys and 299 girls. The curricula of these schools were geared towards university entrance and many thought they neglected practical subjects. Given the large numbers of university-educated teachers holding posts in the schools this bias was not surprising. The emphasis placed on education in an area with few career outlets for young people led to large numbers being educated to secondary level; in 1938 there were 1,469 pupils at this level. The importance placed on education was shown by the 1951 census figures. In the county 13.6 per cent of seventeen- to nineteen-year-olds were in full-time education, compared to an average of 7 per cent for England and Wales. Especial pride was taken in the number of university awards granted by the county council. There were sixty-six in 1951 and 271 ten years later. Later calculations based on the number of awards granted by each county's educational authority from 1965 to 1967, showed that of 1,000 pupils in the county 103 went to university, whereas the national average was 57. Surrey came second with 96.

Education underwent significant changes in the second half of the century. Access to both secondary and higher branches was widened and rendered less hierarchical, primary and secondary demarcated, and greater emphasis placed on the Welsh language. To some extent Cardiganshire had prefigured these developments. For instance, by 1951 it was the first Welsh county to separate primary and secondary education. In the early 1950s half of its secondary schools (called bilateral schools) were not based on the eleven-plus exam, although the others were grammar and modern schools. And in 1950 the county decided to make the teaching of Welsh to O level compulsory. Nevertheless, some felt that traditional education was under siege. Speaking at the 1954 prize day, T. Edgar Davies, headmaster of Llandysul Grammar School, expressed his concern about the present 'machine age' in which 'boys and girls [were] trained to become part of a machine'.[14] Likewise, Principal Ifor Leslie Evans of Aberystwyth felt uneasy about post-1945 educational changes; larger universities were not to his liking. However, under Dr Thomas Parry, principal from 1957, the Penglais site was developed and the 1960s were a period of expansion. This enlargement meant that more students came from outside Wales. Whereas the majority of students (some 66 per cent) in 1960 were Welsh, by 1969 only 37 per cent of the 2,000 were from Wales. Lampeter, which became part of University of Wales in 1971, also grew in the 1960s. In 1993 there were 4,804 students at Aberystwyth and 1,260 at Lampeter.

Alterations in the social fabric were signified by changes in the ownership and condition of buildings. Estates became less remunerative, partly the result of increased taxation. Estate duty was raised from 20 per cent in 1914 to 40 per cent eleven years later. Consequently, many landowners sold property. For tenants, land auctions represented an opportunity to acquire security of tenure, although mortgages could be as onerous as rent. Some of the former landowners' properties were demolished in the 1950s. Hafod's ruins were brought down in 1956, and much of its wood was taken during the world wars. Derry Ormond and Cilbronnau, Llangoedmor, were demolished earlier in the decade. Surviving structures performed various functions. As mentioned above, Highmead became a school, by 1980 Nanteos was a hotel and, after the Second World War, Trawsgoed was taken over by the Ministry of Agriculture. Expansion in government services and commercial activities therefore ensured that some of the county's houses survived. Workhouses, those other architectural emblems of the past, also changed. Like the country houses, their role had long been diminishing. Workhouses did not contain many inmates, the 1909 Royal Commission on the Poor Laws reported that there were 2,331 paupers in the county but only 205 in Cardiganshire's workhouses; most of these were sick and elderly. Only forty-one were able bodied, mainly shepherds, agricultural labourers and servants. Aberaeron workhouse was the first to close in 1914 and was turned into a cottage hospital. Tregaron followed in 1915. After the implementation of the National Assistance Act (1948) the old workhouse at Aberystwyth became a geriatric unit, while Lampeter's became an old people's home and Cardigan's was transformed into flats.

Tourism had long contributed to the county's income. As leisure time and personal transportation increased in the twentieth century, it became even more significant. In turn, concerns about attracting enough tourists multiplied. Aberystwyth's trade is believed to have peaked during the period 1890–1914. Although R. F. Walker has noted that with the First World War 'tourism came to an abrupt end for five years', by the summer of 1918 there was an improvement and the local press compared it to the best pre-war seasons. Similarly, the 1944 August bank holiday was described by the *Welsh Gazette* as being like peacetime. Visitors were confident that the war would end soon,

but had to sleep in shelters and police cells because so much accom-
modation had been taken over by the authorities. Local people also
frequented the coast; in the 1920s some carried sea water, reputed for
its health-giving qualities, home to dip their feet into. Many miners
from south Wales visited New Quay and Aberaeron. Indeed, in 1932
the *Gossiping Guide to Wales* thought that during the summer
Aberaeron was very much a Welsh resort with only the 'occasional
English visitor attracted by the trout fishing in the Aeron'. Even in the
early 1950s Maxwell Fraser praised Cardiganshire resorts, with the
exception of Aberystwyth, for there being 'little attempt to develop on
"popular" lines' and having retained 'great individuality'.[15]

Those very features which enthused Fraser, however, alarmed
others who felt that the county was not capitalizing on the increasing
affluence that characterized the post-austerity period. Therefore, there
were efforts to attract people to inland Cardiganshire. There had
already been attempts to draw visitors to the county's interior when the
first youth hostel in Cardiganshire was founded at Ponterwyd in 1934.
From the mid-1950s the success of pony trekking in Scotland
motivated attempts to promote this activity in Wales. Many hoped that
this activity would help counteract the decline in the number of tourists
who stayed for longer periods. From the 1960s, however, the main
A487 and A44 roads were improved and this facilitated the arrival of
the caravan. By 1978 there were forty-one sites on the coast and
seventy-four in the county as a whole.

All did not welcome the leisure invasion. Even at the turn of the
century one Aberaeron resident, David Samuel, thought that the miners
who visited the coast were all 'blackguards'. Later, as the commercial
and cultural influence of English grew, there were attempts to stop
caravan developments. Locals put forward a number of reasons why
sites north of Clarach should not be enlarged in 1968. The Borth area
had 1,400 caravans, twice the number of those living in the village.
There were economic grounds for limiting these developments. Hotel
bookings were declining and developers built shops on the sites that
had a negative impact on local tradesmen. Moreover, the clubs on these
sites made a mockery of the Sunday-opening regulations. As car
ownership increased, smaller beaches were visited more frequently.
The poet Isfoel, writing about Cwmtydu in 1966, remembered how the
language on the beach was Welsh in the days before the car. Others felt
that litter left by those visiting the county's beaches was polluting the
local environment. In 1964, a group of visitors, led by an RAF officer,
formed a line and cleared Dolwen beach, Aber-porth. The following
year, a comment by judges in the county's best kept village competition that the dirty area around the river at Furnace was 'caused

most likely by visitors' reveals the ambiguous relationship between tourism and the county.[16] Tourism was estimated to have brought £5,000,000 into Cardiganshire during 1969. Weather meant money for a county whose economy relied on tourism. In 1985, the wettest June in fifty years provoked consternation. Yet the rain did not seem to affect bookings as widely reported muggings in Spain deterred tourists from travelling there. Events in far away lands had tangible consequences on the area's economy.

Changes in Cardiganshire's economic structure influenced perceptions of its inhabitants. As fewer people depended on agriculture, the stereotype that cast the Cardi as a farmer who drew a scanty living from the land grew fainter. The number employed in agriculture fell from 10,663 in 1911 to 3,240 eighty years later. By 2001 there were 2,564 employed in the census category 'agriculture, hunting and forestry', compared to 4,969 in the largest group, those employed in the wholesale and retail trades and motor mechanics. Numbers of part-time farmers increased. Yet at the end of the century agriculture was still an important part of the county's economy; money earned on farms and spent locally assisted local businesses. The numbers of agricultural labourers declined at a faster rate than farmers; at the turn of the twentieth century many Irish came to help in the summer. By the final quarter of the century fewer people living in the county had contact with farming life than ever before. They might have lived near farms and eaten food produced there, but the farming cycle did not cross over into their lives in offices or factories. As well as better prospects elsewhere, more mechanization on farms limited the opportunities for labourers to climb the farming property ladder. In the early 1930s many farmers without electricity used old cars to power agricultural machinery.

Scientific developments in the kinds of grass that could be grown enabled small upland farms to become more profitable. George Stapleton secured funds in 1919 to establish a Welsh Plant Breeding Station at Aberystwyth which was inspired by the one at Cambridge. Some thought that Britain would have suffered greater deprivation during the Second World War if this establishment had not been founded. After a fall in agricultural prices from the 1920s to the mid-1930s, the war encouraged the government to support food production. This continued after the war, and the European Economic Community's 'Less Favoured Area' policy aided the county later in the century. Before the Milk Marketing Board (MMB) was founded in 1933, farmers from the area had difficulty reaching the milk market, but the MMB ensured that all farmers had the same price for milk. There was a corresponding increase in the numbers of dairy cattle kept by farmers, especially in southern Cardiganshire. In the late 1940s considerable pride was generated by the fact that the county's cattle had been cleared of tuberculosis. Creameries were established at Felin-fach and Llanio. But they closed in the 1990s after the introduction of milk quotas in 1984 had reduced the profitability of dairy farming. Thereafter, sheep numbers increased as dairy cows declined. Motor transport reduced dependence on the horse, but the famed Cardiganshire cob, celebrated in the paintings of Aneurin Jones, continues to be associated with the area.

Another artist, John Elwyn, the son of a Newcastle Emlyn woollen-mill owner, painted various subjects related to the county. These included people gathered around chapels, landscapes bathed in light and the woollen industry. Textile production was an important industry in Cardiganshire until the 1930s and small rural mills were active in the 1950s. There was a boom period during the First World War as military uniforms were in demand. A massive drop in the price of wool accompanied the end of the war because the government's excess stock of blankets and other items were dumped on the market at low prices. Then, during the interwar years industrial disruption in the mining valleys limited the spending power of those who were traditionally the main purchasers of textile products from the Teifi valley. Equally important, the mills were producing uncompetitive products, such as flannel underwear. Furthermore, the producers did not keep up with changing fashions. Outdated machinery, and difficulties in finding those able to repair it, compounded difficulties. Textile crafts carried on, but on a far smaller scale, in due course becoming a subsidiary of the tourist industry. The woollen mill museum at Drefach-Felindre traces the history of this trade.

A link to another of the county's historic industries is provided by the Llywernog lead-mining museum, near Ponterwyd. Though it never recaptured its mid-nineteenth-century peak, lead mining continued to cause environmental problems. During the First World War pollution in the river Teifi raised the unpleasant prospect of this river sharing the fate of the Ystwyth and Rheidol. Even though the increased price of zinc and lead during the war did not lead to a mining renaissance in Cardiganshire, there was evidently enough activity near the Teifi, in mines like Cwmmawr and Esgairmawr, to pollute the river. Other wartime activity included a failed attempt by Henry Gammon to operate Cwmystwyth as a going concern. Mining in the Pont-rhyd-y-groes area reaped some rewards in 1927 but failed to flourish. Later, during the Second World War, attempts were made to find zinc blende in the county, yet the costs were too burdensome and northern England provided a more accessible source and skilled labour.

Two instances in which the employment of women was discussed in the late 1920s reveal some contemporary opinions about the role of working women. A letter sent to the Cardiganshire Police Committee from the Home Office early in 1927 reminded them of the 'desirability of appointing one or more policewomen where the circumstances justified the course'. The committee decided not to take any action, as they thought it 'was a matter for London and other large cities'. Also in 1927, the county's Education Committee revoked a resolution passed in 1926 stating that where possible women should be appointed head teachers of schools with fewer than forty pupils. They were concerned that some thirty-five of the county's 114 schools would be reserved for women 'at the expense of men teachers'. They noted, however, that there needed to be female teachers in order for 'sewing and cookery' to be taught, men were not expected to provide this aspect of education.[17]

By the late 1950s there was considerable activity in the county, though some ideas, such as the plans made in 1957 to set up a nuclear power station near Llanrhystud, never materialized. An editorial in the *Cambrian News* enthused that Cardiganshire was not a 'quiet rural area' anymore, it was the scene of 'activity and development unprecedented since the old lead mining days'. The paper declared that the county's long period of economic stagnation and isolation was over. There was the Rheidol hydroelectric scheme and the Rheidol valley road was being widened. What was more, a television mast at Blaenplwyf, the water scheme at Teifi Pools and improved sewerage at Llanbadarn Fawr and Lampeter meant that the area was modernizing. Afforestation was another activity that contributed to the bustle. But this brought criticism from farmers who felt that common land should belong to the sheep farmers. There were efforts to bring light industry to the area; the 1961 *County Handbook* published by the county council welcomed all newcomers 'even more so if they can bring their own light industry with them'. It was hoped that small factories would employ some of those who were out of work. The south-west of the county has at times been 'the jobless black spot of Wales' with 16.7 per cent unemployed in 1979; two years earlier 19.8 per cent were jobless. Cardigan town's distance from other centres has been given as a reason for its high level of unemployment.[18]

This distance between the county and other places prompted a Cardiff firm to experiment with aerial transport in 1933, when an insurance assessor from Cardiff flew to Cardigan for a meeting. The journey took fifty minutes; the round trip would have taken almost two days if taken by rail or road. There was considerable excitement in the town when this plane was seen circling Cardigan. In later years, however, the increased use of sky space caused consternation. For, although displays by the Red Arrows entertained Cardiganshire spectators in the late 1970s, at the start of the decade, in October 1970, Concorde caused outrage when it flew at 1,210 miles per hour along the west coast of Wales. These supersonic flights, with their accompanying sonic booms, distressed animals and alarmed people; they were eventually outlawed. Low-flying military aircraft caused similar problems in the 1980s. In 1987 the Ministry of Defence (MoD) confirmed that planes were flying as low as 100 ft, levels which the MoD itself regarded as constituting an unbearable nuisance for the public.

Motorized road vehicles were another twentieth-century transport revolution. Motor traffic appeared on Cardiganshire roads in the first decade of the century. From the summer of 1901 motor taxis plied their trade in Aberystwyth. In the Edwardian period local police forces came under criticism for enforcing speed limits of 20 miles per hour in the countryside and 10 miles per hour in some towns. Some feared that police speed traps, in which police lay waiting in ditches with stopwatches at the ready, would deter tourists. Indeed, in July 1910 the Tal-y-bont Petty Sessions dealt with many speeding visitors, including Sir Arthur Cory Wright of Totteridge who was fined 40 s. and costs. Fifty years later, the car and the Cardi were firm friends. Jac L. Williams described its prevalence among farmers and observed how even the lowly road worker had his own small car.[19] The ability to move swiftly between the county's scattered settlements ensured that the car became an important part of Cardiganshire life. For example, the car facilitated cultural competitions when it enabled some families in the 1970s to compete in more than one eisteddfod a day. In the same way, crime was assisted by fast personal transportation. Yet in 1958, 104 years after the county force had been established, there were only six mobile policemen. The first mobile patrol was established in 1934.

The county's rail network expanded during the first two decades of the century. In 1902 the Vale of Rheidol route to Devil's Bridge opened. At first this railway served the Rheidol mines. Later, the tourist trade ensured it remained open. The Lampeter to Aberaeron railway commenced in 1911. Four years later the service was praised in the *Railway Magazine* which noted that it took fifty minutes to travel between the towns. When it closed in 1951, though, it was not mourned. There was no late evening train, and those trains that ran did so at inconvenient times. In contrast, the termination of the Carmarthen to Aberystwyth passenger service in 1965 provoked resistance. Freight stopped using the line in 1973. The Cardigan to Whitland passenger and goods services ended in 1962 and 1963 respectively; before 1920 staff had been allowed to shoot game from trains on this line. Transporting goods by road was deemed both cheaper and more expedient and this ensured the demise of rail in the area.

Cardiganshire's population increased during the latter part of the century. By 2001 some fifty years of growth meant that there were 74,941 residents, more than ever before; the previous crest of 73,441 in 1871 had been surpassed. This was largely the result of counter-urbanization, but increased student numbers also accounted for the growth. Population decline characterized the first half of the century, and in 1951, the year the Lampeter to Aberaeron railway was discontinued, only 53,278 resided in the area; this was the lowest number since 1811. Census figures provide an indication of the county's population, but the time of year during which they were gathered and changes in the type of data collected mean that census information cannot be compared without some qualifications. In 1921 figures were gathered in June, a time when holidaymakers inflated the total. From the 1981 census, people were recorded on the basis of where they lived instead of where they were on census night. Therefore, temporary visitors would not be classified as inhabitants of the county.

Together with an increasing population, the standard of living and basic amenities in the county improved during the second half of the century. Throughout the interwar years, however, the area had been renowned for its bad housing conditions. The local authority built less new housing, as a proportion of all new dwellings, than any other county in Wales during the period between 1919 and 1940. Some accused the county council of placing greater emphasis on education than health. However, there was some slum clearance such as that carried out in the Mwldan area of Cardigan in 1937. Tuberculosis – the county had the fourth highest rate in England and Wales in 1939 – killed many in the district, including the dramatist Idwal Jones. In 1951, 56 per cent of dwellings in the county were without a toilet; the English and Welsh average was 21 per cent. Half were without piped water and 68 per cent did not have a bath. The coming of electricity, which arrived at Llanddewibrefi in the early 1950s, meant that there were no more jokes about Cardi women who, when visiting their husbands in the mining valleys, tried to blow out the electric light bulb. Yet even at the start of the twenty-first century a greater proportion of Cardiganshire houses were without modern conveniences than the England and Wales average. Dwellings without central heating constituted 14.5 per cent of the total compared to 8.5 in England and Wales. The county still had an aging population. In 2001 the average age in Ceredigion was 40.5 compared to 38.7 in England and Wales; if students were not included this would be somewhat higher. Furthermore, pensioners living alone accounted for 16.4 per cent of households compared to 14.4 per cent in England and Wales.

This aging population contributed to a public relations faux pas by the Welsh miners in 1974, soon after they had compelled the Conservative government to call an election. A Cardiganshire councillor, Gareth Ellis, suggested that the miners should deliver a free ton of coal to 4,000 of the county's pensioners every year. Welsh union leaders – the president of the south Wales area of the National Union of Mineworkers, Emlyn Williams, and the secretary Dai Smith – rejected the proposal. The local press and Ellis responded by highlighting Cardiganshire's unenviable position of having the lowest wage-earning capacity in Wales, and described how, when the coal was piled high in the mining valleys, former miners who retired to the county went cold. The history of those who retired to the county after working in the coal mines has yet to be written. In 1955 the annual report of the Health Executive Council in Cardiganshire noted that cost per prescription in Cardiganshire was 56.15 d. whereas the average in Wales was 51.54 d. Doctors explained that many retired to the county from industrial areas with silicosis and as a result needed supplementary medication.

More has been written about successful migrants from the county than those whose working lives resulted in silicosis. Various Cardis made, or extended, their fortunes in London. David James of Pantyfedwen went to the capital to run a family milk business in the 1920s. He branched out into the entertainment industry, eventually owning thirteen cinemas, and his name lives on in the eisteddfodau, established in the 1960s at Lampeter and Pontrhydfendigaid. Another Cardiganshire man who diversified from the milk trade was Evan Evans from Tregaron who established a petrol station in Bloomsbury. Less well known are entrepreneurs from the county who contributed to the economic life of the south Wales valleys. One, Evan Thomas Jones, moved to Troedyrhiw at the age of fourteen and later started his own bus business. He was credited with having pioneered motor transport in the area.

Warfare had a considerable impact on the lives of Cardiganshire's inhabitants during the twentieth century. Indeed, the possibility of a nuclear clash during the Cold War, in which the Aber-porth RAF base would have been a likely target, cast a shadow that lasted until the end of the century. The way in which the First World War touched all places, no matter how small, is revealed in the columns of the local press where villages – like Felin-fach, Swyddffynnon and Dihewyd – which rarely entered the papers in peacetime were reported as welcoming those who returned or mourning those who did not. There was also relief, such as when two missing men who hailed from

Llandysul were confirmed as being prisoners of war in June 1918. Many villages and towns held eisteddfods and concerts in aid of local funds for soldiers and sailors, and the county contributed many merchant seamen. Large sums were raised through investments in war bonds; the Cardiganshire War Savings Committee's average contribution of £51 was a record in the United Kingdom. Belgian refugees, like the De Kemel family at Aberaeron who were renowned jacks-of-all-trades, contributed to the county's wartime economy. Another Belgian, the painter Valerius de Saedeleer, bestowed some artwork. Unlike the Poles who settled in the county after the Second World War, the Belgians returned to continental Europe either during the latter part of the conflict, like the De Kemels, or after the war; de Saedeleer left in 1921. Others who came to the county during the war included some one hundred and fifty women who were members of the Land Army. Most of these women hailed from Glamorganshire, Denbighshire and Durham. After training in their home counties, they came to work on the county's farms and earned between 7 $s.$ and 15 $s.$ per week. Some stayed in Cardiganshire after the war.

There were conflicts and tensions in Cardiganshire during the war. Some, such as a Talgarreg man who drowned himself in the river Clettwr, committed suicide rather than be conscripted into the army after 1915. One father, who lived near Aber-porth, took his own life in order to prevent his son being conscripted, as the only male in the family the son would be expected to care for his mother. The pacifist Independent minister T. E. Nicholas struggled against the tide of support for the war among the Nonconformist population which had been partly generated by David Lloyd George. One minister at Tregaron argued that if the 'apostle of peace' Henry Richard had been alive he would have supported the war. Councillors and Calvinistic Methodists organized demonstrations which contributed to the ejection of a German lecturer, Dr Hermann Ethé, from Aberystwyth. According to Herbert M. Vaughan, who sat on the county's Appeal Tribunal which considered objections to conscription orders that had been delivered by local tribunals, there were only about six conscientious objectors in the county, although many objected on economic grounds.[20] Farmers also came under fire during the war for not growing enough wheat, preferring instead to grow hay which they then sold at a substantial profit.

Similar accusations were levelled at the farming community in the Second World War. The news that sugar, bacon and butter were to be rationed – bacon to 4 oz a week – from 8 January 1940 contributed to a thriving black market. The remnants of the boat-building trade also benefited as merchant ships needed to be equipped with lifeboats. In addition to legal action against black marketeers, there were cases of what was called 'seditious talk' in the county. One case was brought against an elderly county councillor who allegedly said that if the Germans won the war things would be no worse than they were before. Others were apprehensive about the impact evacuees would have on Cardiganshire society. In 1939 the prospect of Catholic children from Liverpool arriving in the county caused some Nonconformists to complain about the possible detrimental affects of this forced cultural exchange. And Welsh nationalists were concerned at the influence English children would have on native Welsh-speaking children. Their arrival stimulated Ifan ab Owen Edwards to open a private Welsh-medium primary school at Aberystwyth in 1939 which initially catered for seven children. The war encouraged others to voluntarily move to the area. Two women from Wolverhampton were jailed for three months after trespassing in an American base near Aberaeron; when discovered they were in the company of two 'coloured Americans'. In court, Inspector Davies said that these kinds of women 'spread disease which deprived the Army of the services of good soldiers'.[21]

Focusing on the minutiae of wartime life can sometimes highlight the tensions and occlude some of the nobler deeds carried out on the home front. Examples of Cardiganshire's contribution to the war effort include the numerous improvised firing ranges set up by the Home Guard in fields lent by local farmers, the 200 volunteers who gave blood at short notice in the Grand Hotel at Borth in 1944 and the welcome given to the British forces who had fled the continent – there were some 3,000 members of the British Expeditionary Force at Aberystwyth in June 1940. Yet past accomplishments could outshine current efforts. It was noted in 1940 that the response to the National War Savings campaign was not as great as that demonstrated during the previous conflict. Tellingly, some commentators thought that this was due to the county's religious institutions not being as active during this war. Perhaps this reflected a waning population, the declining influence of religious institutions, or the lack of belligerent Non-conformist fervour compared to the previous war. Even then, there were successes in the field of battle that reflected well on the county. The *Welsh Gazette* reproduced a regimental order praising the honourable conduct of the 146th Field Regiment Royal Artillery, a territorial force raised in the county. They were told that their actions at Medinine in 1943 were 'largely responsible for the complete defeat of the Germans' and thus contributed to the final defeat of the Axis in north Africa.[22]

There was a political shift after this war and Labour swept to victory. Cardiganshire, however, did not follow the pattern and remained a Liberal stronghold. Yet Liberals sometimes came to blows with each other in the county. At the beginning of the century Vaughan Davies became a convincing Welsh Liberal supporting old age pensions and the disestablishment of the Established Church in Wales, and even went further than his party in his support of the female franchise. Both the *Cambrian News* and the Aberystwyth Town Council championed votes for women. After Vaughan Davies's elevation to the Lords in 1921 there was a Liberal civil war in the county. This was ignited when Lloyd George's private secretary Ernest Evans was put forward as a Coalition Liberal. In response Llywelyn Williams, an Asquith supporter who had opposed conscription, stood against him. Evans won the battle, partly through the aid of Margaret Lloyd George who wooed some of the 14,000 women who could vote for the first time in the county election. The following year Evans just pipped another Liberal rival, R. H. Morris, by 515 votes. In the third election in as many years, Morris, as Independent Liberal, beat Evans and a Conservative candidate with a majority of 5,078. Morris held the seat until it passed to another Nonconformist lawyer, D. Owen Evans, in 1932. Evans held off Labour and Conservative opposition until 1945 when the barrister E. Roderic Bowen continued the Liberal hegemony by beating a Labour candidate, the academic Iwan Morgan, by over 8,000 votes.

The Labour movement in Cardiganshire emerged from trade union activity that had taken root at the end of the nineteenth century. The Amalgamated Society of Rail Servants established a branch at Aberystwyth in 1898 and the North Cardiganshire Trade Union and Labour Council was founded in 1912. Industrial disputes had an impact on the county's tourist trade in 1911 when a strike by rail workers left holidaymakers stranded. Other strikes in Aberystwyth during the era of late Edwardian industrial distress included those by painters and carters in 1914. And in 1919 a rail strike meant that German prisoners were not dispatched on time from Lampeter station. Towards the end of the First World War there was unprecedented trade union activity throughout the county. The pacifist minister, T. E. Nicholas of Llangybi, talked at Llangeitho about rural workers' unions. Indeed, the fact that the term farm servant was replaced by farm worker around this time indicates how opinions and self images were changing. Wage rates set by the Agricultural Wages Board in 1918 meant that farmers were often eager to employ German prisoners. Yet Labour did not contest the seat until 1931, and did not win it until the 1960s, although L. Rees Hughes, a Carmarthenshire councillor and the first female candidate in a Cardiganshire election, won a respectable 28.2 per cent when she came second in 1959. Various reasons have been put forward to explain this late arrival including the stoking of the county's Liberal tradition as a result of their internal disputes. Another limit on Labour's development could have been the predominance of the socially conservative Calvinistic Methodists.

Bowen's hold on the county seat had started to weaken by 1964. He was seen as being more interested in his legal work and had a cool relationship with his leader Jo Grimmond who was too far to the left for his liking. He was beaten by the Labour candidate Elystan Morgan, who was also a lawyer and had been a member of Plaid Cymru, in the 1966 election by 523 votes. Bowen's assumption that Cardiganshire was innately Liberal was rudely upset. Many felt that a voice to represent the county in Westminster would be more likely to be heard if it was that of a Labour candidate. Unlike 1945, the county had followed a nationwide swing towards Labour; Harold Wilson's party had won 61 per cent of the Welsh vote. Nonetheless, Morgan lost the two 1974 elections to Geraint Howells by over 2,400 votes on both occasions. Like earlier Liberal representatives, Howells had a long tenure, though unlike many earlier legal Liberals, Howells was a farmer and managed a meat company. Morgan also had a farming background, his family having worked on the soil for 400 years. This contributed to his victory in 1970. Both Howells and Morgan won many votes through what P. J. Madgwick called the 'personal vote' in the county. Madgwick noted that in Cardiganshire 'value is placed on acquaintance and service'.[23] When Plaid Cymru won the seat for the first time in 1992, its candidate, Cynog Dafis, had also won votes on the basis of his personal qualities, as well as alliance with the Greens. By dethroning Howells, Dafis achieved the greatest swing in any British constituency during that election. In 1982 and 1987, when the then district of Ceredigion was joined with another part of Dyfed, north Pembrokeshire, to form a new constituency, Dafis had come fourth. Plaid held on to the seat in 1997, when Ceredigion was a separate county, and Dafis's successor, Simon Thomas, one of the founders of Radio Ceredigion, ensured that Plaid Cymru held the county seat at the turn of the twenty-first century.

With the advent of devolution, the county gained another representative, one who sat at the Welsh Assembly at Cardiff instead of Westminster. Dyfed, with the rest of Wales, rejected the troubled Labour government's devolution plans in 1979. Eighteen years later Tony Blair's fresh Labour administration supported devolution, as did Ceredigion and the majority of Welsh voters. In fact, the county cast the second highest percentage of votes in favour of the Welsh Assembly (65.3 per cent), and was one of only three areas in which over 60 per cent backed the move. This shift in the political landscape also led the county acquiring its first female representative, Plaid

Cymru's Elin Jones, a former mayor of Aberystwyth, who won the Assembly seat in 1999.

The lives and concerns of ordinary people are more prominent in accounts of the twentieth century than in earlier periods. Government statistics, newspapers, democracy, the prominence of mass culture and many other factors contributed to this change in focus. In keeping with this emphasis on the people, the county council's *Ceredigion Community Strategy* forecasts that by 2020 the county will be 'a self confident, healthy, caring, bilingual community' with a 'strong local economy' which draws on the 'skills of its people', 'providing opportunities for all to reach their full potential'.[24] The extent to which these goals are attained will no doubt form part of a future history of the county.

Notes

Chapter I

[1] R. Thomas, 'A prehistoric flint factory discovered at Aberystwyth', *Archaeologia Cambrensis*, 67 (1912), 211–16.

[2] J. W. Willis-Bund, 'Reports on Llanio and a church restoration', *Archaeologia Cambrensis*, 43 (1888), 297–317.

[3] Jeffrey L. Davies, 'A bronze vehicle mount from Trawsgoed, Dyfed', *Britannia*, 18 (1987), 277–8.

[4] J. W. James (trans.), *Rhygyfarch's Life of St David* (Cardiff, 1967), pp. 38, 33.

[5] W. J. Rees (trans.) *Lives of the Cambro British Saints* (Llandovery, 1853), p. 506.

[6] Patrick K. Ford (trans.), *The Mabinogi* (Berkeley, 1977), p. 56.

[7] Thomas Jones (trans.), *Brut y Tywysogyon or The Chronicle of the Princes: Red Book of Hergest version* (Cardiff, 1955), pp. 5, 9.

[8] A. W. Wade-Evans, *Welsh Medieval Law* (Oxford, 1909), p. 194.

[9] Owen Jones, Edward Williams and Owen Pughe, *The Myvyrian Archaiology of Wales* (Denbigh, 1853), p. 688; D. P. Kirby, 'The place of Ceredigion in the early history of Wales c.400–1170', *Ceredigion*, 6 (1968–71), 268.

[10] *Red Book of Hergest*, p. 13.

Chapter II

[1] J. E. Lloyd, *The Welsh Chronicles* (London, 1929), pp. 17–19.

[2] Thomas Jones (trans.), *Brut y Tynysogion or The Chronicle of the Princes: Red book of Hergest version* (Cardiff, 1955), p. 32.

[3] Samuel Rush Meyrick, *The History and Antiquities of the County of Cardigan* (London, 1808), p. 14.

[4] J. E. Lloyd, *The Story of Ceredigion (400–1277)* (Cardiff, 1937), p. 26.

[5] *Red Book of Hergest*, p. 57.

[6] Ibid., p. 61.

[7] See Robert S. Babcock, 'Imbeciles and Normans: The *Ynfydion* of Gruffudd ap Rhys reconsidered', *Haskins Society Journal*, 4 (1992), 1–9.

[8] *Red Book of Hergest*, p. 115.

[9] Thomas Jones (trans.), *Brut y Tywysogyon or The Chronicle of the Princes: Peniarth MS. 20 version* (Cardiff, 1952), p. 27.

[10] D. C. Rees, *Tregaron: Historical and Antiquarian* (Llandysul, 1936), p. 70.

[11] *Red Book of Hergest*, p. 93.

[12] Roger Turvey, *The Lord Rhys: Prince of Deheubarth* (Llandysul, 1997), p. 81.

[13] C. A. Ralegh Radford, *Strata Florida Abbey* (Edinburgh, 1980), p. 1; Gwynfor Evans, *Land of My Fathers* (Tal-y-bont, 1992), p. 217.

[14] F. G. Cowley, *The Monastic Order in South Wales, 1066–1349* (Cardiff, 1977), pp. 97–8.

[15] M. R. James (trans.), Walter Map, *De Nugis Curialium: Courtiers' Trifles* (Oxford, 1983), p. 101.

[16] Lewis Thorpe (trans.), Gerald of Wales, *The Journey through Wales and the Description of Wales* (Harmondsworth, 1978), p. 172.

[17] T. Jones Pierce, 'Medieval Cardiganshire: a study in social origins', in J. Beverley Smith (ed.), *Medieval Welsh Society: Selected Essays* (Cardiff, 1972), p. 316; Christopher Tyerman, 'Who went on crusades to the Holy Land?', in B. Z. Kedar (ed.), *Horns of Hattin* (Jerusalem, 1992), p. 15; W. J. Lewis, *A History of Lampeter* (Aberystwyth, 1997), p. 3; *Journey through Wales*, p. 178.

[18] *Journey through Wales*, p. 231.

[19] *Peniarth*, p. 75.

[20] D. H. Williams, *The Welsh Cistercians* (Leominster, 2001), p. 27.

[21] *Red Book of Hergest*, p. 267.

Chapter III

[1] C. J. Spurgeon, 'The castle and borough to 1649', in Ieuan Gwynedd Jones (ed.), *Aberystwyth, 1277–1977* (Llandysul, 1977), p. 37.

[2] R. A. Griffiths, 'Aberystwyth', in idem. (ed.), *Boroughs of Medieval Wales* (Cardiff, 1978), p. 19.

[3] R. H. Hilton, *English and French Towns in Feudal Society* (Cambridge, 1992) pp. 6–7.

[4] Maurice Beresford, *New Towns of the Middle Ages* (Stroud, 1988), p. 284.

[5] E. A. Lewis, 'A contribution to the commercial history of Medieval Wales', *Y Cymmrodor*, 24 (1913), 108–9.

[6] William Rees (ed.), *Calendar of Ancient Petitions Relating to Wales: Thirteenth to Sixteenth Century* (Cardiff, 1975), p. 156.

[7] I. Soulsby, *The Towns of Medieval Wales* (Chichester, 1983), pp. 254–5.

[8] J. W. Willis-Bund (ed.), *Black Book of St David's* (London, 1902), pp. 219–29.

[9] R. R. Davies, *The Age of Conquest: Wales 1063–1415* (Oxford, 1987), p. 171.

[10] R. Ian Jack, 'Wales and the Marches', in H. E. Hallam (ed.), *The Agrarian History of England and Wales, vol. 2, 1042–1350* (Cambridge, 1989), p. 479.

[11] *Calendar of Ancient Petitions*, pp. 88–9.

[12] J. E. Morris, *The Welsh Wars of Edward I* (Oxford, 1901), p. 154.

[13] R. A. Griffiths, 'Gentlemen and rebels in later Medieval Cardiganshire', *Ceredigion*, 5 (1964–7), 146.

[14] Glanmor Williams, 'The collegiate church of Llanddewibrefi', *Ceredigion*, 4 (1960–3), 340.

[15] See Rachel Bromwich (trans.), Dafydd ap Gwilym, *A Selection of Poems* (Harmondsworth, 1985).

[16] L. B. Smith, ' "Cannwyll Disbwyll a Dosbarth": gwyr cyfraith Ceredigion yn yr Oesoedd Canol Diweddar', *Ceredigion*, 10 (1984–7), 229–53.

[17] William Rees, 'The Black Death in Wales', *Transactions of the Royal Historical Society*, 3 (1920), 135.

Chapter IV

[1]   J. E. Lloyd, *Owen Glendower/Owen Glyndŵr* (Felinfach, 1992), pp. 149–54; Ian Fleming, *Glyndŵr's First Victory: The Battle of Hyddgen 1401* (Tal-y-Bont, 2001).
[2]   C. Given-Wilson (trans.), *The Chronicle of Adam of Usk* (Oxford, 1997), p. 145.
[3]   Lloyd, *Owen Glendower*, p. 136.
[4]   Rhidian Griffiths, 'Prince Henry's war: armies, garrisons and supply during the Glyndŵr rising', *Bulletin of the Board of Celtic Studies*, 34 (1987), 168.
[5]   Glanmor Williams, *Owain Glyndŵr* (Cardiff, 1993), p. 44.
[6]   Lloyd, *Owen Glendower*, p. 153.
[7]   *Adam of Usk*, p. 145.
[8]   W. Rees, *South Wales and the March 1284–1415* (Oxford, 1924), p. 274.
[9]   Richard Rex, *The Lollards* (Basingstoke, 2002), p. 70.
[10] E. D. Jones, 'Lewis Glyn Cothi', in A. O. H. Jarman and Gwilym Rees Hughes (eds), *A Guide to Welsh Literature*, 2 (Swansea, 1979), p. 254.
[11] Eurys Rowlands, 'The continuing tradition', ibid., p. 308.
[12] 'Church restoration', *Archaeologia Cambrensis*, 5 (1888), 317–9.
[13] Richard Suggett, 'Tŷ John Morgan and its roof: the medieval king-post in Cardiganshire', *Ceredigion*, 11 (1988–92), 425–32.
[14] *The Episcopal Registers of the Diocese of St David's 1397–1518* (London, 1917), pp. 542–7.
[15] *Calendar of the Patent Rolls Henry VI*, 5 (London, 1901), pp. 151–2.
[16] *Poetical Works of Dafydd Nanmor* (Cardiff, 1923), pp. 14–15.
[17] Ffransis G. Payne, *Yr Aradr Gymreig* (Cardiff, 1975), p. 59.
[18] R. A. Griffiths, 'After Glyndŵr: an age of reconciliation?', *Proceedings of the British Academy*, 117 (2001), 159.
[19] H. T. Evans, *Wales and the Wars of the Roses* (Stroud, 1995), p. 131.
[20] Miri Rubin, *The Hollow Crown* (London, 2005), p. 318.

Chapter V

[1]   See Immanuel Wallerstein, *The Modern World-system* (London, 1989).
[2]   W. J. Lewis, 'Some aspects of lead mining in Cardiganshire in the sixteenth and seventeenth centuries', *Ceredigion*, 1 (1950–1), 179.
[3]   Dillwyn Miles (ed.), *The Description of Pembrokeshire by George Owen of Henllys* (Llandysul, 1994), p. 95.
[4]   Lucy Toulmin Smith (ed.), *The Itinerary in Wales of John Leland in or about the years 1536–1539* (London, 1906), pp. 118, 124.
[5]   Leonard Owen, 'The population of Wales in the sixteenth and seventeenth centuries', *Transactions of the Honourable Society of Cymmrodorion* (1959), 99–113.
[6]   R. Ian Jack, 'The cloth industry in medieval Wales', *Welsh History Review*, 10 (1980–1), 443–60.
[7]   Caroline A. J. Skeel, 'The Welsh woollen industry in the sixteenth and seventeenth centuries', *Archaeologia Cambrensis*, 77 (1922), 225.
[8]   E. A. Lewis, *Welsh Port Books 1560–1603* (London, 1927) pp. 310–11; Thomas Phaer, 'Anglia Wallia', *Archaeologia Cambrensis*, 2 (1911), 429.
[9]   W. Ogwen Williams, 'Some notes on Tudor Cardiganshire', *Ceredigion*, 6 (1968–71), 142.

[10] W. Ambrose Bebb, *Cyfnod y Tuduriaid* (Wrecsam, 1939), p. 34.

[11] W. Llewelyn Williams, 'The union of England and Wales', *Transactions of the Honourable Society of Cymmrodorion* (1907–8), 95.

[12] George Owen, 'The dialogue of the government of Wales', *Pembrokeshire* (London, 1906), pp. 92–3; W. Llewelyn Williams, *The Making of Modern Wales* (London, 1919), p. 80; *Welsh Gazette*, 18 March 1937; Williams, 'Some notes', 149.

[13] Philip S. Edwards, 'The parliamentary representation of the Welsh boroughs in the mid-sixteenth century', *Bulletin of the Board of Celtic Studies*, 27 (1976–8), 425–39.

[14] J. Gwynfor Jones, *The Welsh Gentry, 1536–1640* (Cardiff, 1998), pp. 95–132.

[15] Gilbert Burnet, *The History of the Reformation of the Church of England*, 1 (London, 1841), pp. 391–2.

[16] Glanmor Williams, *Wales and the Reformation* (Cardiff, 1997), p. 279.

[17] Joseph Joseph, 'Gwyn of Trecastle', *Archaeologia Cambrensis*, 13 (1867), 66.

[18] Miles (ed.), *Description of Pembrokeshire*, pp. 208–19.

[19] Peter Burke, *Popular Culture in Early Modern Europe* (London, 1978), p. 270.

[20] Ralph Flenley (ed.), *Register of the Queen's Majesty's Council (1535) 1569–1591* (London, 1916), p. 105.

Chapter VI

[1] Geraint H. Jenkins, *The Foundations of Modern Wales, 1642–1780* (Oxford, 1993), p. 43; Roy Lewis and Sandra Wheatley, 'Exploring the residential structure of Early Modern Aberystwyth', *Ceredigion*, 12 (1993–6), 21–32.

[2] Thomas Richards, *A History of the Puritan Movement in Wales* (London, 1920), p. 136.

[3] Nigel Smith (ed.), George Fox, *The Journal* (Harmondsworth, 1998), p. 228; John Lewis, *Eyaggeloigrapha* (London, 1659), p. 11.

[4] E. G. Bowen, 'The Teifi valley as a religious frontier', *Ceredigion*, 7 (1972–5), 5.

[5] Philip Jenkins, 'Seventeenth-century Wales: definition and identity', in Brendan Bradshaw and Peter Roberts (eds), *British Consciousness and Identity: The Making of Britain, 1533–1707* (Cambridge, 1998), p. 233.

[6] John Lewis, *Contemplations upon these times, or the Parliament explained to Wales* (London, 1646), pp. 10, 22.

[7] J. Roland Phillips, *Memoirs of the Civil War in Wales and the Marches 1642–9*, 1 (London, 1874), p. 234.

[8] Ibid., p. 355.

[9] 'Wales under the Commonwealth', *Old Wales*, 1 (1905–6), 226.

[10] W. J. Lewis, *'The Gateway to Wales': A History of Cardigan* (Carmarthen, 1990), p. 115.

[11] R. H. Morris (ed.), Edward Lhuyd, *Parochialia*, 3 (London, 1909–1911), p. 89.

[12] William Waller, *Essay on the Value of the Mines* (London, 1698), pp. 4–5, 12.

[13] Richard Blome, *Britannia* (London, 1673) pp. 267, 269.

[14] W. J. Lewis, 'Some of the freeholders of Cardiganshire in 1632', *Ceredigion*, 3 (1956–9), 92.

[15] Melville Richards, 'Is Coed Uwch Hirwern in 1651', *Ceredigion*, 4 (1960–3), 387; Gerald Morgan, 'Women in early modern Cardiganshire', *Ceredigion*, 13 (1997–2000), 18.

[16] Lewis, *Contemplations*, p. 27; William E. A. Axon, 'Welsh folk-lore of the seventeenth century', *Y Cymmrodor*, 31 (1908), 116; Lhuyd, *Parochialia*, p. 88; Axon, 'Welsh folk-lore', 121–2; Lhuyd, *Parochialia*, pp. 81, 90.

[17] Moelwyn I. Williams, 'A Cardiganshire will: a mirror of life in the parish of Henfynyw circa 1656', *Ceredigion*, 4 (1960–3), 202–4; Richards, 'Is Coed Uwch Hirwern', 387.

[18] Thomas Dineley, *The Account of the Official Progress of His Grace, Henry, the First Duke of Beaufort through Wales in 1684* (London, 1888), p. 249; Lhuyd, *Parochialia*, p. 4.

[19] Lhuyd, *Parochialia*, p. 86; E. A. L., 'The goods and chattels of a Cardiganshire esquire in 1663', *Cardiganshire Antiquarian Society Transactions*, 11 (1936), 28–9.

[20] John Speed, *Wales: The Second Part of John Speed's Atlas* (London, 1970), p. 113; Blome, p. 267; Dineley, p. 247.

Chapter VII

[1] H. M. Vaughan, 'Household accounts of a Welsh peeress in the eighteenth century', *Historical Society of West Wales Transactions*, 5 (1915), 294; J. M. Howells, 'The Crosswood estate, 1547–1947', *Ceredigion*, 3 (1956–9), 70; W. Edmunds, 'Peterwell', *Archaeologia Cambrensis*, 7 (1861), 157–8.

[2] Francis Jones, 'The Society of Sea Serjeants', *Transactions of the Honourable Society of Cymmrodorion* (1967), 61.

[3] *Bye-gones*, 4 (1895–6), 468.

[4] R. E. Bevan, 'Extracts from two old diaries concerning Llanarth', *Cardiganshire Antiquarian Society Transactions*, 4 (1926), 93.

[5] Tom Beynon (ed.), 'Howell Harris' visits to Cardiganshire', *Cylchgrawn Cymdeithas Hanes y Methodistiaid Calfinaidd*, 24 (1944), 125.

[6] George Eyre Evans (ed.), *Lloyd Letters (1754–1796)* (Aberystwyth, 1908), p. 29.

[7] Hugh Owen (ed.), *Additional Letters of the Morrises of Anglesey (1735–1786)*, 2 (London, 1949), pp. 688–9; Erasmus Saunders, *A View of the State of Religion in the Diocese of St David's* (London, 1721), pp. 17, 31–2.

[8] Bevan, 'Extracts', p. 74; Robert Redfield, *Peasant Society and Culture* (Chicago, 1956).

[9] Gerald Morgan, *Circulating Schools in Cardiganshire 1738–1777* (Aberystwyth, 1991), pp. 2, 6, 7.

[10] A. H. Williams (ed.), *John Wesley in Wales 1739–1790* (Cardiff, 1971), p. 94; Daniel Defoe, *Tour Through the Whole of the Island of Great Britain*, 2 (London, 1962), p. 59.

[11] George Eyre Evans (ed.), *Cardiganshire* (Aberystwyth, 1903), p. 4; *A Descriptive Account of the Devil's Bridge* (Hereford, 1796), p. 30.

[12] B. G. Charles, 'The Highmead Dairy', *Ceredigion*, 5 (1964–7), 76.

[13] M. J. Baylis, 'A portrait of Thomas Makeig of Penlan-fawr, 1721–66', *Ceredigion*, 5 (1964–7), 56–7.

[14] Bevan, 'Extracts', 77.

Chapter VIII

[1] *Carmarthen Journal*, 13 June 1817.

[2] *Cambrian*, 26 July 1806.

[3] Morgan Ebenezer Morgan, *Cipdrem ar Hanes Tregaron a'r Cylch* (Llanbedr Pont Stephan, 1911), p. 37.

⁴ David Williams, *The Rebecca Riots* (Cardiff, 1971), p. 116.

⁵ Thomas Davies (gol.), *Bywyd ac Ysgrifeniadau y Diweddar Barch. D. Rees, Llanelli* (Llanelli, 1871), p. 406.

⁶ Francis Jones, 'Cardiganshire election songs', *Ceredigion*, 5 (1964–7), 42–6.

⁷ J. E. Lloyd, *The Story of Ceredigion (400–1277)* (Cardiff, 1937), p. 1.

⁸ I. G. Jones, 'Cardiganshire politics in the mid-19th century', *Ceredigion*, 5 (1964–7), 14.

⁹ *Carmarthen Journal*, 12 January 1866.

¹⁰ *Cambrian News*, 29 November 1872.

¹¹ Ibid., 19 April 1895.

¹² *Carmarthen Journal*, 12 April 1850.

¹³ *Cambrian News*, 12 October 1877.

¹⁴ Ibid., 7 March 1890.

¹⁵ Ibid., 9 January 1885; D. C. Davies, 'The fisheries of Wales', in William R. Owen (ed.), *Liverpool National Eisteddfod 1884 Transactions* (Liverpool, 1885), p. 301.

¹⁶ *Carmarthen Journal*, 18 September 1818.

¹⁷ *Census of England and Wales 1891: Preliminary Report and Tables* (London, 1891), p. 27.

¹⁸ *Carmarthen Journal*, 7 May 1841.

¹⁹ *Yr Ymofynnydd*, 2 (1869), 25.

²⁰ *Y Drysorfa*, 13 (1859), 328.

²¹ *Yr Ymofynnydd*, 13 (1860), 9–10.

²² *Report of the Commissioners of Inquiry into the State of Education in Wales*, 2 (London, 1847), p. 150.

²³ *Cambrian News*, 5 January 1872.

²⁴ D. T. W. Price, *A History of Saint David's University College Lampeter*, 1 (Cardiff, 1977), p. 152.

²⁵ G. Jones, *Enwogion Sir Aberteifi* (Dolgellau, 1868), pp. 52–3.

Chapter IX

¹ W. Jones-Edwards, *Ar Lethrau Ffair Rhos* (Aberystwyth, 1963), p. 20.

² *Cardiff Times*, 19 November 1904; *Tarian y Gweithiwr*, 9 February 1905; *Cambrian News*, 20 April 1906.

³ Daniel Thomas, *Dail yr Hydref* (Dinbych, 1916), p. 27; Kate Davies, *Hafau fy Mhlentyndod ym Mhentref Pren-gwyn* (Llandysul, 1970), pp. 46–7.

⁴ *Cardigan and Tivyside Advertiser*, 14 October 1949.

⁵ Donald Davies, *Those Were the Days*, 2 (Cardigan, 1992), p. 39; D. Ben Rees, *Hanes Plwyf Llanddewi Brefi* (Llanddewi Brefi, 1984), p. 220.

⁶ T. Llew Jones, *Fy Mhobl i* (Llandysul, 2002), pp. 41–5.

⁷ John Williams and Eben Davies, *Fferm a Ffair a Phentre* (Aberystwyth, 1958), p. 18; *Cambrian News*, 7 January 1974.

⁸ David Jenkins, Emrys Jones, T. Jones Hughes and Trefor M. Owen, *Welsh Rural Communities* (Cardiff, 1962), pp. 1–117.

⁹ *Cambrian News*, 2 March 1906.

¹⁰ *Cardigan and Tivyside Advertiser*, 5 October 1979; *Cambrian News*, 4 March 1977.

¹¹ *Cardigan and Tivyside Advertiser*, 5 May 1972; Gwilym Jenkins, *Ar Bwys y Ffald* (Tal-y-bont, 2001), p. 23.

¹² *Welsh Gazette*, 30 May 1905.

[13] *Cardigan and Tivyside Advertiser*, 6 June 1958.

[14] *Carmarthen Journal*, 24 December 1954.

[15] R. F. Walker, 'Tourism in Cardiganshire', in Geraint H. Jenkins and Ieuan Gwynedd Jones (eds), *Cardiganshire County History Vol. 3: Cardiganshire in Modern Times* (Cardiff, 1998), p. 313; *Welsh Gazette*, 8 August 1918; ibid., 10 August 1944; *Gossiping Guide to Wales* (Oswestry, 1932), p. 51; Maxwell Fraser, *Wales*, 2 (London, 1952), p. 329.

[16] Lyn Evans, *Portrait of a Pioneer: A Biography of Howell Thomas Evans* (Llandybïe, 1982), p. 147; Isfoel, 'Cwmtydu', *Y Cardi: Cylchgrawn Cymdeithas Ceredigion*, 1 (1966), 17; *Cardigan and Tivyside Advertiser*, 27 August 1965.

[17] *Welsh Gazette*, 20 January; ibid., 5 May 1927.

[18] *Cambrian News*, 9 May 1958; *Cardiganshire: The County Handbook* (1961), p. 7; *Cardigan and Tivyside Advertiser*, 2 February 1979.

[19] Jac L. Williams, 'Sut mae hi?', *Cymdeithas Ceredigion Llundain*, 15 (1959–60), 13.

[20] Herbert M. Vaughan, 'Cardigan appeal tribunal', *Wales*, 7 (1947), 171–80.

[21] *Welsh Gazette*, 28 December 1944.

[22] Ibid., 1 June 1944.

[23] P. J. Madgwick, Non Griffiths and Valerie Walker, *The Politics of Rural Wales: A Study of Cardiganshire* (London, 1973), p. 214.

[24] *Ceredigion 2020: Ceredigion Community Strategy*, www.ceredigion2020.org.uk, p. 8.

Select Bibliography

ab Alun, Afan, *Cestyll Ceredigion* (Capel Garmon, 1991).

Baker-Jones, Leslie, *Princelings, Privilege and Power: The Tivyside Gentry in their Community* (Llandysul, 1999).

Ballinger, John, *Gleanings from a Printer's File* (Aberystwyth, 1928).

Barnes, David Russell, *People of Seion: Patterns of Nonconformity in Cardiganshire and Carmarthenshire in the Century Preceding the Religious Census of 1851* (Cardiff, 1995).

Bevan, Teleri, *Years of my Time: Glimpses of a Cardiganshire Upbringing* (Llandysul, 1997).

Bick, David E., *Lewis Morris and the Cardiganshire Mines* (Aberystwyth, 1994).

Bowen, E. G., *A History of Llanbadarn Fawr* (Llanbadarn Fawr, 1979).

Carr, Tina, *Pigs & Ingots: The Lead/Silver Mines of Cardiganshire* (Tal-y-bont, 1993).

Clarke, Gillian, *Banc Siôn Cwilt: A Local Habitation and a Name* (Newtown, 1998).

Cumberland, George, *An Attempt to Describe Hafod* (Aberystwyth, 1996).

Davies, David J., *Hanes, Hynafiaethau ac Achyddiaeth Llanarth, Henfynyw, Llanllwchaiarn a Llandyssilio-gogo* (Caerfyrddin, 1930).

Davies, Donald, *Those Were the Days: A History of Cardigan, the Locality and its People*, 2 vols (Cardigan, 1991–2).

Davies, Evan, *Hanes Plwyf Llangynllo* (Llandysul, 1905).

Davies, Hettie Glyn, *Edrych yn ôl: Hen Atgofion am Geredigion* (Lerpwl, 1958).

Davies, J. L. and Kirby, D. P. (eds), *Cardiganshire County History vol. 1: From the Earliest Times to the Coming of the Normans* (Cardiff, 1994).

Davies, Kate, *Hafau fy Mhlentyndod ym Mhentref Pren-gwyn* (Llandysul, 1970).

Davies, Llinos M., *Crochan Ceredigion* (Aberystwyth, 1992).

Davies, T. J., *Nabod Bro a Brodorion* (Abertawe, 1975).

Davies, William Jenkin, *Hanes Plwyf Llandyssul* (Llandysul, 1896).

Davis, Paul R., *A Company of Forts: A Guide to the Medieval Castles of West Wales* (Llandysul, 2000).

Edwardes, David, *Plwyf Nantcwnlle, Hen a Diweddar* (Lampeter, 1913).

——*Reminiscence of the Rev. D. Edwardes* (Shrewsbury, 1914).

Ellis, T. I., *Crwydro Ceredigion* (Abertawe, 1977).

Evans, George Eyre, *Cardiganshire* (Aberystwyth, 1903).

——*Lampeter* (Aberystwyth, 1905).

Evans, Henry, *Adgofion gan "Henafgwr"* (Lampeter, 1904).

Evans, J. T., *The Church Plate of Cardiganshire* (Stow-on-the-Wold, 1914).

Evans, John, *Hanes Methodistiaeth rhan ddeheuol sir Aberteifi o ddechreuad y "Diwygiad Methodistaidd" yn 1735 hyd 1900* (Dolgellau, 1904).

Harris, John (ed.), *Fury Never Leaves Us: A Miscellany of Caradoc Evans* (Bridgend, 1985).

Horsfall-Turner, E. R., *Walks and Wanderings in County Cardigan* (Bingley, 1902).

Howells, Edryd, *Dim ond pen gair: Casgliad o Ddywediadau Ceredigion* (Aberystwyth, 1990).

Hughes, John, *A History of the Parliamentary Representation of the County of Cardigan* (Aberystwyth, 1849).

Inglis-Jones, Elisabeth, *Peacocks in Paradise* (Llandysul, 2001).

James, David B., *Ceredigion: A Natural History* (Bow Street, 2001).

Jenkins, David, *The Agricultural Community in South-West Wales at the Turn of the Twentieth Century* (Cardiff, 1971).

Jenkins, G. H. and Jones, Ieuan Gwynedd (eds), *Cardiganshire County History vol. 3: Cardiganshire in Modern Times* (Cardiff, 1998).

Jenkins, Gwilym, *Ar Bwys y Ffald: Atgofion Amaethwr o Ogledd Ceredigion* (Aberystwyth, 2001).

Jenkins, J. Geraint, *Ceredigion: Interpreting an Ancient County* (Llanrwst, 2005).

Johnes, Thomas, *A Cardiganshire Landlord's Advice to his Tenants* (Bristol, 1800).

Jones, Ben A., *Y Byd o Ben Trichrug* (Aberystwyth, 1959).

Jones, Evan, *Y Mynydd Bach a Bro Eiddwen* (Aberystwyth, 1990).

Jones, Francis, *Historic Cardiganshire Homes and their Families* (Newport, Pembs., 2000).

Jones, Glyn Lewis, *Llyfryddiaeth Ceredigion 1600–1964: A Bibliography of Cardiganshire*, 3 vols (Aberystwyth, 1967).

Jones, Griffith, *Enwogion Sir Aberteifi* (Dolgellau, 1868).

Jones, Ieuan Gwynedd (ed.), *Aberystwyth, 1277–1977* (Llandysul, 1977).

Jones, J. Islan, *Yr Hen Amser Gynt: Atgofion Ceredigion* (Aberystwyth, 1958).

Jones, Ruth, *Atgofion Ruth Mynachlog sef Ruth Jones* (Llandysul, 1939).

Jones, Sally, *Allen Raine* (Cardiff, 1979).

Jones-Edwards, W., *Ar Lethrau Ffair Rhos: Atgofion Mwnwr* (Aberystwyth, 1963).

Knowles, Anne Kelly, *Calvinists Incorporated: Welsh Immigrants on Ohio's Industrial Frontier* (Chicago, 1997).

Lewis, L. Haydn, *Penodau yn Hanes Aberaeron* (Llandysul, 1970).

Lewis, W. J., *Cardiganshire Historical Atlas* (Aberystwyth, 1969).

——*Born on a Perilous Rock: Aberystwyth Past and Present* (Aberystwyth, 1980).

—— *'The Gateway to Wales': A History of Cardigan* (Carmarthen, 1990).

——*A History of Lampeter* (Ceredigion County Council, 1997).

Lloyd, John Edward, *The Story of Ceredigion (400–1277)* (Cardiff, 1937).

Lloyd, Thomas and Turnor, Revd, *General View of the Agriculture of the County of Cardigan* (London, 1794).

Mathias, Idris, *Last of the Mwldan* (Llandysul, 1998).

Meyrick, Samuel Rush, *The History and Antiquities of the County of Cardigan* (London, 1808).

Moore-Colyer, R. J. (ed.), *A Land of Pure Delight: Selections from the Letters of Thomas Johnes of Hafod, Cardiganshire, 1748–1816* (Llandysul, 1992).

Morgan, Gerald, *A Welsh House and its Family: The Vaughans of Trawscoed* (Llandysul, 1997).

——*Ceredigion: A Wealth of History* (Llandysul, 2005).

——(ed.), *Nanteos: A Welsh House and its Families* (Llandysul, 2001).

Phillips, Bethan, *Peterwell: A History of a Mansion and its Infamous Squire* (Aberystwyth, 1997).

——*Pity the Swagman: The Australian Odyssey of a Victorian Diarist* (Aberystwyth, 2002).

Phillips, John Roland, *A List of the Sheriffs of Cardiganshire, from A.D. 1539 to A.D. 1868* (Carmarthen, 1868).

Rees, D. Ben, *Hanes Plwyf Llanddewi Brefi* (Llanddewi Brefi, 1984).

Rees, D. C., *Tregaron: Historical and Antiquarian* (Llandysul, 1936).

Richards, Thomas, *Atgofion Cardi* (Aberystwyth, 1960).

Saer, D. J., *The Story of Cardiganshire* (Cardiff, 1912).

Thomas, Peter, *Strangers from a Secret Land: The Voyages of the Brig Albion and the Founding of the First Welsh Settlements in Canada* (Llandysul, 1986).

White, Eryn M., *Praidd Bach y Bugail Mawr: Seiadau Methodistaidd De-Orllewin Cymru* (Llandysul, 1995).

Williams, Benjamin, *Enwogion Ceredigion* (Caerfyrddin, 1869).

Williams, David, *Y Wladfa Fach Fynddig, Situated in the Parishes of Llanddewibrefi and Llanfairclydogau* (Dinbych, 1963).

Williams, John and Davies, Ebenezer Richard, *Fferm a Ffair a Phentre* (Aberystwyth, 1958).
Wmffre, Iwan, *The Place Names of Cardiganshire*, 3 vols (Cardiff, 2003).
Yardley, Evan, *The Life of a Cardiganshire Seaman* (Aberystwyth, 2001).

Local Periodicals

Aberystwyth Studies
Y Cardi: Cylchgrawn Cymdeithas Ceredigion
Cardiganshire Antiquarian Society Transactions
Ceredigion: Journal of the Ceredigion Antiquarian Society
Cymdeithas Ceredigion Llundain

Newspapers

Aberystwyth Observer
Cambrian
Cambrian News
Y Cardi
Cardigan and Tivyside Advertiser
Carmarthen Journal
Welsh Gazette

Unpublished Theses

Aubel, Felix, 'Cardiganshire parliamentary elections and their backgrounds 1921–32' (University of Wales, Lampeter, M.Phil., 1989).
Bentley, Gemma, 'A survey and evaluation of sources for the First World War and Cardiganshire' (University of Wales, Aberystwyth, M.Sc. (Econ.), 1999).
Benbough-Jackson, Mike, 'Locating a place and its people: Ceredigion and the Cardi, *c.*1760–2004' (University of Wales, Lampeter, Ph.D. 2004).
Birtwistle, Michael, 'Pobl y tai bach: some aspects of the agricultural labouring classes of Cardiganshire in the second half of the nineteenth century' (University of Wales, Aberystwyth, MA, 1981).

Davies, A. M. E., 'Poverty and its treatment in Cardiganshire, 1750–1850' (University of Wales, Aberystwyth, MA, 1968).

Davies, Gareth Huw, 'An investigation into the factors influencing rural depopulation, with particular reference to education, especially in Ceredigion' (UWIST, M.Sc., 1984).

Thomas, Gwilym Ivor, 'The growth and decline of Cardiganshire shipbuilding from 1740–1914, with special reference to Llansanffraid' (University of Wales, Lampeter, M.Phil., 1995).

Index